Communicating
Change

Communicating Change

How to Win Employee Support for New Business Directions

TJ and Sandar Larkin
Larkin Communication Consulting
New York, New York

McGraw-Hill, Inc.
New York   San Francisco   Washington, D.C.   Auckland   Bogotá
Caracas   Lisbon   London   Madrid   Mexico City   Milan
Montreal   New Delhi   San Juan   Singapore
Sydney   Tokyo   Toronto

Library of Congress Cataloging-in-Publication Data

Larkin, TJ and Sandar
    Communicating change : how to win employee support for new
  business directions / TJ and Sandar Larkin.
        p.   cm.
    Includes bibliographical references and index.
    ISBN 0-07-036452-4
    1. Communication in personnel management.   2. Industrial
  relations.   3. Organizational change.   I. Larkin, Sandar.
  II. Title.
  HF5549.5.C6T15   1994
  658.4'5—dc20   93-29248
                                                                         CIP

    4 5 6 7 8 9 0   DOC/DOC   9 0 9 8 7 6 5

ISBN 0-07-036452-4

*The sponsoring editor for this book was Caroline Carney, the editing supervi-
sor was Joseph Bertuna, and the production supervisor was Suzanne W.
Babeuf. It was set in Palatino by McGraw-Hill's Professional Book Group
composition unit.*

Printed and bound by R. R. Donnelley & Sons Company.

To: Donald P. Cushman
Professor of Communication
State University of New York at Albany

*Many others have dedicated their work to
Professor Cushman. We are only two of a
large group deeply touched by the power of
his teaching, and warmth of his friendship.*

Contents

Preface   ix
Introduction   xi

Part 1. Communicate Directly to Supervisors

1. **Target Supervisors**   **1**

2. **Don't Go Directly to the Front Line**   **12**

3. **Don't Trickle Down through Middle Management**   **19**

4. **Middle Managers: Improving Their Communication**   **27**

5. **Communicating Customer Service**   **40**

6. **Communicating New Technology**   **48**

7. **Communicating a Downsizing**   **61**

8. **Communication Training Is Not the Answer**   **75**

9. **Making Supervisors Number One Priority**   **81**

Part 2. Use Face-to-Face Communication

10. If It's Not Face-to-Face, It's Not
    Communication   86

11. Video   96

12. Briefing Meetings   107

13. Company Newspaper   117

14. Suggestion Schemes   126

15. Employee Attitude Surveys   134

16. Putting Your Communication to the Test   144

Part 3. Communicate Relative Performance of Local Work Area

17. Your Employees Don't Care About the
    Company   152

18. Communicating Quality: Better or Worse
    Than Competitor's   165

19. Communicating Quality: Looking In-House   175

20. Communicating Customer Service
    Performance   185

21. Stop Communicating Values   209

22. If You're the Boss, Communicate
    Performance   220

23. How to Communicate When Everything
    Is Uncertain   227

Appendix   239

Glossary   245
Index   247

Preface

Most of the advice given to senior managers telling them how to communicate change is wrong.

This advice usually boils down to "more": more videos, more training, more senior manager road shows, more briefing meetings, more newsletters, and more employee surveys. What we have isn't working. Why would anyone want more of it? By "not working," we mean something very specific: These communication methods are not reaching and changing the way our frontline employees act.

Our business is helping managers communicate change. Over the years, we have given our share of bad advice. But together, with our clients, we have eventually discovered a better way to communicate. This book puts that experience on paper.

The most dangerous mistake when advising managers is spending too much time in the executive board room and too little on the front line. A discussion with almost any forklift driver, bank teller, stamping press operator, drivers' license record keeper, department store sales clerk, or telephone equipment installer will reveal the truth about employee communication: Frontline employees distrust information from senior managers, don't believe employee publications, hate watching executives on video, and have little or no interest in corporatewide topics. The boundary of the frontline worker's world is his or her local work area. If the communication doesn't break through this boundary, it is wasted.

Learning this lesson over and over, in banks, factories, mines, stores, public and private organizations, we eventually arrived at three facts of employee communication, which form the three divisions of this book.

Violate these facts, and in most cases, we believe your communication will fail. How to apply these facts is what this book is about.

Acknowledgments

We are grateful to: The Conference Board and the American Management Association in New York; The Confederation of British Industry, The Information Society, and the Institute of Personnel Management in London; and the Australian Human Resources Institute in Melbourne. These organizations allowed us access to their libraries and files, and their assistance is greatly appreciated. Research published by the International Association of Business Communicators and TPF&C proved especially valuable.

We thank friends, Louis Goldring and David Brenner, for reading and commenting on an early draft.

Books do not appear unless a publisher believes in them. We were fortunate to receive the support of Ms. Caroline Carney, our editor at McGraw-Hill.

TJ owes a special debt to his thesis adviser, Dr. Anthony Heath, at the University of Oxford; and his dissertation adviser, Dr. David C. Ralph at Michigan State University. It is now almost 15 years since TJ was their student, but their advice and teaching are still remembered and appreciated.

Anthony Loquet of Deakin University in Melbourne has our gratitude for showing faith in our work from the beginning.

Collectively we thank our parents: Susan and Stanley Cheerlips; Happy and Tom Larkin.

And Matthew Reghenzani.

TJ and Sandar Larkin

Introduction

This book is about the best ways to communicate change to employees in large companies. There are three facts:

1. Communicate directly to supervisors.
2. Use face-to-face communication.
3. Communicate relative performance of the local work area.

Two theories support these facts:

Communication Should Change Behavior

After receiving the communication, employees should return to their jobs and perform better than before. This change should be observable and immediate.

If the communication changes behavior, it's good communication; if it doesn't, it's bad communication. All the usual standards for evaluating communication must go: improving morale, keeping employees informed, building an identification with the company. Those phrases cover up the truth: The communication isn't working, isn't doing anything, isn't changing the way they act.

Communication should have one goal: improving performance. It should change the way employees do their jobs.

Communication Should Be
Receiver-Oriented

Aristotle told us, in 350 B.C., if communication is to change behavior, it must be grounded in the desires and interests of the receivers. In more than 2000 years since, there have been no major changes to the central idea. To be noticed, communication must contain something that interests the receivers; to change behavior, it must touch one of their values. Not what interests CEOs, not what touches CEOs, but what interests and touches frontline employees.

Our current communication is designed to please head office. It's about them. Senior managers read it and like what they see. But it doesn't change employees. Typically our communication comes from the wrong source (senior managers instead of first-line supervisors) using the wrong method (print or video instead of face to face) carrying the wrong message (corporate instead of local work area performance). The communication is not oriented toward its receivers and consequently does not change the way they act.

At this moment the Voyager spacecraft is moving at least 25,000 miles an hour into an outer space destination unknown. Aboard is a message. A description of Earth and its inhabitants written in binary code, zeros and ones. We have no idea where this message is going or what sort of intelligence may find it. No idea if they will understand it. If understood, no idea what they will do as a result. Too much of our communication to employees is like that.

The problem becomes critical when communicating change. Informing them is not enough—we are out to change them. Improving customer service, raising quality, implementing new technology, reducing costs, introducing new operations: We want employees to receive the communication, return to their jobs, and change. Too often, they return to their jobs and carry on exactly as before.

Between 1983 and 1993, half of the world's largest companies, measured by sales, were displaced from the top ten list.[1] During the same period, about 40 percent of U.S. companies fell off the Fortune 500 list. Most of this movement occurred because these companies did not change fast enough.[2]

This book is not about what you should change to—that's your business. This book is about how to communicate that change to your frontline employees, whatever it is.

Part 1, "Communicate Directly to Supervisors," stresses the importance of targeting first-line supervisors when communicating a major change. A warning is given against communicating directly to frontline workers. And several methods for improving communication from middle managers are discussed. Targeting supervisors is the theme in the chapters showing how to communicate customer service, new technology, and downsizing.

Part 2, "Use Face-to-Face Communication," is a criticism of our current communication methods: videos, briefing meetings, company newspapers, suggestion schemes, and employee attitude surveys. While these methods may reach middle managers, we argue they do not reach, and more importantly do not change, frontline workers.

Part 3, "Communicate Relative Performance of the Local Work Area," concentrates on content. What should we communicate? The topic with the greatest power to change employees is performance, specifically comparing their local work area with other similar areas. Communicating the relative performance of local work areas is the primary theme in the chapters on quality and customer service. Communicating values is strongly discouraged. Chapter 23 answers the frequently asked question: How can I communicate when everything is uncertain?

The appendix is a table summarizing all the practical communication examples used in the book. A glossary provides definitions of key terms.

References

1. *Fortune*, August 22, 1983, pp. 170–171; and *Fortune*, July 26, 1993, pp. 81–82.
2. Tom Peters, "Get Innovative or Get Dead: Part One," *California Management Review*, vol. 33, no. 1, fall 1990, pp. 9–26.

1

Target Supervisors

It's time for the big announcement. The employees have filled the cafeteria. The CEO approaches the podium and delivers a rousing, change-urging speech building up to a conclusion asking for everyone's support.

Following the speech, the communication campaign begins. Videos are sent to all locations. A two-way satellite hookup goes live for handling employee questions. The company newspaper is sent to all employees' homes and is dedicated entirely to news of the change. Teams of executives sweep through all locations carrying a more personalized message: how the change will affect you.

Adding a little razzmatazz, posters with the change slogan are hung in the elevator lobbies, and cardboard pyramids displaying the change logo are ready for everyone's desk.

All of this is wrong. Not only will it fail—it is positively harmful. Of the many sins committed here, the mortal one is failing to use supervisors to introduce the change to frontline employees.

The unwritten assumption of the foregoing communication campaign is that employees are most likely to change if they hear the message first from a head office source: CEO, company newspaper, video, or poster. This assumes that the head office is also the most desired and credible source in employees' eyes. And this is wrong.

Ask employees who they want their information from and the answer is almost always the same: their immediate supervisor. U.S., U.K., and Canadian employees all prefer communication from their supervisor (see Figs. 1-1, 1-2, and 1-3).[1]

Target managers

Figure 1-1. United States: Employees' preferred source of information. *(Source: Ref. 1.)*

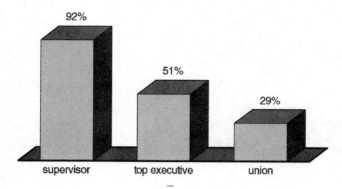

Figure 1-2. United Kingdom: Employees' preferred source of information. *(Source: Ref. 1.)*

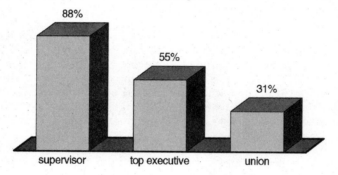

Figure 1-3. Canada: Employees' preferred source of information. *(Source: Ref. 1.)*

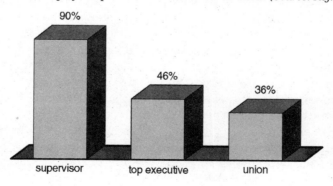

(percents do not add to 100 because employees could choose more than one source)

Research on Employees' Preferred Source of Information

The research is screaming out. The IABC/TPF&C studies in 1980, 1982, 1984, and 1990 all found supervisors as the preferred source of information for U.S. and Canadian employees.[2] The U.K. Industrial Society, and research by Crossan, verified the preference of supervisors among British employees.[3,4] The same result was found with Australian employees in Mackay's and Hainey's research.[5,6]

Research within companies arrives at the same conclusion. General Motors found their employees wanted to hear not from the union, and not from senior managers, but from those managers closest to them (see Fig. 1-4).[7] General Tire & Rubber, Hewlett-Packard, Cadbury Schweppes, General Electric, ICI, and AT&T, all found supervisors as the preferred source of information.

We Are Not Paying Attention.   As if deaf, we practitioners insist on launching from the top, somehow convinced that the employees will be more favorably impressed with the change if they hear it first from senior executives.

There is some loyalty and admiration for executives among many middle and senior managers. This dissipates fast as you head toward the front line. On the front line, loyalty and admiration are replaced with suspicion.

The former director of corporate communications for GM, Alvie Smith, says that, in businesses today (not just GM), there exists "a

Figure 1-4.   General Motors: Employees' preferred source of information. *(Source: Ref. 7.)*

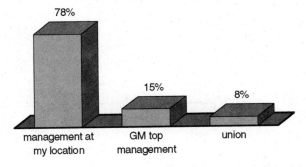

strong undercurrent of anger, resentment, fear and mistrust among employees."[8]

The evidence supports Smith's opinion. With a predominantly front-line sample, the research and consulting firm Wyatt found that 70 percent of U.K. employees felt the information they were receiving from management was often misleading.[9] In the United States and Canada, according to a Lou Harris & Assoc. study, only 38 percent of office workers are confident that management is honest in dealings with them.[10]

Studying cynicism in the workplace, Philip Marvis and Donald Kanter found 43 percent of workers are cynics and that these people are not just suspicious, they firmly believe management lies and is trying to cheat them. Cynics were found to be most prevalent among blue-collar workers in manufacturing and employees in lower-paying service jobs.[11]

Notice that we are not talking about a few scattered loonies here. The research says somewhere around 40 percent of frontline employees think management is not telling the truth. Compare this with the GM research showing 83 percent of employees rank their supervisor as their most believable source.[12] Or look at Dennis Taylor's research with Australian employees showing 96 percent believing their supervisor is always or normally telling the truth.[13]

Communication has the best chance of changing frontline behavior if it comes from the most desired and credible source, and that is not the CEO—it's the immediate supervisor. The first words your employees hear about the customer service campaign, the new product line, the quality drive, the cost-cutting exercise, should come from the lips of the person they most know and trust.

The Best Way to Communicate Change

When the change is major. When the future of the company depends on it. When senior executives with sweaty palms look each other in the eye saying, "We've got to get this one right," then:

Do not communicate the change directly to frontline employees (explained more fully in Chap. 2).

Do not rely on communication trickling down through middle management (Chap. 3).

Do not assume frontline employees will change based on information they receive from videos, briefing meetings, or the company newspaper (Chaps. 10 to 13).

Instead, when change is critical, the first priority must be targeting first-line supervisors. Establish direct, two-way communication between supervisors and senior managers. Figure 1-5 shows what we mean: Rely on traditional communication methods (for example, briefing meetings, company newspaper, video) to reach middle managers. But, in addition, plug the communication directly into the supervisor level as well.

Remember, this is not a recommendation for communicating day-to-day changes. Here we are talking about major, once every two or three years, type of change. Methods for improving the communication of day-to-day operating changes are discussed in Chap. 4, "Middle Managers: Improving Their Communication."

The following section shows how to target supervisors when communicating a major change.

Figure 1-5. Communicating a major change.

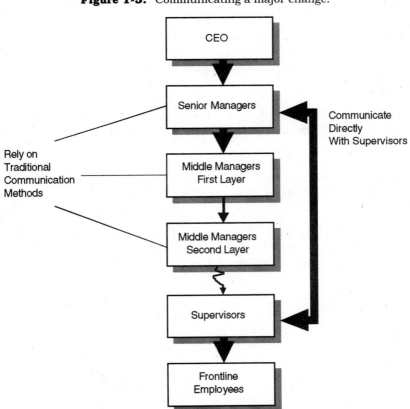

Targeting Supervisors: An Example

An offshore oil company was communicating a major change in their maintenance operation.

The long-established tradition was for each offshore platform to contain its own operating and maintenance crews—anywhere from 40 to 60 people living and working on each offshore platform. Recently, however, management had decided that permanently locating an entire maintenance crew on every platform had become unnecessary. Efficiencies could be gained if maintenance crews were centralized onto a few large "host" platforms.

When operators needed maintenance, the new plan called for them to radio their host platform, requesting a maintenance crew. The maintenance crew would board a helicopter, fly to the platform needing service, do their work, and return to the host platform or go to the next platform requiring maintenance. The plan allowed a 25 percent reduction in maintenance employees and a similar reduction in catering employees, such as cooks and cleaners.

Rumors of this change created intense anxiety offshore. Terminating employees is always emotional. Added to this was apprehension among operators about running platforms without full maintenance crews onboard and wariness among maintenance workers about having to learn and maintain equipment on a variety of differently configured platforms.

The communication plan had two parts: supervisors' briefings at the start of each shift and a supervisors' opinion report intended primarily for the CEO.

Supervisors' Briefings

During the months of planning for this change, supervisors attended half-hour briefing sessions. These occurred just before supervisors left shore to work their week-long shift on a platform. Senior managers ran the briefings, covering topics such as:

Approximate number of terminations being considered

Criteria for selecting employees to be terminated

Estimated size of severance package

Training planned for maintenance workers servicing unfamiliar platforms

Two points are important here: First, we did not communicate directly to frontline employees. In their extremely anxious frame of mind, they would not have believed a word any senior manager said. It is worth remembering that, in 1988 just prior to Eastern Airline's bankruptcy, executives communicating with employees occasionally met with spitting and punching. When frontline workers are nearing panic, you don't gather them in a large group for a presentation. The best chance of communicating occurs when you use the most trusted and desired source of information, their supervisor.

Second, we did not rely on this critical information trickling down through the management layers. Supervisors were targeted for privileged communication. The senior managers who conducted the briefings were the people planning the change, and they were three layers of management above the supervisors. As we will discuss in Chap. 3, if you count on the information cascading down, you can count on being disappointed. It simply won't make it.

Supervisors' Opinion Reports

A *supervisors' opinion report* is an unbiased listing of supervisors' dominant worries concerning the change. The goal here is to add supervisors' concerns to those of the CEO.

The supervisors' opinion report is made from one-on-one, anonymous interviews with supervisors. The first round of these interviews revealed four major supervisor worries:

1. That operating crews would be left alone, without full maintenance crews. This concern was addressed by giving operating supervisors a new right: the opportunity to pick their own crews.

2. That maintenance crews would lack the full set of skills required for working on several different platforms. Maintenance supervisors said this could be overcome if they could choose their own crews.

3. That lines of authority were unclear. The new organizational chart failed to make clear who was the ultimate authority when a maintenance crew was aboard a satellite platform: the operating supervisor or the maintenance supervisor.

4. That refineries had not been told to expect approximately 10 percent less production resulting from increased pumping downtime during the transition to centralized maintenance.

The *supervisors' opinion report* is shared with the supervisors, managers in charge of the change, and, most importantly, the CEO.

Unless this report goes to the CEO, these supervisors' concerns will never be addressed. Or, at best, the supervisors' concerns will not be looked at until the final moments before implementation.

Why? Because the managers planning the change are all looking up, not down.

The atmosphere surrounding this type of change is one of tremendous pressure: millions of dollars at stake, terminating employees, changing an established tradition that has worked well for 20 years. Here careers are on the line. Running through the veins of each and every manager working on this change is the question: "How will the senior executives evaluate my handling of this major change?" In this tense atmosphere the concerns of supervisors are lost.

All eyes are up. For the managers planning the maintenance operation change in the offshore oil company, the priorities were set by the expectation of what questions the CEO and senior executive committee would ask at the next progress meeting:

Can you justify the 25 percent manpower cut?

Is it too little? Too much?

Are the union negotiations going to produce a severance payout so large that it eats all the savings?

Does the change have the support of the government regulatory agencies? Does it meet the company's safety standards?

Has the price of new helicopters been deducted from the savings figures?

The CEO and executives were not going to ask:

Oh, and by the way, are we changing the rostering system so that supervisors have greater say getting the crews they want?

That concern would never cross the mind of the CEO. Supervisor concerns are an absolute bottom priority when all eyes are up. Without the supervisors' report, at best, some middle manager would eventually have been given the task of juggling rosters designing a system allowing greater supervisor discretion in crew selection. If done at all, it would happen moments before the launch.

But that would have been too late. For months now frontline employees had been going into the control room asking their supervisor, "What do you think of this change to centralized maintenance?" And the supervisor's been answering, "It's [profanity deleted]." He's saying that because for months *his* major concerns with the change have not been answered.

Your opinion leaders, your most critical receivers, the ones who determine the behavior of the rest of your employees, have turned against the change. There is one and only one solution: the major concerns of supervisors must become major concerns of the CEO. And that's what the supervisors' opinion report does: It puts supervisors' concerns onto the CEO agenda and, by so doing, makes them a top priority among the change managers.

Supervisors' briefings give supervisors access to senior managers planning the change; and the supervisors' opinion report makes a direct upward communication link with the CEO. The purpose of these measures is improving communication to supervisors, the result is winning their support, and the reward is supervisors' bringing the rest of your employees with them.

Best Practical Advice in Communication

In 1962, Everett Rogers wrote *Diffusion of Innovations*.[14] It is, we believe, the most important practical work in the field of communication.

Many of Rogers's ideas originated from his research into the best ways to communicate change in less-developed countries. For example, Rogers, working with governments and aid organizations, helped communicate agricultural innovations such as higher-yielding crop seeds and health innovations such as boiled drinking water.

The standard approach involved sending in experts, holding presentations, and explaining the benefits of the new technique to everyone. (In other words, what we almost always do when communicating change in large companies.) This did not work. Over and over, villagers rejected the change, opting instead for their traditional ways. Rogers recommended not sending in the expert. The expert was considered a stranger with no track record in the village and thus was viewed with suspicion. Worst of all, the outside expert using new terms, claiming new power, discrediting long-established traditions, was seen by the existing opinion leader as a potential rival.

Rogers saw that our communication was sabotaging our attempts to introduce change to these people. Instead, Rogers said, identify the village opinion leaders (for example, elders, chiefs, witch-doctors), acknowledge their superior status, and ask them, and only them, to listen to the new ideas. Rogers went on to say that we should modify the changes according to opinion leader suggestions and then rely solely on the opinion leaders to do the direct, face-to-face communicating with villagers.

Thirty years later, Roger's ideas are still dominating work in diffusion. One recent example is in Uganda. Government agencies there were having little luck encouraging villagers to use condoms in the fight against AIDS. Following Rogers, they reined the experts back in, and instead invited respected village storytellers to come to Kampala. Once there, experts and storytellers exchanged information about village habits and AIDS. Storytellers returned to their villages, and condom use surged.

Supervisors are the opinion leaders for frontline employees. They are the only people who can change frontline behavior. Supervisors are not just one of the receivers—they are the receivers. The consultants, the CEO, the VP for marketing or finance are never going to change the way frontline employees act. Only the supervisor can do that. Once we understand this, it becomes clear that communicating across an organization is not like spreading butter across a slice of bread. Instead, communication involves targeting the key receivers, the ones who can make it happen. Your success in communicating change to the front line depends on your success in communicating to supervisors.

References

1. Julie Foehrenbach and Karn Rosenberg, "How are We Doing?" *Journal of Communication Management*, vol. 12, no. 1, 1983, pp. 3—11.

2. Karn Rosenberg, "What Employees Think of Communication: 1984 Update," *Communication World*, May 1985, pp. 46–50. The TPF&C 1990 survey results are in Julie Foehrenbach and Steve Goldfarb, "Employee Communication in the '90s," *Communication World*, May/June 1990.

3. The Industrial Society, edited by Sue Webb, *Blueprint for Success: A Report on Involving Employees in Britain*, London, May 1989.

4. Des Crossan, "A Company Employee Communications Strategy," *Management Decision*, vol. 25, no. 3, 1987, pp. 28–34.

5. Hugh Mackay, *The Communication Climate in Australian Organisations*, Australian Institute of Management—New South Wales Division, 1980.

6. G. Hainey, "High Information Sharing Companies: What Their Employees Think," *Work and People*, vol. 10, no. 1, 1984, pp. 17–22.

7. "Local Managers + Information = Key Internal Communicators," *Employee Relations and Human Resources Bulletin*, Report no. 1672, sec. 1, September 21, 1988, pp. 1–6.

8. Alvie Smith, *Innovative Employee Communication*, Prentice-Hall, Englewood Cliffs, N. J., 1991, pp. ix–x.

9. Wyatt, *Wyatt Work UK: UK Benchmark of Attitudes to Work*, London, 1989.

10. Lou Harris & Assoc. study quoted in Gary W. Kemper, "Managing: Corporate Communication in Turbulent Times," *Communication World*, May–June 1992, pp. 29–32.

11. Philip H. Marvis and Donald L. Kanter, "Combatting Cynicism in the Workplace," *National Productivity Review*, vol. 8, no. 4, autumn 1989, pp. 377–394.

12. *Employee Relations and Human Resources Bulletin*, op. cit., p. 2.

13. Dennis W. Taylor: *Employee Information Sharing*, Department of Employment and Industrial Relations, Australian Government Publishing Service, Canberra, 1982, p. 67.

14. Everett M. Rogers, *Diffusion of Innovations*, Free Press, New York, 1983.

Communicatn. involves targeting the key receivers, the ones who can make it happen.

2
Don't Go Directly to the Front Line

Many sincere attempts to improve communication are poorly conceived. None more so than CEOs establishing direct communication links with frontline employees.

The chairman at Dana Corporation, in a campaign called "A Letter to the Chairman," encouraged any employee with a comment or question to contact him directly. Frontline employees at Hasbro, a toy maker, were invited to contact their CEO through a program called "Write to the Top." At Steelcase, the president and chairman provided employees with their home telephone numbers. Moving higher tech, the CEO at Portland Maine insurance company, UNUM Corporation, encouraged any of his 5,500 employees to contact him through the electronic mail system; the CEO attempted to personally answer all inquiries by the following morning.

These measures are well-intended, but they are also mistakes. The blame rests firmly on the shoulders of communication professionals: professors, consultants, and senior executives in human resources and public affairs. It is the CEOs' responsibility to improve communication—it is the communication professional's job to show them how. And establishing a direct communication link with frontline employees is a step backward.

These campaigns are wrong for two reasons. First, they are more symbolic than real; and frontline employees, having little love for the symbolic, quickly become disillusioned. Second, and much worse, these campaigns weaken the relationship between frontline employees and their supervisors.

The A Letter to the Chairman campaign at Dana Corporation resulted in 3000 letters a year. If the chairman were to personally answer each letter—and that was the promise—he would be answering more than eight letters a day, every day of the year. And certainly employees want more than a form-letter response—they want action. They want their forklift repaired, a new collating photocopy machine, a paper-recycling program, flexitime, a failed promotion reviewed, more car parking spaces, a daycare center, additional sick days due to lingering illness, and better maintenance on the stamping presses. And the expectations for action are high; after all, they're talking to the *chairman* now. In most companies, what they get is usually something like the hypothetical letter shown in Fig. 2-1.

This response will make them angry. In their eyes it will appear to be the epitome of a bureaucratic management brushoff. "Now I get it. It's all a con. Management doesn't really care—it's just a show." "Even the CEO doesn't really give a damn."

And that is the good outcome. The bad outcome is when the CEO actually does something. For now there is absolutely no reason for a

Figure 2-1. Hypothetical response to employee inquiry.

From the Office of the CEO

Dear Bob Jones:

Thank you for your recent inquiry concerning additional car parking spaces for second-shift employees. I have turned your request over to Ms. Mary Lewis in the Grounds and Maintenance Department. Ms. Lewis will make a thorough examination of parking requirements and availability, and, in due course, provide you with a complete response.

Your concern for the company and its more efficient operation is greatly appreciated and I encourage you to write again in the near future.

Sincerely

CEO

frontline employee to communicate with his or her supervisor. "Why talk to her? When I want to know something, or want something done, I talk to the CEO—directly."

Imagine the shock for a supervisor telling an operator that the stamping presses will only undergo preventative maintenance every 1500 hours, and the operator replies, "Oh yeah, I think it should be every 1000, and so does the CEO. I just called her at home."

Establishing a direct link with frontline employees sounds good in speeches. It paints a picture of openness, breaking down bureaucracy, getting things done. But the pretty picture is not the reality. The reality is that this is a bad idea. If the CEO doesn't act, employees are disillusioned and discouraged; but worse, if the CEO does act, the relationship between the supervisor and employee is weakened.

The Pelz Effect

CEOs seem convinced their communication can change employees. A study of 164 CEOs in Fortune 500 companies, by A. Foster Higgins & Co., shows that 97 percent of these CEOs believe their communication affects employee job satisfaction, and 75 percent believe it affects employee job performance.[1] This is grand self-delusion. There is absolutely no evidence that communication from CEOs in large companies significantly affects employee behavior. CEO interviews in the company newspaper, on videos, giving presentations in the plants, or encouraging direct links through electronic mail or letters do not change the behavior of large numbers of frontline employees. Only in the most rare circumstances, a company on the brink of financial disaster with an extraordinarily charismatic CEO, does this type of communication have any chance of making lasting impressions on employees.

A wealth of evidence, however, shows that increasing the power of your supervisors increases both satisfaction and performance among frontline employees. This relationship was first discovered by Donald Pelz working at the University of Michigan in 1952, and it is commonly referred to as the *Pelz effect*.[2]

Pelz did his important research with 10,000 employees from the Detroit Edison Company, an electrical utility. The purpose was finding what types of leadership styles would cause employees to be most satisfied with their supervisors. To obtain high satisfaction, should a supervisor be formal or informal, autocratic or participative, management oriented or frontline oriented?

What Pelz found shocked him: What mattered most was not the supervisor's leadership style but whether the supervisor had power.

Specifically, it mattered most whether the supervisor had influence in decisions made at higher levels of management. If the supervisor had upward influence, the subordinates expressed high satisfaction with their supervisor. The leadership style had little effect. Employees want to work for someone who is connected. Someone who has a voice in decisions.

Studying almost 30 years of research on the Pelz effect, Fredric Jablin referred to it as "one of the most widely accepted propositions about organizational communication...."[3]

Karlene Roberts and Charles O'Reilly discovered additional effects from working for someone you believe has power.[4] According to their research, working for a powerful supervisor is associated with:

Increased trust in the supervisor

Increased desire for communication with the supervisor

Increased belief in the accuracy of information coming from the supervisor

The most recent research is showing even broader implications: The quality of the relationship between supervisor and employee influences the employee's feelings about the entire company.

The researcher, Paul Nystrom, was searching for the causes of organizational commitment. He looked at years in the job, seniority, job level, and organization size; and he came up with nothing. Then he looked at the quality of the relationship with one's boss and found this was three times more powerful in predicting organizational commitment than the other variables.[5]

Most startling is the research at GE and Hewlett-Packard. The conclusion of this research, involving thousands of employees at both companies, is: "The better the manager's communication, the more satisfied employees are with all aspects of their work life."[6]

Looking at Hewlett-Packard employees, for example, Brad Whitworth, manager of employee communication at H-P, separated those employees who expressed positive opinions of communication with their supervisors, from those employees expressing negative opinions of supervisor communication. Predictably, Whitworth found those H-P employees who reported poor communication with their supervisor also had lower job satisfaction. But unpredictably, he also found those employees who had poor communication relationships with their supervisors also had lower opinions of:

Overall management

Training

Pay

Benefits

Working conditions

Operating efficiency

Corporate policies

Company image

There is no rational reason why a poor communication relationship with a supervisor should go hand in hand with a lower opinion of company benefits. But that is exactly what GE and H-P found.

But, finally, does the relationship between employees and supervisors also affect performance? Yes.

The classic study was done by Lawshe and Nagle in 1953 working with the International Harvester Company (now Navistar).[7] Lawshe and Nagle studied 14 work groups, measuring two variables: employee satisfaction with their supervisor and work group productivity. The correlation was a shocking .86 (where 1 is perfect).

Recent research by Phillip Clampitt and Cal Downs examined communication and productivity in a U.S. savings and loan company.[8] Clampitt and Downs asked the employees to remember some communication incident that caused them to improve their work. Seventy percent of these employees mentioned face to face communication with their supervisors. Communication with much lower impact on performance included communication with co-workers, meetings, memos, and corporate information.

In conclusion, we know employees are more satisfied with their supervisors when they believe those supervisors have power; and we know that employees who are satisfied with their supervisors think better of the entire company and do better work.

The supervisor's power is strengthened when she or he is treated as a privileged sender and receiver of information. This is why companies such as Johnson & Johnson and Nissan (United Kingdom) discourage almost all direct communication from the corporate level to frontline employees. Employees should get important information from their supervisors, not the CEO. The Pelz effect and most communication research suggests these companies have got it right.

Conclusion

Now you can understand our insistence: It is not an employee's communication relationship with the CEO or head office that matters;

rather it is his or her communication with his or her supervisor that is paramount.

When we enter an organization as consultants, the first thing the client does is load us full of past copies of the company newspaper, their team briefing manual, adoption rates from their suggestion scheme, videos of the CEO, results from attitude surveys, mission statements, declarations of corporate values—none of this matters. Only one thing matters: the quality of the communication between employees and their supervisors. You improve that relationship by ensuring that the supervisor has a voice in decision making, and making sure the supervisor has something to say, that she or he has privileged access to information. None of this is helped by establishing a direct link between frontline employees and senior management.

For more than 10 years now, Tom Peters has been pleading with us to practice "management by wandering around." Undeniably a good idea, but there is an assumption here: the person wandering around knows something the others don't. This requires communication targeting supervisors and discourages direct links with frontline employees, particularly when communicating an important change.

Take your deeply felt beliefs about equality and leave them in the political domain where they belong. As the Pelz effect shows: You are not doing your frontline employees a favor by convincing them their supervisor knows nothing more than they do.

Even the CEO presentation to the troops, announcing the big change, contains within it the seeds of poor communication. Any time supervisors sit shoulder to shoulder with frontline employees, treated as equals, you have made a mistake. Sitting supervisors shoulder to shoulder with frontline employees is evidence of your failure to recognize their superior status. And no one needs that recognition more than first-line supervisors, 60 percent of whom don't even think of themselves as management, according to research by Lester Bittel and Jackson Ramsey.[9]

The prestige of an *exclusive* supervisors' meeting with senior executives enhances their power and consequently strengthens their relationship with their people. Most of all it is the first step toward winning their support for your change.

Establishing a direct communication line to frontline employees will not help communicate your change. You are destroying supervisors' information superiority and consequently weakening their ties to their people. Worst of all, you have failed to recognize the status of your supervisor and in the process made an enemy of the person you need most. You will not change the behavior of frontline employees without their strong support. And communicating with supervisors as if they were just another employee is not a good start.

Reference

1. A. Foster Higgins & Co. study reported in "CEOs Say They Neglect Employee Communications," *Public Relations Journal*, May 1990, p. 13.

2. Donald C. Pelz, "Influence: A Key to Effective Leadership in the First-Line Supervisor," *Personnel*, vol. 29, November 1952, pp. 209–217.

3. Fredric M. Jablin, "Superior's Upward Influence, Satisfaction, and Openness in Superior-Subordinate Communication: A Re-examination of the Pelz Effect'," *Human Communication Research*, vol. 6, no. 3, spring 1980, pp. 210–220.

4. Karlene H. Roberts and Charles A. O'Reilly III, "Failures in Upward Communication in Organizations: Three Possible Culprits," *Academy of Management Journal*, vol. 17, no. 2, 1974, 205–215.

5. Paul C. Nystrom, "Vertical Exchanges and Organizational Commitments of American Business Managers," *Group & Organization Studies*, vol. 15, no. 3, September 1990, pp. 296–312.

6. GE and Hewlett-Packard research in Brad Whitworth, "Proof at Last," *Communication World*, December 1990, pp. 28–31.

7. C. H. Lawshe and B. F. Nagle, "Productivity and Attitude Toward Supervisor," *Journal of Applied Psychology*, vol. 37, 1953, pp. 159–162.

8. Phillip G. Clampitt and Cal W. Downs, "Employee Perceptions of the Relationship Between Communication and Productivity," *The Journal of Business Communication*, vol. 30, no. 1, 1993, pp. 5–28.

9. Lester R. Bittel and Jackson E. Ramsey, "The Limited, Traditional World of Supervisors," *Harvard Business Review*, July–August 1982, pp. 26–36.

3

Don't Trickle Down through Middle Management

You won't make it.

Asea Brown Boveri (ABB), a manufacturing company headquartered in Zurich, employs 240,000 people worldwide and specializes in power distribution and transmission equipment.[1] The CEO personally launched a campaign called, "Cash Race," intended to improve accounts receivables. Two thousand employees around the world work in accounts receivables. The CEO decided to personally visit many of them to check on Cash Race progress. On arriving, he found:

> These people hadn't even heard of the program, and it should have been their top priority. When you come face to face with this lack of communication, this massive inertia, you can get horrified, depressed, almost desperate.

Somewhere between the CEO and the front line the message bogs down. The accusatory finger is usually pointed at middle managers. GM refers to them as the "frozen middle," GE as the "cement layer," and Polaroid as the "muddle in the middle." Almost half of all human resource executive tell "horror stories" about communicating change through layers of middle management, according to research by Alan Frank.[2]

Why don't messages move down management layers like a marble rolling down steps? Why? Because the middle steps grab the marble, drain its content, and transform it into a little piece of power.

Middle Management: Transforming Information into Power

Middle managers are power sponges. A fascinating study by a European research group called "Decisions in Organizations" looked at the legally prescribed power of employees compared to their real everyday power.[3] *Legal power* referred to an employee's proper influence in decision making as determined by the company's formal rules, policies, and regulations. *Real power* referred to the actual influence employees exerted in numerous company decisions studied by the researchers. Middle managers proved to be the undisputed masters of absorbing unofficial power (see Fig. 3-1).

Research by Miller and Longair shows roughly 40 percent of middle managers' time is taken up moving messages through organizational layers.[4] But as we have just shown, this is no neutral transfer of information; the messages are withheld or modified in ways enhancing middle managers' power.

Here are two examples:

A large bank, roughly 10,000 employees with 500 branches, was introducing many new financial products and practices. Progress, however, was slowing as branches began complaining they couldn't keep up. Staff turnover at the branches was nearing 50 percent, and the experienced couldn't teach the novices fast enough. The branches sent a message to head office: Stop the changes.

The first thing we noticed was the horrendous communication in circulars sent from head office departments to branches. Figure 3-2 shows an example from a typical head office circular.

Figure 3-1. Percent increase of real power over legal power. *(Source: Ref. 3.)*

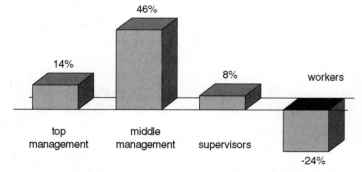

The communication describing new products and procedures was fantastically and needlessly complex. Fixing these circulars involved finding five experienced branch staff employees who could write, bringing them to head office, and giving them two weeks' intensive training in technical writing. After their training, the circular in Fig. 3-2 was reissued as shown in Fig. 3-3.

Reaction to the new circulars at the branches was euphoric. As weeks passed, the writers became better and better, and circulars clearer and clearer. But enthusiasm for the new circulars was not shared by head

Figure 3-2. Original circular.

```
Circular No. 440/91

Real Property Mortgage


Except where an existing mortgage can be upstamped
to secure a further advance, mortgage documents
are to be prepared in all instances where real
property is offered as security by a borrower, a
borrower in conjunction with a third party or a
third party (refer clause 4.08 Notes on Mortgage
Documents - Real Property).


The Bank's new real property mortgage is not a
third  party document.  Where the property offered
as security is owned by a third party or a third
party in conjunction with a borrower, a guarantee
is to be prepared in addition to a mortgage, for
execution by any mortgagor who is not a borrower.
The borrower is named as the Principal Debtor in
the guarantee.


The booklet Memorandum of Common Provisions of
Mortgage (No. 7522) is to be handed to a mortgagor
upon request.  As the original of the common
provisions of the real property mortgage has been
registered at the Titles Office, it is not
mandatory with the exception of advances that in
future will be regulated under the Credit Act, that
a booklet be provided to each mortgagor.
```

Figure 3-3. Circular rewrite.

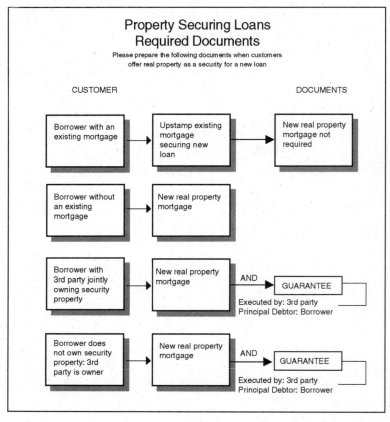

Property Securing Loans
Required Documents
Please prepare the following documents when customers
offer real property as a security for a new loan

CUSTOMER   DOCUMENTS

| Borrower with an existing mortgage | → | Upstamp existing mortgage securing new loan | → | New real property mortgage not required |

| Borrower without an existing mortgage | → | New real property mortgage |

| Borrower with 3rd party jointly owning security property | → | New real property mortgage | AND → | GUARANTEE |
Executed by: 3rd party
Principal Debtor: Borrower

| Borrower does not own security property: 3rd party is owner | → | New real property mortgage | AND → | GUARANTEE |
Executed by: 3rd party
Principal Debtor: Borrower

office departments. Head office memos began making their way to the CEO saying the new circulars were: demeaning, reducing serious topics to pretty pictures, treating staff like children, and detracting from the dignity of banking.

Even though 87 percent of branch staff employees ranked the new circulars the best change made by the bank that year in an employee survey, head office departments were encouraging a return to the old system.

Support for the old-style circulars becomes understandable when you see how the traditional communication actually worked. Branch staff, unable to understand the circulars, would telephone head office departments, verbally prostrating themselves, admitting imbecility, and begging for tidbits of interpretation. Conducting even routine transactions became impossible without knowing someone in head office, someone willing to explain what the circular really said.

The operation of 500 branches depended on a couple dozen head office managers who really did know how things were supposed to be done. And every incoming phone call was a reaffirmation of their experience, wisdom, and tolerance of the ignorance of others. These calls went from hundreds under the old circulars to dozens under the new ones.

In a moment of startling honesty, one of these managers said, "It took me a long time to learn the language of the banking profession, and it disturbs me to see some in this bank have no respect for this." Translated, this means: "Those people don't know what the hell's going on, I'm the guy who tells them, and that's the way I like it."

Maintaining the power of middle managers can be very expensive. Philip Crosby Associates Inc. surveys show British banks waste more than 50 percent of their operating costs because of error-prone procedures.[5] But, in this case, middle managers preferred maintaining power to improving communication—despite the costs.

It should now be clearer why a marble rolling down steps is such an inappropriate analogy for messages moving through middle management. Each person handling the message reconstructs it in ways enhancing his or her power. When, if, it reaches the front line, it is less a datum of information and more a means of control.

Here is another example: $communication\ for\ middle\ managers = control$

A large manufacturing company began a 15 percent cost-cutting drive. The plant cafeteria was to take its share of the cuts. A middle manager responsible for this change sent the memo in Fig. 3-4 to his plant supervisors.

Many of you will think this memo is simply a case of bad writing: too much jargon. This assumption is not only wrong but encourages useless spending. If this were bad writing, it could be fixed by training. Spending money and time on communication training programs would, under this assumption, improve the communication. The flaw, however, is that this is not bad writing. This is good writing. Brilliant writing, given the intentions of the writer.

Let's work through what happens when this memo arrives on the desk of plant supervisor Carol.

Carol reads it, has no idea what it means, calls Harold, and learns that "advanced catering technology" means microwave ovens and "a more flexible approach to the span of hours of remaining cafeteria staff" means split shifts.

Now *she* gets to deliver the news that her workers are going to take pre-prepared meals out of a freezer and heat them in microwave ovens and that management does not consider this to be a lowering of present service (so as not to violate their collective-bargaining agreement). And, best of all, the night-shift cafeteria staff, doing only washing up, is going

Figure 3-4. Harold's memo to supervisors.

MEMO

To: All Plant Supervisors

From: Harold Smith
               Operations Manager

Re: Plant Cafeteria
               Operating Cost Reductions

Operating expenses in the cafeteria are to be
reduced by eliminating the positions of some
third-shift cafeteria workers. A firm commitment
is made that these reductions will not lower the
quality of our present service.

As compensatory measures, advanced catering
technology and a more flexible approach to the
span of hours of remaining cafeteria staff are
to be established.

to work an eight-hour shift broken into two parts, 11 p.m. to 3 a.m. and then 6 a.m. to 10 a.m., with three unpaid hours in the middle.

Both Harold and she realize that all hell will break loose when the workers understand what's about to happen. But Harold, through very skillful writing, has ensured that, when it hits the fan, it does so on the front line as far as possible from his office.

There will be a blowup. But Harold has tried to control the description of the blowup that will inevitably circulate through the company. "Did you hear about all the trouble Carol is having with her crew?" And not: "Did you hear about all the trouble Harold caused with his memo?" Harold has constructed the message so the cause of the explosion is associated with his supervisor and not with himself.

Some will think we've read too much into this example. To those readers, we ask you to imagine the following situation: Harold is at home; it's his turn to cook dinner for the children; someone phones Harold and asks him to sub for a tennis match at the club; Harold writes a note. Does he say:

"Dear Children,

Please take the hardened animal fiber from the heat-absorbing chamber and accelerate its molecules in the advanced catering technology.

No, he doesn't say that. Harold writes: "Take the hamburgers out of the refrigerator and cook them in the microwave." Harold can write perfectly clearly when he wants the receivers to understand.

This is why communication training is frequently so far off the mark. These managers can write. They are experts at it. It would take years for them to teach a typical communication trainer what they know. The "poor" communication is an intentional shield protecting the manager from the explosion. The ability to write clearly has nothing to do with what's happening here.

Harold's memo is the opposite of what should be done. Bad news should come loud and clear from middle or senior management. This recommendation is not based on some concept of justice. It's not that Harold, making more money than Carol, should take the heat. No, the justification is practical. All your communication should aim to protect the supervisor's relationship with her or his crew. That relationship is all you have to change frontline behavior. Beginning by giving it a swift kick is hardly a good start. Absorb the heat at some level above the supervisors. There are many successful companies where frontline employees hate middle managers; there are none where frontline employees hate their supervisors.

When the change is big, and everything depends on it, you can't afford to risk that the communication will not make it, not reach supervisors and the front line. Prepare the message carefully, and take it directly to first-line supervisors.

Communicating smaller, but still important, changes requires improving middle management communication. This is the topic in Chap. 4.

References

1. Asea Brown Boveri example from William Taylor, "The Logic of Global Business: An Interview with ABB's Percy Barnevik," *Harvard Business Review*, March–April 1991, pp. 91–105.

2. Allan D. Frank, "Trends in Communication: Who Talks to Whom?" *Personnel*, vol. 62, no. 12, December 1985, pp. 41–47.

3. "Participative Decision Making: A Comparative Study," *Industrial Relations*, vol. 18, no. 3, fall 1979, pp. 295–309.

4. J. Miller and R. Longair, *New Directions in Middle Management–A Dilemma?* The Australian Institute of Management, Victoria, Melbourne, 1986.

5. Philip Crosby Associates, Inc., survey quoted in, "Quality Overview: It's an Old World in More Ways Than One," *Business Week*, Special Edition, 1991, pp. 26–28.

4

Middle Managers: Improving Their Communication

Do not lose sleep at night worrying how you are going to get information into middle management. Worry how you are going to get it out.

Middle manager satisfaction with communication, although not good, is higher than that of supervisors, and considerably higher than that of hourly or clerical workers. Communication research conducted by TPF&C consultants Julie Foehrenbach and Steve Goldfarb[1] shows that middle managers are more likely to believe that:

The company is trying hard to keep them informed.

The information they receive is accurate, candid, and tells the whole story.

Their company is a better communicator than most.

Why are middle managers relatively more satisfied with communication? Networks. Middle managers have built semiformal links with individuals in departments throughout the company. These networks provide them not with rumors but with informal access to formal information and plans.

Research by Jules Harcourt, Virginia Richerson, and Mark Wattier studied the communication practices of 871 U.S. middle managers,[2] 16 percent of whom said their most important source of information was formal channels; 21 percent said the grapevine; and by far the largest group, 62 percent, said their most important information source was their intentionally constructed network.

Information is moving in and through middle management. It is not moving out.

When the change is major, solve the problem by cutting a direct communication link from senior managers to first-line supervisors. When the change is less critical, involving day-to-day operations, a direct link between senior managers and supervisor is neither desirable nor practical.

Improving the communication of day-to-day change requires getting more information out of your middle managers. Here are two ways to do that: a transmission check and a supervisor evaluation of manager communication.

Transmission Check

A *transmission check* means you call supervisors and make sure they received and understood the message.

Here is an example from a manufacturing company having problems communicating industrial relations (IR) information.

Every three years the company renegotiates its collective-bargaining agreement with its union. The problem was that first-line supervisors were frequently violating parts of the agreements, especially those parts changed in the most recent negotiations.

Supervisors said these violations were caused by poor communication. They were not told of the changes. Most of what they knew they had heard from their subordinates. The union, supervisors claimed, did a better job communicating the new agreements than did management.

The industrial relations managers denied this accusation of poor communication, claiming completed agreements were faxed to supervisors only hours after ratification by the rank and file.

This faxing did indeed occur, but whether it could be called "communication" was another question. Fig. 4-1 shows a sample clause from an agreement concerning required communication of terminations, typical of what the industrial relations department managers would fax to supervisors.

If you think we selected an example (Fig. 4-1) with particularly poor communication, you are wrong. James Suchan and Clyde Scott examined 196 collective-bargaining contracts involving a wide range of unions, from the Teamsters and the UAW to the Motion Picture Guild.[3] Using a readability instrument called the *Gunning Fog Index*, they tested

Figure 4-1. Sample clause from a termination agreement.

```
    Required Notification Prior to
  Termination Not Resulting From
       Employee Negligence


  A definite decision, made by the employer,
  that the employer no longer wishes the job
  the employee has been doing done by anyone
  (and this is not due to the ordinary and
  customary turnover of labor, or to negligent
  discipline-attracting behavior on the part of
  the employee) and that decision may lead to
  termination of employment; in such cases the
  employer shall be required to hold
  discussions with the employees directly
  affected and where applicable with their
  union.
```

the amount of education required to read and understand a typical clause in a typical agreement. The answer was 18 years of education: high school, college, and 2 years of graduate study. Three percent of the agreements could be understood by someone with only a high school education. Either we must send all our supervisors back to university for masters degrees or we try improving the communication.

A transmission check is one way to improve communication. The manufacturing company described in this example decided to randomly call supervisors on the phone and test the quality of communication reaching them.

Each call asked supervisors to answer five true-false questions concerning the most recent changes. Scores from individual supervisors were kept secret. Scores from all supervisors at a particular plant were aggregated, averaged, and reported by plant. As a result, no one knew the score of any individual supervisor, but everyone knew the score of each plant and therefore the performance of the industrial relations manager responsible for communication at that plant.

Figure 4-2 shows the results from the first test, with four of the five plants missing at least three questions. This chart was shared with all supervisors and higher managers. An unhappy CEO ordered the test repeated with new questions the following week. With the retest, four plants answered all questions correctly, and one plant missed, on average, two questions. Almost 150 percent improvement in communication in one week.

IR managers prepared for the second test by sending every supervisor a one-page summary describing the major contract changes in very clear words. (The same kind of summaries they routinely use when communicating with senior executives.) Some IR managers personally visited supervisors, asking for any questions. One manager recorded a telephone message highlighting the major contract changes.

Communicating the test results caused IR managers to improve their communication. And this was done without training, multitiered cascading team meetings, or organized formal presentations with dozens of overhead transparencies. More than anything else, what is required to improve communication is pressure—pressure on middle managers to improve their communication with supervisors.

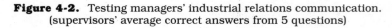

Figure 4-2. Testing managers' industrial relations communication. (supervisors' average correct answers from 5 questions)

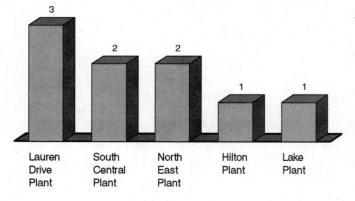

No Managers Believe They Are Poor Communicators

Managers do not say:

> My people are pretty much in the dark; I don't listen to their problems and rarely tell them about upcoming changes. I need to work on this.

Instead they say:

> They realize my door is always open.
> I've been in their shoes; I understand their problems.
> My ear's to the ground. I don't get out there as often as I should, but when it matters, it happens.

However, interviewing their subordinates, first-line supervisors, does not confirm the managers' down-home, folksy, it-happens assurances.

Instead, supervisors relate example after example of frustration and embarrassment. Neither listened to nor informed of major changes. Where their usual response to frontline questions is: "I don't know."

Making these stories of frustration and embarrassment even more poignant is the fact that supervisors generally like their managers. Confirming our experience, Lester Bittle and Jackson Ramsey's research involving 6000 supervisors found 63 percent of supervisors said their boss was "one of the better things about my job."[4]

Complaints of poor communication are not simply symptoms of poor interpersonal relationships. Take the complaints for exactly what they are: desperate pleas to be included, listened to, and told what's going on. And perhaps more than anything, to be saved the embarrassment of admitting to their own subordinates, the frontline employees, that they are not connected and have no influence.

Supervisors don't know what's going on, and this has not escaped the attention of frontline employees. In the United States only 57 percent of frontline employees believe their supervisors are well informed.[5]

Once the supervisor is perceived as lacking information and therefore power—it's over. Improving customer service, quality, cutting costs, adopting new technology, merging operations, all require changing employees. Changing employees requires a strong supervisor.

Managers need to take off their warm blanket of self-approval and have a hard look at their communication competence. If they do, they'll see subordinates do not agree with their rosy assessments. Evidence for this is shown in Fig. 4-3.[6]

Figure 4-3. Managers see fewer problems. *(Source: Ref. 6.)*

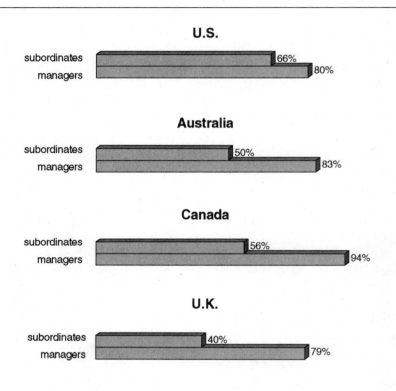

The company keeps employees well informed;
asks about employee problems; recognizes good work.
(% answering favorably)

Using the chart in Fig. 4-3 to compare communication in different countries is dodgy. These studies asked slightly different questions, to different sorts of samples, on different scales. But one conclusion is inescapable: Managers grossly overestimate the quality of their communication.

With a more precise design, James Larson and his colleagues researched 360 matched pairs of managers and subordinates in 50 organizations.[7] Larson asked the manager and one of the manager's real-life subordinates to evaluate the quality of the manager's feedback. The correlation was .17 (where 0 = no relationship and 1 = a perfect relationship). According to this study, what a manager thinks about the quality of her or his communication doesn't mean anything. The manager's opinion tells us almost nothing about what her or his subordinates think of this feedback.

Judi Brownell researched how well managers listen.[8] Brownell asked 144 managers in six hospitality organizations to rate their own listening ability. Brownell then collected about 6 subordinates for each manager and asked them to rate their manager's listening ability. Zeroing in on the bottom 25 percent of managers (managers whose subordinates had given them a score of 4.3 or less on a 7-point scale), Brownell found 94 percent of these bottom-scoring managers rated themselves at the top of the scale as good or very good listeners.

Emerging from this research is a clearer view of why it is so hard to change communication behavior: Because no one really thinks they have a problem. Of course, there are communication screw-ups where managers admit they didn't have enough time to communicate, or the change happened too quickly, or the communication job was delegated to someone who forgot. But all these communication accidents don't add up to—I'm a poor communicator.

Thus the futility of training, videos, lectures, posters encouraging managers to improve communication. It's not relevant—they don't have a communication problem. No manager believes he or she is a poor communicator. And they are never going to until there is an objective test.

Supervisor Evaluation of Manager Communication

Here is the experience of a manufacturing company attempting to improve middle management communication by asking supervisors for an evaluation of their managers' communication.

The company has eight almost identical plants, each employing about 1000 employees. Within each plant the management structure is roughly the same (Fig. 4-4).

Each supervisor received a one-question questionnaire asking for an evaluation of his or her manager's communication (Fig. 4-5).

Supervisors remained anonymous, and results were returned directly to the consultants, so no one in the company handled the supervisors' questionnaires.

Figure 4-4. Plant organizational structure.

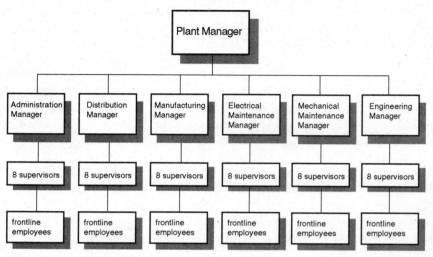

Figure 4-5. Sample questionnaire sent to all supervisors.

Please circle one number that best describes the quality of communication with your manager.

poor   excellent

1   2   3   4   5   6   7   8   9   10

comments

Results were published in a booklet, containing:

One bar chart showing the average score for each plant

Eight bar charts, one for each plant, showing the average score for each department manager at that plant

Supervisors' comments (Concerned that comments might identify particular supervisors, all comments were printed but aggregated by department, so, for example, comments about engineering managers at all eight plants were randomly shuffled and lumped together under the general title "Engineering Managers.")

The results booklet was distributed to all supervisors, department managers, plant managers, and the CEO. Figure 4-6 shows the first bar chart with the average score for each plant.

Also shown here is a sample of one of the eight bar charts, the one for the Grange Plant, with average scores for each department manager (Fig. 4-7).

The CEO made it clear that low-scoring managers were not to be scolded or punished. What he wanted was improvement. Praise and blame would be reserved for six months later when the evaluation would be repeated. Then emphasis would be placed on improvement, from low scorers as well as high scorers.

Two weeks after publishing the results, 100 randomly selected supervisors were phoned and asked for their assessment of effects.

Figure 4-6. Communication evaluation: Average scores by plant.

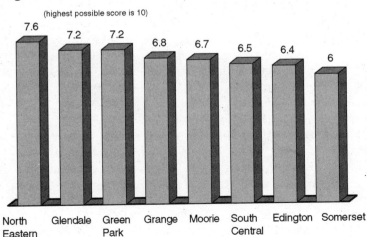

Figure 4-7. Communication at Grange plant: Average scores by department.

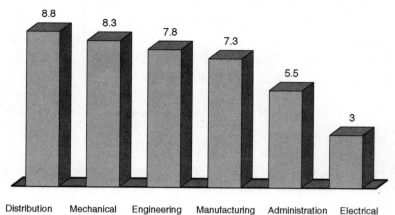

Seventy-three percent said communication had significantly improved. The most frequently mentioned effects, accounting for about 90 percent of mentioned changes, were:

1. Managers began having lunch almost everyday with supervisors.
2. Managers started daily rounds, checking in with supervisors, for a few minutes, asking about problems or questions.
3. Many managers began operating from a desk moved onto the shop floor rather than from their offices in the management suite.

And here we have something very important to say: These are exactly the right actions for improving communication to supervisors. Not one manager, among 48 of them, began a department newsletter, put up posters praising the virtues of communication, called in trainers to help with team building, asked supervisors to elect a representative to sit on a consultative committee, installed quality circles, a suggestion scheme—none of those contrivances.

These managers did immediately and precisely what it takes to improve communication: They increased face-to-face, frequent, informal communication.

Managers know how to improve communication with supervisors. They do not need training, manuals, or communication programs. They need pressure.

These results landed like a bomb. Never before had managers been evaluated by subordinates, and never had any evaluation been shared with so many employees. The CEO and supervisors thought the evaluation was great. However, the evaluation was not well received by department managers or plant managers. The primary criticism from department and plant managers was that the results booklet was shared with too many people. Department managers thought only department managers should see the results; plant managers thought only plant managers should see the results—none of these people thought results should have been shown to the CEO or supervisors. It was not so much the evaluation that angered them but sharing the results with superiors and subordinates.

The angry reaction was sufficiently intense for the eight plant managers to call a meeting and unanimously recommend to the CEO that the consultants never be hired again—even though 73 percent of *their* supervisors reported an immediate and significant improvement in communication. That this was a painful experience for many low-scoring managers is beyond doubt. That change of this magnitude could be achieved so immediately without widely sharing results is equally beyond doubt.

Xerox has conducted similar subordinate evaluations involving communication in one of its business groups.[9] The average improvement in a manager's score during the three years of the program was 3.4 percent.

Why did the manufacturing company in this example see a 73 percent improvement while Xerox was getting 3.4 percent? The Xerox evaluation results were shown only to the evaluated manager (not to the manager's boss or subordinates). Each manager received his or her average score, as given by subordinates and, for comparison purposes, an aggregated average score for all Xerox managers in the business group. No one, other than the evaluated manager, saw an individual score.

Reporting results privately does not create enough pressure to overcome a lifetime of poor communication habits.

Opponents accused the evaluation of embarrassing managers. We see it differently. The evaluation did not create more embarrassment. It merely shifted the embarrassment to more powerful and vocal people. Do you think not being listened to, or told about changes, is not embarrassing for supervisors?

> Hey, that new two-ton overhead crane is almost up. Didn't you tell them it's not big enough for our loads?

> There's a bunch of crates on the loading dock. Union rep says they're putting up a flexible manufacturing system here. Is that true?

> Those stems on the fasteners from that new supplier are an inch too long. I'm torching every one of them off. Can't you do something?

"They don't seem to listen to me." "I don't know anything about that." "The manager's too busy to see me." Don't these answers count as embarrassment? Or is it the case that, for an embarrassment to count, it must be felt by a manager?

A company's ability to change has become a requirement for survival. The changes that matter most involve the delivery of service or quality of production. But changing the behavior of frontline employees requires strong supervisors armed with good communication.

With plant closings and termination programs occurring everywhere, we ask if shifting embarrassment to often college educated, well paid, white collar workers, is not a price worth paying.

Everyone Is Looking Up

Edward Lawler, Lyman Porter, and Allen Tennenbaum examined the types of interactions managers find most rewarding.[10] Lawler and his colleagues asked 105 managers at five organizations to record all their face-to-face interactions. Managers were then asked to evaluate these interactions: Were they valuable, satisfying, interesting?

The highest-evaluated interactions were self-initiated contacts with a superior. The lowest evaluations went to other-initiated contacts with a subordinate. In other words, the face-to-face sessions managers put at the bottom involved subordinates coming to them with questions or comments.

In direct opposition to what managers typically say, where they most want to be is in the boardroom with the other suits and ties. Perhaps naturally, they want to be included with the brass—not pestered by first-line supervisors.

Contempt for these managers is inappropriate. Looking up is a way of life in large organizations. The evidence is clear: Seventy-five percent of senior managers believe the company listens to their ideas, only 40 percent of supervisors think so. And worse, only 35 percent of supervisors believe the company acts on their ideas and suggestions, according to research by Towers Perrin.[11] A transmission check or a supervisor evaluation of manager communication is a powerful step to redirecting the attention of managers back down to the front line, where our services are delivered and products made.

References

1. Julie Foehrenbach and Steve Goldfarb, "Employee Communication in the 90s," *Communication World*, May/June 1990.

2. Jules Harcourt, Virginia Richerson, and Mark J. Wattier, "A National Study of Managers' Assessment of Organization Communication Quality," *Journal of Business Communication*, vol. 28, fall 1991, pp. 348–365.

3. James Suchan and Clyde Scott, "Unclear Contract Language and Its Effect on Corporate Culture," *Business Horizons*, January–February 1986, pp. 20–25.

4. Bittle and Ramsey, op. cit., p. 31.

5. Foehrenbach and Goldfarb, op. cit., p. 3.

6. Manager and subordinate agreement chart (Fig. 4-3): U.K. data from *Working Together: The Way Ahead: Workplace Communication and Employee Involvement in Yorkshire and Humberside*, a joint TUC, CBI, and ACAS exercise, March 1986, pp. 1–16; Canadian data from David A. Peach and R. Dale Oliver, "Employees and Managers—Seeing Things Differently," *Business Quarterly*, fall 1985, pp. 39–43; Australian data from Verena Marshall and Ron Cacioppe, "A Survey of Differences in Communication between Managers and Subordinates," *Leadership & Organization Development Journal*, vol. 7, no. 5, 1986, pp. 17–25; U.S. data from Foehrenbach and Goldfarb, op. cit., p. 3.

7. James R. Larson, Mary Ann Glynn, C. Patrick Fleenor, and M. Peter Scontrino, "Exploring the Dimensionality of Managers' Performance Feedback to Subordinates," *Human Relations*, vol. 39, no. 12, December 1986, pp. 1083–1102.

8. Judi Brownell, "Perceptions of Effective Listeners: A Management Study," *The Journal of Business Communication*, vol. 27, no. 4, fall 1990, pp. 401–415.

9. Xerox evaluation results reported in Norman Deets, and Richard Morano: "Xerox's Strategy for Changing Management Styles," *Management Review*, vol. 75, no. 3, March 1986, pp. 31–35.

10. Edward E. Lawler III, Lyman W. Porter, and Allen Tennenbaum, "Managers' Attitudes Toward Interaction Episodes," *Journal of Applied Psychology*, vol. 52, no. 6, 1968, pp. 432–439.

11. Towers Perrin research quoted in Alvie L. Smith, "Getting Managers Off Their Butts and Into the Communication Game," *Communication World*, January 1992, p. 32–37.

5
Communicating Customer Service

They are on their way back from the mountain resort. The CEO and executive committee locked themselves in for a week. Now they're coming back, and they have a new idea: *Commitment to Customers*.

A specially constituted task force composed of employees from all organizational levels will drive the campaign. The task force will visit top-performing customer service companies, for example, American Express, Disney, Nordstrom, Dell Computers, and Delta Air Lines. Then they will hold focus-group discussions with the company's customers; followed by talks with employee groups discovering barriers to service. And finally the report: *Recommendations from the Commitment to Customers Task Force*.

One of these recommendations is to make customer service a top communication priority. Usually this involves demonstrating senior management commitment through mission statements, company newspaper articles, a massive customer service training program—all accented with logos, posters, pins, and videos.

This communication will not work.

It is critical to remember the communication theory described in the introduction: *receiver orientation*. For communication to succeed, it must be grounded in the values of the receivers. All the communication described above will be received very positively by the people who went to the mountain. The people who deliver the service will see it as one massive piece of hypocrisy.

Put yourself in the receiver's shoes. Imagine you are the manager at a branch of a large bank. (Here the term *branch manager* is being used in the same sense as first-line supervisor). Task force representatives are coming to your branch to talk with you and your staff about ideas for improving customer service. Many of these are the same head office people who, in the last six months, have:

Reduced the number of tellers at your branch by a third

Eliminated a policy of replacing absent tellers with relievers

Ran full-page newspaper ads announcing the new Visa Business Card, when your branch had never heard of it, had never seen one, had no brochures nor applications, can't answer customer questions, and there's nothing in the product manual

Just issued a new company telephone book so out of date that bunches of people listed had retired years ago

Apparently contracted out branch cleaning because for two weeks now complete strangers carrying mops are showing up each evening with permission-to-enter forms signed by head office managers

The people who've spent the last six weeks traveling the country, going to Disney World, having lunch with AMEX executives, flying Delta, and shopping at Nordstrom are coming with their new idea. From the people who never actually serve a customer, their latest and greatest idea: *Commitment to Customers.*

The view of the Commitment to Customer campaign is dramatically different looking up from the bottom, than down from the top.

Our experience, interviewing branch managers and tellers, has revealed a very consistent picture. Branches see themselves as small outposts, understaffed, underfunded, struggling to serve customers. Whose largest obstacle is a fat, egocentric, out-of-touch head office.

There is not much research into the relationship between branch managers and their bank head office, but an interesting study was conducted by Rita Martenson at the University of Gothenburg in Sweden.[1] She asked 53 Swedish branch managers to describe the relationship with their head office. Seventy-one percent of these branch managers said their relationship with head office was clearly negative or neutral or that they preferred not to comment, probably because they were too afraid to say anything (Fig. 5-1).

The largest barrier to communicating customer service is the perceived hypocrisy of it all. The people with big offices and big salaries providing pathetic service are now demanding superlative service from those with little offices and little salaries. The branch managers have little reason to begin back flips upon hearing that the customer service task force is coming to town.

Figure 5-1. Branch managers describe relationship with head office.
(Source: Ref. 1.)

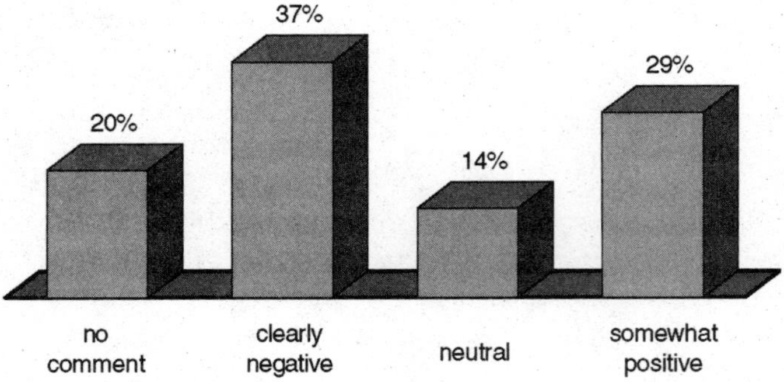

```
    37%

20%                              29%

              14%


no        clearly              somewhat
comment   negative   neutral   positive
```

Communicating *Commitment to Customers* isn't going to work. It isn't going to change behavior.

Improving Head Office Customer Service

Improved customer service should start with the people who went to the mountain. Head office should commit itself to improving its service to branches.

Perhaps the smartest, most ignored words in the management literature come from Karl Albrecht and Ron Zemke, in their book *Service America*: "If you're not serving the customer, you'd better be serving someone who is."[2] It would be hard to find wisdom less practiced. Begin communicating your customer service here: Communicate the quality of head office customer service to your branches.

The example we're about to show is from a banking client. Taking a couple of weeks, operating costs close to zero, the communication immediately improved head office customer service and prepared the ground for eventually improving service to the bank's external customers. For a description of this second part, communication improving service to external customers, see Chap. 20.

Three steps were involved: measuring the quality of head office service, reporting the results, and repeating the measure.

First, head office service was measured by asking branch managers to anonymously give quality scores to head office departments on a one-page questionnaire (Fig. 5-2).

In addition to the questionnaire, 50 branch managers were interviewed providing their opinions of head office service, with the usual

Figure 5-2. Evaluation form completed by branch managers.

Head Office Department	Quality of Service 10 = excellent 1 = poor
Accounting	
Branch Maintenance	
Corporate Finance	
Credit Cards	
Information Systems	
International	
Marketing	
Personnel	
Public Affairs	
Small Business	
Treasury	

qualification that anything they said would be repeated but under no circumstances attributed to specific individuals.

Second, the questionnaire results were reported to the CEO, all branch managers, and head office department heads (Fig. 5-3).

Included with this bar chart of questionnaire results was a *Head Office Service* news sheet. This news sheet gave the results from the interviews and provided the reasons behind the evaluation scores (Fig. 5-4).

The third step involved repeating the questionnaire six weeks after its first administration. This second evaluation brought an average score of 6.9, showing a 25 percent improvement in head office service in six weeks.

Figure 5-3. Head office customer service evaluation by branch managers.

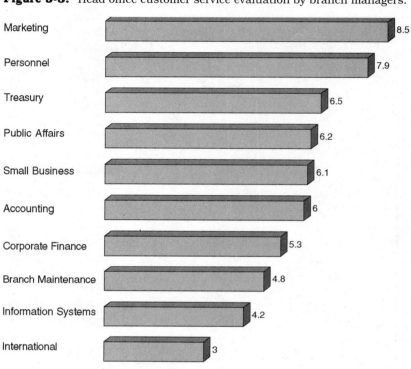

Communicating results such as the bar chart in Fig. 5-3 makes things happen. Senior managers, heading up large departments, don't want to see their department at the bottom of any list. Especially one representing the CEO's top concern, customer service, and especially regarding an activity, customer service, over which managers do have control. A poor financial performance in the Credit Cards Department might result from economic conditions such as high unemployment and interest rates; but when your dismal performance results from the refusal of your people to answer telephone calls—that's your fault. Everybody understands that.

This communication works. Every call to Credit Cards is being answered within three rings; Information Systems (IS) decided to turn some employees into client reps, so any question or problem at a branch would go through the one IS contact; International decided that every

Figure 5-4. Head office service newsletter.

CEO Promises Head Office Will Do Better

-------- -- ---- --- ---   ----- -- ------- ------- ------   ------- --------- -- ---
-------- -- ---- --- ---   ----- -- ------- ------- ------   ------- --------- -- ---
-------- -- ---- --- ---   ----- -- ------- ------- ------   ------- --------- -- ---
-------- -- ---- --- ---   ----- -- ------- ------- ------   ------- --------- -- ---

Marketing Reps. Visiting Branches -
Reason for Top Score

-------- -- ---- --- ---   ----- -- ------- ------- ---
-------- -- ---- --- ---   ----- -- ------- ------- ---
-------- -- ---- --- ---   ----- -- ------- ------- ---
-------- -- ---- --- ---   ----- -- ------- ------- ---

Refusing to Answer Telephones Puts Credit Cards on Bottom

-------- -- ---- --- ---
----- -- ------- ------
------- -------- -- -----
--- --- ----- -- -------
-------- ------

-------- -- ---- --- ---
----- -- ------- -------
------- -------- -- ---
--- --- ----- -- -------

Personnel Scores High,
New Staff Wardrobe is Well Received

-------- -- ---- --- ---   ----- -- ------- ------- ---
-------- -- ---- --- ---   ----- -- ------- ------- ---
-------- -- ---- --- ---   ----- -- ------- ------- ---
-------- -- ---- --- ---   ----- -- ------- ------- ---
----- ---- ---- -----   -- --- ----- ------ --------

Claiming "Elitist Attitude" Managers Downgrade International

-------- -- ---- --- ---   ----- -- ------- ------- ------   ------- --------- -- ---
-------- -- ---- --- ---   ----- -- ------- ------- ------   ------- --------- -- ---
-------- -- ---- --- ---   ----- -- ------- ------- ------   ------- --------- -- ---

manager would spend one day a quarter working at a major branch selling international products over the counter; Branch Maintenance would require the owners of the cleaning businesses to pass an interview with the branch manager before being awarded a contract. And many other changes were made, all within a couple of weeks of publishing the evaluation. Changes that branch managers noticed, enough changes in their minds to raise the evaluation of head office service by 25 percent.

This communication is six pieces of paper. A one-page questionnaire, a one-page bar chart, and a four-page news sheet. No pins, buttons, posters, slogans, logos, videos, speech-making-touring CEO, and most of all no organized, cascading, team-building, brain-storming, talk fests, lead by charismatic, motivating, empowering facilitators. Cut all that out. It's only a pretense of communication. It's not real communication because it doesn't change behavior—it's just talk.

Pass This Test before Taking Customer Service to the Front Line

This chapter has not talked about communicating the importance of customer service to frontline employees, tellers, for example. Because the idea presented here must be mastered first: No customer service campaign will work until branch managers perceive that an effort is being made to improve service to them. Without this first step your branch manager, or first-line supervisor, will sabotage your efforts to improve service to customers. Communicating customer service is particularly difficult because of the blatant hypocrisy perceived in the message. Branch managers, the people who determine how tellers behave, don't think they get good customer service, and, until they do, no message will work.

Whether you are ready to begin communicating customer service to the front line depends on passing this test: Go to your branch managers and ask them what head office has done in the last couple of months to improve its service to the branches. If branch managers can't, off the top of their heads, list two or three actions, then you aren't ready. Your message will be received as hypocrisy, and branch managers behind your back, but in front of their staff, will trash it. Tellers will get the drift that this is one more goofy idea from the ivory tower. Your money, time, training, and communication will be wasted. There will be no behavior change.

Send a message that customer service begins in head office. Not by writing a silly mission statement hung on a wall somewhere. Instead, use the news sheet described in this chapter to run a picture of the General Manager International Department apologizing to branch managers for their score and their reputation of arrogance. Let the GM International explain how she's going to fix this problem by requiring all International managers to spend one day a quarter at major branches selling foreign drafts, letters of credit, forwards, telegraphic transfers, travelers checks, and the rest. A mission statement is a waste of time—

a GM International apologizing for a score of 3 on a 10-point scale is a clear message that the CEO really has made a commitment to customers. And the first customers to receive better treatment are the employees closest to the front line.

References

1. Rita Martenson, "Focus on the Retail Bank Market: Can You Trust Branch Managers' View of It?" *International Journal of Bank Marketing*, vol. 4, no. 4, 1986, pp. 23—38.
2. Karl Albrecht and Ron Zemke, *Service America! Doing Business in the New Economy*, Dow Jones-Irwin, Homewood, Ill., 1985, p. 106.

6
Communicating New Technology

We were in a coal preparation plant, where coal is separated from dirt, interviewing a supervisor, when an excited, hourly paid plant worker burst through the door: "There is a big semi out there and a bunch of people from Goodrich unloading tall piles of brightly colored rubber squares and heading toward the screen house. What the hell's going on?" The supervisor, looking flustered and embarrassed, replied, "I don't know."

Later, the plant manager told us he had purchased rubber-polyethylene screen panels replacing the old wire ones used to size coal into big and small chunks prior to the dirt separating treatments. Concerning the poor communication, he said, "Slipped through the cracks," but, he continued, "It will all come good because they'll love these new panels: quieter, longer lasting, and easier to replace."

This poor communication may severely limit the productivity gains from this investment. According to manufacturing experts Robert Hayes, Steven Wheelwright, and Kim Clark, often the biggest gains from capital investment come not from the thing bought but from the "learning" that occurs surrounding the thing.[1] What determines the level of productivity improvement is whether the people on the floor begin to study, experiment, and fine-tune the new machine or technology. And whether this new investment causes them to rethink the operation of other machines.

The contribution from the new screens depends on whether the supervisors experiment with different conveyor speeds for the feeding belts, aperture settings of feed trays, screen slope and vibration, and downstream effects on magnetite solutions in the separation tanks.

The supervisor in this example has two legitimate options: He can supervise the operation of the new screens, that is, replacing cracked or broken panels and periodically stopping the belts to remove coal stuck in panel holes. Or he can begin to study the new screens and surrounding operations. In one factory examined by Hayes, Wheelwright, and Clark, two-thirds of the productivity gain from capital investment came not from the machines purchased but from the subsequent "learning." The fine-tuning that occurred as a result of the investment.

But in this example, the supervisor's first experience with the new equipment was wrapped in shame and embarrassment. Yet another admission in front of his crew that he is not connected, is not involved in important decisions, and simply doesn't know what's going on. When exciting things happen, there's not too much reason to burst into the supervisor's office—he doesn't know. It is hard to imagine communication less inclined toward subsequent experimenting and learning.

The plant manager's failure to communicate is not an insignificant "slip through the crack" that "will all come good." Rather, his failure to communicate, following Hayes, may have limited the productivity gain from these new screens by as much as 66 percent.

Testing Your Communication of Capital Investments

Perhaps you need this chapter—perhaps you don't. Here is a test. Pick out two or three current capital investment applications submitted by plant managers to your senior executives. Walk onto the floor and ask supervisors if they know anything about these requested purchases.

Here is our experience using this test with a mining client.

At a meeting of the managers heading the various departments (mechanical, electrical, plant, engineering, production, and administration), we asked, "Do you usually get supervisors' advice before requesting new capital equipment." The answer: "It's informal, but it happens." The managers said all the right things about communicating with operating and maintenance supervisors and involving people in decision making.

The following day, the CEO gave us a dozen or so capital equipment applications waiting on his desk for approval, and we headed onto the floor to find supervisors who knew about these requested purchases.

Figure 6-1. Partial results: supervisor awareness of possible new equipment.

Requested Equipment	Number of Supervisors Knowing Anything About this Request
GEC 1172 High Voltage Circuit Breaker (used in draglines)	0
Gemco Auger Drill to be mounted on a Challenger Tractor	0
Grove RT760 Rough Terrain Crane	0
replacing Bostrum truck seats with Isenringhausen	1
Cat 785 rear dump truck	0

The mine has roughly 1000 employees, and each requested investment would affect approximately 15 to 20 production or maintenance supervisors. Figure 6-1 shows partial results.

We spoke with roughly 30 supervisors, any one of whom may have been affected by, say, 5 of these intended purchases. Out of a possible 150 yes answers ("yes, my manager told me about the possibility of buying that piece of equipment"), we found 4 yes answers. About 3 percent awareness of these capital equipment applications.

Returning to the department managers and sharing these results gave birth to a bizarre meeting where the managers explained that, in fact, they do communicate with supervisors concerning the purchase of new equipment, but the particular instances we examined were aberrant.

A sampling of the excuses is presented in Figure 6-2.

And now we are at the very heart of the problem. Deep down, managers believe they are communicating. In 10 years of communication consulting, not one manager has ever said he or she was a poor communicator. Not one. They admit to the occasional screw-up, but overall, everyone, without exception, believes they are basically good communicators. Even when you push their noses into it, as in the example

Figure 6-2. Managers' reasons for poor communication.

Equipment	Reasons
GEC 1172 High Voltage Circuit Breaker	that's a very technical piece of circuitry, I didn't think they could contribute much
Gemco Auger Drill to be mounted on Challenger Tractor	a fluke, the communication got lost, production thought maintenance did it, maintenance thought engineering did it, engineering thought production did it
Grove RT760 Rough Terrain Crane	not much different than the P&H lattice boom crane they use now - so no real reason to consult
replacing Bostrum truck seats with Isenringhausen	deadline for submission was 4 pm Friday, and I didn't see the money was available until 2 pm, so only had time to mention it to one supervisor
Cat 785 rear dump truck	that's a beaut truck and it's not a good idea to get their hopes up before receiving final approval

above, it can all be explained away as atypical aberrations from what is usually good communication.

In the face of countless everyday instances of poor communication, managers wrap themselves in a warm blanket of self-approval. These people are never going to change their communication behavior themselves because, deep down, they don't believe they have a communication problem.

Proposed solutions may take many different forms, but one characteristic is certain: It will be something forced onto protesting managers from above.

The Type of Communication Missing When Introducing New Technology

The failure to communicate with supervisors concerning new equipment and technology is causing the same problem over and over—not that the equipment or technology is wrong but that it is poorly configured for the company's particular people and working conditions. Eventually the machine or procedure can be made productive, but the failure to communicate greatly lengthens the time between introducing the change and its functioning at full potential.

When it comes to new equipment and technology, the managers-engineers believe the answers are in the data, not in the people. A meticulous study of the facts, equipment specifications, will eventually reveal the correct purchase.

From this perspective, communication is unnecessary, or something you do after the decision to persuade others of your wisdom. The only really necessary conversation is between the manager and the numbers.

This narrow allegiance to a single perspective blinds the managers to another equally important issue: the appropriateness of this equipment or technology for your particular situation and your particular people. The latter perspective obtainable only by speaking with the experts on this subject—the first-line supervisors.

A new front-end loader rolled into the maintenance yard. The maintenance supervisor, shocked to see it, walked around, looked underneath, and said, "Hoses hanging too low and not strong enough to take our high temperatures." For the next year that machine had 29 percent availability due mostly to broken and melted hoses.

New belly-dump trucks arrived to the complete surprise of production and maintenance supervisors, but after a two minute inspection, one maintenance supervisor, worried about the common lubrication tank, explained, "This truck is going to have cross-contamination problems. The design of the lube tank allows metal flecks from the brake system to be carried to the transmission, engine, hydraulics, and throughout the whole truck." It was one year before the new trucks were out of the workshops long enough to carry the tonnage of the old trucks they were meant to replace.

The failure to communicate with supervisors prior to purchasing means we are bringing new equipment and technology into our companies that are incompatible with our people and working conditions. Not necessarily that the purchase is wrong—simply not configured properly. This failure to communicate not only delays the return on the investment but at times endangers the people as well.

While interviewing a mobile electric drill operator at a large open-cut mine, we watched him take a plastic coffee spoon, break off the handle, pinch the scoop, and jam it into a recessed safety button which caused the drill to move forward on its tanklike tracks. This is a big drill, perhaps 10 meters long, that crawls forward until it's over a marker, drills a hole that is subsequently filled with explosives and blasted, enabling easier digging by the electric shovels. When we asked him why he sabotaged this obvious safety feature, he said, "I'm 5 foot 4 inches tall. I can't press that button, and still see beyond the control panel to the outside window. It's driving without looking or jamming the button."

If the drill hits a rock and knocks the operator down, it could crawl over a 10-meter bench or perhaps fall 80 meters into the mining pit. Safety inspectors, rummaging through the debris, will find the jammed safety button and attribute the accident's cause to operator error. But surely part of the blame rests with the managers who year after year after year purchased mobile drills with the same control panel problem.

And why do engineers fail to include these kinds of modifications in their specifications for desired equipment? Because this kind of information is only obtainable through discussions with those closest to the machine operation. No amount of studying the drill's specs could ever tell you that these control panels are inappropriately designed for short operators and would risk the lives of perhaps half of any possible female operators. You either have some long careful talks with your supervisors about how your operators are using your current equipment—or you don't know. It doesn't matter if your degree is from MIT, Cal Tech, Carnegie Mellon, or the moon; there is one and only one way to get that kind of information: talking to the people who know the front line.

Supporting our anecdotal evidence is a brilliant study by David Meister on how engineers design.[2] Meister collected 44 engineers (mechanical, electrical, and design) with an average of 15 years engineering experience each, and asked them to perform a design task.

Engineers, for example, were asked to design an air traffic control radar console. These designs were completed over 10 sessions. During each session, the researchers made themselves available to answer questions and provide additional information that might be requested.

What Meister found was an "obsession with hardware" and an almost total reluctance to "consider operator or human factors in making decisions fundamental to system configurations."

Shockingly, mechanical and electrical engineers did not ask a single question concerning the operator's use of the equipment (design engineers did only slightly better). Meister reports there were almost no questions involving:

Number of operators using the console

Skill level of operators

Training available for operators

Task structure (where the task fit in terms of other functions and operations)

Task duration (estimate of time required to perform a task)

Task criticality (consequence of a task's being performed incorrectly or not at all)

The engineers didn't ask questions about the people or the task. They concerned themselves almost solely with laying out what goes where. And when faced with an issue absolutely requiring information about an operator, they had a little talk with themselves. Meister explains that, when an engineer faces a situation where human factors are unavoidable, "He says to himself, in effect, 'If I were the operator, how would I prefer the design to be laid out?'"

Meister went on to show that the engineers disliked receiving advice, had little respect for information from people without engineering degrees, and were averse to information presented verbally (preferring graphs, pictures, and tables). None of this suggests that an engineer-manager is going to voluntarily collect the type of communication essential for the smooth implementation of new equipment or technology. In other words, these managers are not going to talk to and seriously consider the opinions of supervisors.

Permit us one final example, almost unbelievable, to help drive this point home.

Interviewing supervisors in an underground coal mine, we were present while they berated the judgment of the engineers up top. We offered a meager defense and were told, "Go over there and sit in the LHD." An LHD is a load-haul-dump vehicle used to carry coal from the face to a conveyor belt transporting coal to the surface. The vehicle is long but not tall so as to avoid scraping on the roof, and the seat is reclined at perhaps a 10-degree pitch.

Doing as we were told, we found it almost impossible to sit in the seat. Everyone underground must by law wear a lamp attached to a hard hat and a self-rescuer, a gas-cap-type device worn in an emergency. Both the lamp battery and self-rescuer are hooked on a wide leather belt worn around the waist. But there is no place for these attachments on the reclined seat. So the supervisors forced us to sit in the LHD and defend the engineers who bought this vehicle with the two metal containers, each liter-sized, jamming into our lower back. Upon getting up, they reminded us that we had been there minutes—their crews do eight-hour shifts like that.

Thinking this must be a one-off fluke, we were subsequently shocked to find a study of underground haulage vehicles by the Institute of Occupational Medicine, showing that almost no LHDs had seats accommodating the driver's battery and self-rescuer.[3]

For you see, when the engineer who bought this vehicle sat in the seat, on the surface, or in the supplier's showroom, he wasn't wearing a hard-hat lamp or self-rescuer. And therefore he didn't feel any problem. It's as simple as that. As Meister found in his research, upon confronting a human factor question, the engineer has a little talk, not with a real operator, but with himself: "Does this seat feel good to me? OK, I'll buy it."

It is impossible to overestimate the severity of this failure to communicate with those closest to the operation. The researcher J. Judeikis, studying 350 underground coal mine fatalities involving mobile face equipment, found 13 of those fatalities (or on average 3 deaths every two years) involved poorly designed seats.[4]

These examples result from a failure to communicate with supervisors. It is not so much that engineers-managers buy the wrong equipment or technology as that they don't demand modifications in the equipment to make it better suited to their particular operators, service crews, and conditions. You can't ask for changes required by people and situations you know nothing about.

And this is why management interview after management interview, like a broken record, ends up with, "I think our new equipment was the right decision, but it sure took longer than we expected before it was operating up to plan." In other words, once the inappropriately configured machine was eventually made right for our people and conditions, then we started to get some return on our investment. Our experience, and that of Hayes and Clark, suggests that time interval may be a year.[5]

Eventually, our supervisor at the coal preparation plant will forget about not having been told about the new screens, and his feelings of embarrassment in front of his crew will subside. After a while he may begin to treat the new screens with some personal ownership. Perhaps this will take six months, maybe a year. If the communication had been right, that ownership could have begun on day 1.

A system is required that will force engineer-managers to communicate with supervisors prior to purchasing new equipment and technology.

Supervisor Advice Forms As Part of Capital Investment Applications

Some CEOs are now requiring all capital equipment applications to include *supervisor advice forms*. For an example of a supervisor advice form, see Fig. 6-3.

The number of supervisor advice forms required depends on the cost of the proposed equipment or technology. Usually one form for every $50,000 up to $300,000; then one additional form for every additional $100,000. So a $300,000 purchase requires documented communication with 6 supervisors; a million dollar investment requires proof of communication with 13 supervisors.

Unless an application has the necessary number of supervisor advice forms, it will be rejected. And occasionally, senior managers call supervisors to verify their response and request elaboration.

The reaction from supervisors has been wildly enthusiastic. This has not been the case for engineer-managers. Take power from a manager and give it to a superior, and you get an unhappy manager—give it to a subordinate and you get an outraged manager.

The two major complaints from managers are: the burden of additional paperwork and degeneration into rule by committee.

First, paperwork. Have another look at that form. It requires a supervisor to sign his or her name and check one of three boxes. The typical capital equipment application, for our mining clients, on a half million dollar investment, is running 25 to 50 pages. Included are: justification, alternatives considered, quotation and specifications, condition report on equipment being replaced, return on investment with discounted present value analysis, and often more. In this context a half dozen signatures and checkmarks seem a small additional requirement.

Second, degeneration into rule by committee. This complaint is more serious. Here the CEO must make it clear: The requirement is communication, not agreement. Supervisors should not have veto power over capital investments. Their opinion is required, not their consent.

The Japanese, in our opinion, have hit the right relationship between communication and decision-making power. Comparing communica-

Figure 6-3. Supervisor advice form.

Supervisor Advice Form

supervisor _____

department _____

opinion (check one)

[ ]   do not purchase

[ ]   purchase with
               modifications

[ ]   purchase as
               described

supervisor recommended modifications

----

tion in Japanese and U.S. companies, Richard Pascale found the Japanese gather as much as three times more information from frontline sources before making important decisions. Three times more, that is, than U.S. managers.[6,7]

But Pascale, and other researchers such as David Plowman and Bill Ford, found the Japanese do not have more participative decision making.[8] The Japanese gather more frontline information, but in the end, the power to decide remains with the manager.

And this is all we are saying: Demand that managers communicate with first-line supervisors, but leave the power to decide in their hands.

If all the supervisors disagree, and the manager remains convinced, and it's a good application, approve it. The rejection by supervisors may be incorrect, the investment may still be a good one, but, when this happens, it flags a critical need for follow-up communication.

One of our clients ordered Komatsu dozers in the face of unanimous opposition by both production and maintenance supervisors. Among many of our clients there is enormous frontline allegiance to Caterpillar.

When all your supervisors reject a significant capital investment, that signals a crucial need for follow-up communication. In this case, a team of supervisors were taken to a neighboring mine using Komatsu dozers. There they spoke with very satisfied supervisors and had the opportunity to inspect and operate the Komatsu machines. In the following week, supervisors were gathered for presentations by Komatsu sales reps and technical specialists. Finally, management explained that because two nearby mines would be using their equipment, Komatsu had agreed to maintaining a local warehouse of most often needed replacement parts.

We don't recall any supervisors changing their minds. But their hostility to Komatsu was significantly weakened.

Some will call this pandering. But any experienced manager knows the power of these people to sabotage your performance. You don't want to get into a situation where, every time those Komatsu dozers are down for repairs, a smiling supervisor sees this as a vindication of his superior judgment.

Consider the alternative to this "pandering": New Komatsu dozers arriving on site, a complete surprise to everyone on the floor, supervisors flying into a rage, cursing the machines and management, screaming obscenities in front of operators and maintenance workers that the new dozers are [profanity deleted], that they will be "a [profanity deleted]" to operate and service, and that this is proof positive the manager doesn't "know [profanity deleted]" about earth-moving equipment. That little scene is not a good start for your multimillion dollar investment.

Supervisor advice forms and subsequent communication can stop that from happening.

Verbal Warnings Don't Work

Telling managers they should communicate with supervisors prior to introducing new equipment and technology will not work. They believe in their hearts they are communicating now.

The way engineer-managers make decisions is deeply rooted in their education and professional enculturation. No casual platitudes ("You know, Jim, you really should get more people involved in this decision") are going to make any difference. The barriers to communication are too entrenched for that.

Besides, most of these communication related platitudes are just plain wrong (Fig. 6-4).

CEOs shake their heads in dismay. Experience has taught them that introducing this new equipment and technology is not going to be easy. Instinctively they can feel the brewing disaster. Waiting to once again be the victim of poorly communicated change.

Figure 6-4. Platitudes are wrong.

Communication Platitude	Error
get everyone involved	don't get everyone involved, that's a wild free-for-all, get supervisors involved
make sure you talk with an operator	don't talk with any operators before speaking with supervisors
strive for consensus	that's ridiculous; supervisors are not engineers, most lacking the same professional commitment, they don't carry briefcases home at night filled with the professional literature, get their opinion not their permission

Our contribution here is to convince CEOs of the futility of verbal warnings. No amount of verbal cautioning ("Are you sure you've communicated these changes to frontline employees?") will make any difference. Any and all words will fail. Set up a system enforcing communication or give it up.

One such system is supervisor advice forms required of all major capital investment applications.

References

1. Robert H. Hayes, Steven C. Wheelwright, and Kim B. Clark, *Dynamic Manufacturing: Creating the Learning Organization*, Free Press, New York, 1988.

2. David Meister, *Human Factors: Theory and Practice*, The Bunker-Ramo Corporation, Wiley Interscience, 1971, especially Chap. 7, "The Engineer and the Human Factors."

3. Institute of Occupational Medicine, E. C. Kingsley, S. Mason, et al., *Investigation of Underground Haulage and Transport Systems*, December 1980, pp. 1–286. Cited in Elaine G. Aiken and Richard S. Fowkes, Pittsburgh Research Center, Internal Report 4656, *Human Factors in Mining: An Annotated Bibliography*, Bureau of Mines, Pittsburgh, Penn., September 1987, accession number 3016.

4. J. Judeikis (MSHA, Triadelphia, W. Va.), personal communication, 1980, cited in Mark S. Sanders and James M. Peay, *Human Factors in Mining*, Bureau of Mines Information Circular 9182, U.S. Department of the Interior, Chap. 6, "Design of Controls, Equipment, and Tools," pp. 55–81.

5. Robert H. Hayes and Kim B. Clark, "Why Some Factories Are More Productive Than Others," *Harvard Business Review*, September/October 1986, pp. 66–73.

6. Richard T. Pascale, "Zen and the Art of Management," *Harvard Business Review*, March–April 1978, pp. 153–162.

7. Richard T. Pascale, "Communication and Decision Making Across Cultures: Japanese and American Comparisons," *Administrative Science Quarterly*, vol. 23, 1978, pp. 91–110.

8. David Plowman and Bill Ford, "Employee Participation in Japan," in *Democracy and Control in the Workplace*, edited by Ed Davis and Russell Lansbury, Longman Cheshire, Melbourne, 1986, pp. 296–312.

7

Communicating a Downsizing

When eliminating a large number of jobs, our communication usually answers the wrong question. We are preoccupied with explaining "why." Instead, communication efforts should focus almost entirely on "Who goes?" and "How much will I get?"

Words about the world's being a more competitive place and that this is a time of constant change and about painful decisions made to secure a stronger future matter to no one, except the senior executives who write them. Terminated employees are never going to say, "I was really angry and hurt, but, after reading about how the world is a more competitive place, now I kind of understand why they had to do it."

Worse, all these words get in the way. In this atmosphere of fear and suspicion employees are desperate for particular information:

How many people are going?

What's the criteria for selecting them?

When do the terminations happen?

How much is the severance package?

Almost any other words are static.

Employees deserve to be told why, but limit this to one sentence. A fact. And consistently use this one sentence, over and over, whenever the question arises. Here are examples from three companies terminating employees.

This company is manufacturing LDPE plastic at a price 15 percent higher than our major competitors, ICI and Hoechst.

We have employed the same number of people since 1984 but now carry 23 percent fewer rail passengers.

Today the company pumps 57 percent less oil than in 1985.

Above everything else communicate the severance package. Publicly, employees sign up for the "I hate the company" attitude, but privately thoughts are on buying into a Pizza Hut franchise, owning a gas station, leasing a neighborhood pub. These employees are not desperate for management rationales and justifications but for facts about the severance benefits.

More employees want out than you imagine. In normal economic times, more than 80 percent of employees leaving their jobs do so voluntarily.[1] British Telecom offered a generous severance package hoping to coax 33,000 employees to leave voluntarily—45,000 raised their hands to go.[2] Many employees want to leave. Give them the information they need.

David Schweiger and Angelo Denisi did a superb study of employee communication in two merging Fortune 500 firms.[3] Schweiger and Denisi kept tract of questions asked by worried employees. In order of frequency, employee questions concerned:

1. Layoffs and severance benefits

2. Other benefits

3. Transfers

4. Integration plans

5. Compensation

6. Background information on the merger

Employees' last concern, background information, is what typically takes center stage in our communication. This preoccupation with justifying terminations and providing rationales is not what's needed. Employees want to know about the money.

Unfortunately, communicating benefits is something most companies do poorly.

Poor Benefits Communication

A large number of companies are unsure or believe their benefit communication is not working. Buck Consultants estimates as many as 43 percent of large companies have these worries.[4]

This insecurity is well founded. Olivia Mitchell has done a careful study of how much employees know about their pension plans.[5] Her research involved 637 employees working for 551 different U.S. companies. Mitchell's worrying results are presented in Fig. 7-1. Somewhere around 50 to 70 percent of employees fail to understand even the most basic facts of their pension plans. These results are for average employees. Results for frontline workers would be worse as Mitchell's data show lower scores for minorities, less-educated, and lower-income employees. Our communication of the big picture is no better than the details. Asking in very general terms, "Do you understand your pay and benefits programs?" less than 50 percent of U.K. employees said yes, according to IABC/TPF&C research.[6] Even though the cost of health care benefits per employee increased 80 percent between 1987 and 1991,[7] Hay Group researchers, Ronald Grey and Peter Gelfond, found employees are, in general, unaware that company-supplied benefits are an increasing cost to employers.[8]

Figure 7-1. Employee knowledge of pension plan. *(Source: Ref. 5.)*

number of employees with defined contribution, DC, pension plans - who knew they had DC plans	49%
knew their employers contribute money to their pension (DC sample only)	48%
knew the amount of employer contribution depends on the employee's salary (DC sample only)	29%
knew that both years of service and age were requirements for early retirement (DB, defined benefits, sample only)	32%
knew age at which early retirement is possible (DB sample only)	29%

When terminating large numbers of employees, what we most need to communicate, the severance package, is the sort of communication we do poorly. Two reasons explain this poor benefit communication: the failure to target supervisors and the lack of a simple how-to-do-it model.

Severance Communication Should Target Supervisors

When communicating a severance package, don't think about a document; think about the likely communication event. How are employees going to get this information?

Let's get this straight: Frontline employees are not going to take your carefully constructed document (perhaps something called *Employees' Guide to Severance Benefits*), read it, highlight the bits they don't understand, call the Human Resources Department with questions, and verify all this information with an independent financial counsellor. That's what managers would do, not the frontline employees.

A research group lead by Mark Peterson investigated where employees turn when faced with an unfamiliar problem.[9] Across all four countries studied (United States, United Kingdom, Japan, and Hong Kong), the results were nearly identical. When faced with a problem they can't solve, employees turn to (in order):

1. Supervisor's advice

2. Experienced coworker's advice

3. Unwritten company policy

4. Company-supplied manuals

Employees aren't going to turn to *Employees' Guide to Severance Benefits*—they're going to turn to their supervisor. Why should they turn to your document—rarely have they understood what you sent them before. And even thumbing the pages will quickly reveal legal and numerical content, thereby guaranteeing impenetrability.

The probability that your lawyers and accountants will write a document frontline employees can understand is not worth considering. Even the managing partners of the 105 largest accounting firms in the United States think accountants can't write. Research by Douglas Andrews and Norman Sigband shows 70 percent of these managing partners believe accountants fresh from university are incapable of clear writing.[10]

Among Fortune 500 vice presidents, 89 percent say communication coming across their desks lacks clarity; and 87 percent of these vice presidents say it lacks conciseness.[11] If Fortune 500 vice presidents are struggling with the company's written communication, what possible chance do frontline employees have?

It's impossible to overestimate the chasm between what we write and whom we write for. Have a look at three facts reported in The Conference Board study on *Literacy in the Work Force*[12]:

Up to 10 percent of American workers are either functionally illiterate or, just, marginally literate.

One out of five young adults, 21 to 25 years old, cannot locate gross pay on a weekly pay stub.

More than half of participating companies in a government study said their employees were unable to use fractions and decimals in mathematical computations.

These people could not, and are not, going to sit down with a calculator and financial dictionary and work their way through the *Employees' Guide to Severance Benefits*.

Nor are they going to call the Human Resources Department with questions. It is unnatural for people to seek advice from those of whom they are most afraid and suspicious. Remember, this is a large termination program, not a topic where Personnel is seen as an innocent bystander.

In this stressful time, employees will turn to the authority they most know and trust, their supervisors.

Our primary communication goal must be equipping supervisors with a basic understanding of how the termination program will work and a few essential facts underlying the severance package.

And, more then anything, our communication must give supervisors confidence. Enough confidence for them to stop the preposterous rumors that will inevitably run wild on the front line:

Plant manager in fabrication said it was OK for Tom to stay with the company but give his severance pay to Mary, so she's leaving with double severance.

They got a list of all the people who have cost the company a lot in medical benefits, and all them are going to be fired first.

These may be laughable. But it's not funny on the front line. In the high drama of plant closing and terminations, these rumors play havoc with people's lives and productivity. In addition to giving supervisors facts, we must give them confidence. The confidence to say, "Don't be ridiculous. This is how terminated employees are going to be selected...."

Supervisors must be our number 1 communication priority. No matter what we do, the supervisor will be at the center of the communication. Employees will put them there. If you want to successfully communicate a large termination program, there is no alternative to targeting supervisors.

Model for Communicating a Downsizing

A simple model for communicating a termination program to supervisors is described in these four sections: (1) how to say it, (2) what to say, (3) handling supervisors' questions, and (4) testing supervisors' knowledge.

How to Say It

Break the message into discrete topics such as who will go, how much money will they get, termination timetable, and how to get more information.

For each topic arrange a seminar with a small group of supervisors (10 to 15) lead by a senior manager involved in the termination planning.

Produce a booklet, say, a dozen pages, for each topic. Use that booklet to guide the senior manager–supervisor seminars, encouraging supervisors to ask questions and write the answers in their own booklets.

The booklets should not look like anything your company has ever produced before. Here are some tips:

Ruthlessly eliminate every possible word.

Leave lots of empty white space.

Avoid sentences and punctuation.

Whenever possible, draw diagrams rather than words.

Put in only facts—nothing else.

Make the book 4 by 6 inches so it will fit in a supervisor's shirt pocket.

Use a plastic cover to resist grease and dirt.

And whatever you do, don't try to paint a positive picture:

~~In each and every case the company has tried its best to accommodate employee wishes in establishing...~~

~~We appreciate the efforts from all of you during the years to have made this such a successful company but in these times...~~

~~After careful consideration and a great deal of painful deliberation on the part of senior management, it is with regret...~~

Do not title the first booklet *Processes and Criteria for the Selection of Terminated Employees*; instead title it *Who Will Go*. This title is saying: This is not like anything we've ever sent you before—you're actually going to be able to understand this. Beginning with the title we are trying to give supervisors confidence. Confidence they can understand this important change.

Most senior and middle managers will neither like nor understand these booklets. Managers read, and these booklets cannot be read, in the traditional sense. They are not stand-alone documents. The booklets only make sense as aides to a conversation. But that is as it should be. Supervisors don't read. They receive information and give information verbally. The booklets are meant as guides to two conversations: (1) the seminar between senior managers and supervisors and more importantly (2) the inevitable discussions between supervisors and their crews:

> No way, you're not going to get all that money in cash. That figure there is your total pension amount, but the company is going to keep almost half that amount until you retire....See, have a look here at page 6 in this booklet...."

Finally, this information should be communicated in discrete chunks. Don't overload supervisors. Companies using these four topics—who will go; how much money will they get; termination timetable; and, how to get more information—usually do one topic a week, over a one-month period.

What to Say

The most important things to get right are the rules for determining who will be terminated and, most important, the severance package.

Look, for example, at a sample page from the booklet *Who Will Go* (Fig. 7-2).

What is most important here is the simplicity of the termination rules. The termination program must break down to a few simple rules. The company is reducing the work force by 1500 employees. First, the company will ask for early retirements, then ask for voluntary resignations,

Figure 7-2. Sample page from booklet *Who Will Go.*

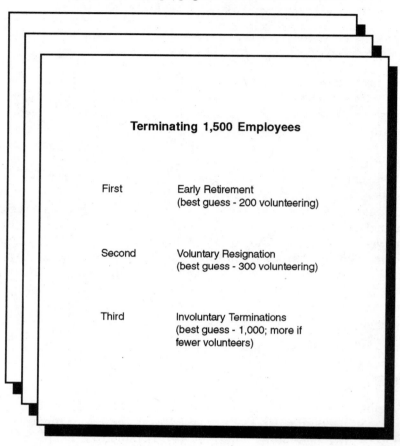

Terminating 1,500 Employees

First   Early Retirement
                         (best guess - 200 volunteering)

Second   Voluntary Resignation
                         (best guess - 300 volunteering)

Third   Involuntary Terminations
                         (best guess - 1,000; more if
                         fewer volunteers)

and then they will force out as many as it needs to hit the 1500 target. If the rules are too complicated to communicate clearly, don't try communicating something complicated—change the rules.

Another sample page from the booklet *Who Will Go* shows an explanation of the selection procedure for terminated employees (Fig. 7-3).

Again, if your termination rules are too difficult to explain in this style—change them. Communication is not something you think about after the policy is made. What is capable of being communicated must help shape the formulation of policy in the first place.

Three important studies have examined the best ways to communicate a downsizing.[13,14,15] All three arrive at the same critical conclusion:

Figure 7-3. Sample page from booklet *Who Will Go.*

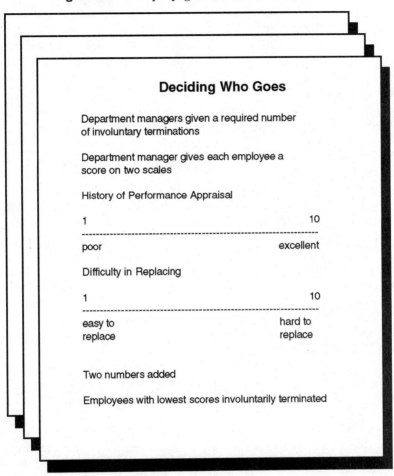

Deciding Who Goes

Department managers given a required number
of involuntary terminations

Department manager gives each employee a
score on two scales

History of Performance Appraisal

1   10
----
poor   excellent

Difficulty in Replacing

1   10
----
easy to   hard to
replace   replace

Two numbers added

Employees with lowest scores involuntarily terminated

The uncertainty surrounding terminations is more destructive to employees and the company than the actual terminations. The uncertainty creates more damage than the downsizing. This means communication can significantly lessen the pain from large-scale terminations. How? Make certain employees understand what's going on. Make clear and simple rules. And communicate them with the simplicity shown in these examples.

Communicating the severance package is perhaps the most difficult topic of all.

Usually the financial managers of the pension fund collaborate with the Human Resources Department producing a several-page document called *Personal Severance Benefits Statements*. These statements, given to each employee affected by the terminations, typically include personal financial information such as: pension benefits, unpaid leave benefit, and severance benefits.

Our experience with these documents is universally bad. They are designed for the convenience of the issuing company—meeting *their* need for standardization, computerization, and protection from litigation.

Communication doesn't get a thought.

Our attempts to sit down with the legal/financial people and revise these forms have been unsuccessful. Communication is not one of their priorities. Our solution has been to hire temporary workers, give them color highlighters, and set them to work highlighting different amounts on these statements in different colors. For example, employer contribution to pension balance is highlighted in red, employer-contributed severance benefit is highlighted in yellow, employee contribution to pension balance is highlighted in green, and so on.

When each employee receives his or her personal severance benefits statement, amounts are already highlighted. This technique allows us to abandon financial terminology. The key to deciphering the colors is described in the booklet. See, for example, the page from the booklet *How Much Will I Get?* (Fig. 7-4).

This is not a good time for near-panic frontline employees to become initiated with the intricacies of our financial lexicon. What they want to know is how much cash they can have. They cannot get on with their lives and their work until they know.

Often, the termination communication seems meant for the terminators. Preoccupied with self-serving justifications, using technical vocabulary only understood by senior managers, with bizarrely complicated rules meant to maximize managers' goals. This can backfire. The way you terminate can so damage the company that the anticipated benefits disappear. Surveying approximately 300 U.S. companies *downsizing* (terminating employees), Right Associates found 75 percent reported no improvement in financial performance; 66 percent reported no improvement in productivity.[16]

The way you terminate determines what you are to become: a confused rumor-filled mass of people uncertain what's happening to them or a company that knows what it's doing.

The two most important topics to communicate are who will go and how much will they get. Put your communication effort into these two topics.

Figure 7-4. Sample page from booklet *How Much Will I Get?*

Understanding the
Personal Severance Benefits Statement

Amount Highlighted in Red

you can't have any of this as cash

company keeps this until you retire

Amount Highlighted in Yellow

you can have some of this as cash

company takes tax out before you get it

most of us will lose about 35% of it to tax

Amount Highlighted in Green

you can have all this as cash

you already paid the tax on this

perhaps you should put this money in an IRA
(see page 10)

Handling Supervisors' Questions

In addition to the senior manager–supervisor seminars, it is often good to establish a supervisor-dedicated telephone hot line:

Hire a small outside consulting firm with downsizing experience to answer the calls.

Consultants act as go-betweens, taking the supervisors' questions to company managers for answers.

Consultants return supervisors' calls explaining the answers.

Hot line operates 9 a.m. to 9 p.m., seven days a week.

Supervisors remain anonymous.

On average, companies receive about one call each week from each supervisor involved with the terminations.

The hot line works because supervisors understand it's for them, it's anonymous, and it relies on verbal, as opposed to written, communication.

Testing Their Knowledge

There is no reason to believe that any of the preceding steps will work unless you also test supervisors' knowledge.

We recommend this format:

Booklets are distributed to supervisors on Friday.

Seminars for supervisors are conducted Monday morning, one hour before shift start-up; seminar concludes with a 20-question exam.

Exam is corrected immediately; any supervisor missing five or more questions is required to stay for an additional remedial session.

After the remedial session, these supervisors retake a similar exam.

This format is repeated each week with the introduction of each new topic: who will go; how much will they get; termination timetable; and how to get more information.

Figure 7-5 shows some typical questions with correct answers circled. If supervisors can't answer these questions, don't let them onto the floor. Employees are depending on them. No matter how good your communication, it means nothing without this test. It is the test that causes the learning.

Figure 7-5. Testing downsizing communication.

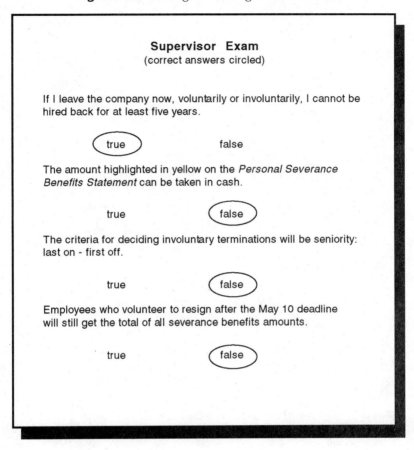

Supervisor Exam
(correct answers circled)

If I leave the company now, voluntarily or involuntarily, I cannot be
hired back for at least five years.

(**true**)   false

The amount highlighted in yellow on the *Personal Severance
Benefits Statement* can be taken in cash.

true   (**false**)

The criteria for deciding involuntary terminations will be seniority:
last on - first off.

true   (**false**)

Employees who volunteer to resign after the May 10 deadline
will still get the total of all severance benefits amounts.

true   (**false**)

Usually about 20 percent of supervisors fail the test. Only very rarely
does any supervisor fail the retest, and these individuals usually have a
learning or language problem requiring special attention.

We have a come a long way from aimlessly flinging words out of head
office, landing who knows where, affecting who knows whom. Here we
have targeted supervisors; written booklets specifically with supervisors in mind; conducted senior manager–supervisor seminars; run a
supervisor-dedicated telephone hot line; ascertained exactly how much
supervisors know; and finally made a stand—unless they know this
information, supervisors can't return to work. Terminating a large number of employees is too important to handle any other way.

References

1. Robert J. Samuelson, "Americans' Loyalty to Work," *Across The Board*, vol. 27, nos. 1 and 2, January/February 1990, pp. 9–10.

2. "Redundancies: Friendly Firing," *The Economist*, March 13, 1993, p.70.

3. David Schweiger and Angelo Denisi, "Communication With Employees Following a Merger: A Longitudinal Field Experiment," *Academy of Management Journal*, vol. 34, no. 1, 1991, pp. 110–135.

4. Buck Consultants, *Wall Street Journal*, July 26, 1988, p. 1.

5. Olivia S. Mitchell, "Worker Knowledge of Pension Provisions," *Journal of Labor Economics*, vol. 6, no. 1, 1988, pp. 21–39.

6. Foehrenbach and Rosenberg (IABC/TPF&C), op. cit., p. 11.

7. A. Foster Higgins & Co. quoted in M. Freudenheim, "I.B.M. Forms Company to Sell Employee-Benefit Services," *New York Times*, May 8, 1992, p. D5.

8. Ronald J. Grey and Peter A. Gelfond, "The People Side of Productivity: Responding to Changing Employee Values," *National Productivity Review*, vol. 9, no. 3, summer 1990, pp. 301–312.

9. Mark F. Peterson, Peter B. Smith, Michael H. Bond, and Jyuji Misumi, "Personal Reliance on Alternative Event-Management Processes in Four Countries," *Group & Organization Studies*, vol. 15, no. 1, March 1990, pp. 75–91.

10. J. Douglas Andrews and Norman B. Sigband, "How Effectively Does the 'New' Accountant Communicate? Perceptions by Practitioners and Academics," *The Journal of Business Communication*, vol. 21, no. 2, spring 1984, pp. 15–24.

11. James C. Bennett and Robert J. Olney, "Executive Priorities for Effective Communication in an Information Society," *The Journal of Business Communication*, vol. 23, no. 2, 1986, pp. 13–22.

12. The Conference Board, *Literacy in the Work Force*, by Leonard Lund and E. Patrick McGuire, Report #947, 1990.

13. Schweiger, op. cit.

14. Jeanette A. Davy, Angelo Kinicki, Christine Scheck, and John Kilroy, "Acquisitions Make Employees Worry: Companies Ease the Pain Through Effective Communication," *Personnel Administrator*, vol. 34, no. 8, August 1989, pp. 84–90.

15. David T. Bastien, "Common Patterns of Behavior and Communication in Corporate Mergers and Acquisitions," *Human Resource Management*, vol. 26, no. 1, spring 1987, pp. 17–33.

16. Right Associates survey reported in "Pink-Slip Productivity," *The Economist*, March 28, 1992, p. 79.

8

Communication Training Is Not the Answer

Our quality circle program failed. Reason: Supervisors couldn't let go, couldn't facilitate, didn't empower.

Team briefing meetings failed. Reason: Supervisors didn't include local-level information with the corporate stuff.

Mission statement flopped. "We Build Our Future Through Service to Customers, Fellow Employees, and Shareholders"—never took off. Reason: Supervisors were too cynical, didn't get on the band-wagon, lacked commitment and motivation.

CEO videos of half yearly financial results not getting through. Reason: Supervisors didn't show it, and, when they did, they refused to study the accompanying briefing sheet, so were unable to lead a reasonable group discussion.

All of this is wrong. Dead wrong. These communication programs fail because they violate the three facts of employee communication: They do not target supervisors as privileged receivers of information, they are not face to face, and they do not focus on performance in the local work area. The preceding failures have nothing to do with supervisors. It's the communication that needs fixing, not the receivers.

Thinking that supervisors are the problem leads to thinking training is the answer. If supervisors can be trained to empower, be participative rather than directive, conduct meetings, lead group discussions, make presentations, then it follows the preceding communication programs would succeed. No. If every supervisor in your company had a Ph.D. in communication, those programs would still fail. If your communication does not conform to the three facts of employee communication, it will fail—training won't make any difference.

Where Did Anyone Get the Idea Supervisors Don't Know How to Communicate?

We had just completed a guest lecture in an MBA class when a student approached and asked, "I would like to do communication training for supervisors in the mining industry. Do you have any advice?" We did. "Don't."

Let's take an example. It's 2 p.m., and head office calls urgently requesting an additional 50 tons. Mining these tons would take until 6 p.m., but the shift ends at 3 p.m., and the mine does not have forced overtime. In this situation, we asked the student how he would advise a supervisor to communicate with his or her crew?

Gather them in a group and ask for three hours' overtime?

Privately ask the king-pin worker, hoping he'll persuade the others?

Build a little coalition, asking only the workers you know probably want the money?

Request as a personal favor?

Promise a reward—knocking off early the next day?

Try ordering it?

Before we go any further, let's mention the implications. If you get it right, company gets the tons, and head office is pleased. However, if you get it wrong, no tons, and head office and customer are disappointed. But if your approach makes the crew angry, they will take the overtime but have a mechanical breakdown, so you'll pay for no tons. And, if they decide to teach you a lesson, they'll take the overtime, have a mechanical breakdown, and call a 24-hour strike the following day, citing "belligerent management attitude."

To our amazement, when confronted with this example, the MBA student looked unphased and began rambling on about Maslow's higherarchy of needs and the Hawthorn experiments. Stunned, we explained that social science, all of it, was irrelevant in the face of problems this practical. Switching track, the student said, "Well, then I'd offer to pitch in and help!" Great answer. With the possible exception of hiring scabs, there is nothing more heinous to a unionized work force then management attempting to get on the tools. That infringement can shut a mine down for weeks. And worse, could get you killed. A study reported in *Mine Safety and Health* showed that almost 70 percent of supervisor fatalities in underground coal mines occur when supervisors attempt nonsupervisory work.[1]

Where did anyone (including us at one time) get the idea supervisors don't know how to communicate with their people?

When supervisors are in our world, seated around a table in a carpeted conference room, you can deceive yourself that you can teach them how to communicate. But when in their world—on the floor of a steel mill, aluminum smelter, forms-processing area of an insurance company—it never crosses your mind to begin telling them how to talk to their own crew. Instinctively, you ask questions, try to stay out of the way, watch, and think not of changing but of assisting their communication. If that MBA student goes underground, they'll eat him alive. He has the wrong attitude. You interview supervisors to find out how the company can better communicate with them—not to tell them how to do their job.

And what is the right answer? Give a dozen experienced supervisors the problem laid out here, and you'll always get the same answer: "It depends on the crew." Supervisors will tell you, in their world, there are no general principles of communication (which is why social science can't function at this level of concreteness)—it all depends on the people. A supervisor with a new crew would probably tell head office he couldn't get the tons. When breaking in a new crew, there is too much to lose to risk a failure. Supervisors don't master general principles of communication; they learn something much more difficult, they learn particular crews. They learn to predict the behavior of unique collections of people. That over time many supervisors get better at this is undeniable; that they eventually end up with a catalog of proven communication rules is simply false.

When Is Communication Training Useful?

Companies have made large commitments to communication training for supervisors (Fig. 8-1).[2]

Figure 8-1. Percent of U.S. companies with supervisor training programs in communication. *(Source: Ref. 2.)*

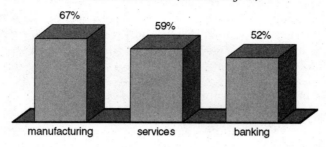

The question is: How much of this is worth having? If the training is meant to breathe life into communication programs that violate the three facts of employee communication, get rid of it.

There is no training that will enable companies to treat supervisors as if they were just any other employee, successfully use print or video, and get corporate values or financial information through to frontline employees. This training does not exist.

Communication training to resuscitate quality circles, employee participation programs, consultative committees, briefing meetings, videos, employee reports, and value campaigns is not worth having. The failure of these programs has nothing to do with supervisors' communication skills. You can teach them to speak like Billy Graham, facilitate like Henry Kissinger, and develop the sensitivity of Mother Theresa, and these programs will still not work. Your message will not reach frontline employees. Violations of the three facts of employee communication cannot be overcome through training.

This does not mean all communication training is a waste. There are at least two instances where communication training makes good sense.

First, training is effective where there is a change in the local work area beyond supervisors' usual experience. For example, beginning performance appraisal of frontline employees or starting a termination program. In these cases you train supervisors to handle one-on-one interactions, which may be new to them.

Second, communication training is worth keeping whenever supervisors say it is. We must begin treating supervisors not as remedials mucking up our grand communication programs but as experts in frontline communication. We watched as hundreds of supervisors in a large electrical utility boycotted a training course, *How to Communicate*

With Employees, launched in support of a companywide team-building program. Perhaps they thought they knew something about how to communicate with employees. How many Fortune 500 CEOs would attend training called *How to Run a Really Big Company*?

Acknowledging supervisors as experts in frontline communication does not mean training is unnecessary. Martina Navratilova takes tennis lessons. Rather, it means we stop treating supervisors as communication imbeciles responsible for the failure of our otherwise magnificent communication programs. If supervisors say some training is good, assume they know what they're talking about.

Training is neither the cause nor solution of our most frequent communication failures. The problem lies in our disregard for the three facts that underlie any successful attempt to communicate change to frontline employees.

Don't Train Poor Communicators

Suppose you have targeted a supervisor as a privileged receiver of information. Provided the supervisor with increased face-to-face information from middle management. Communicated the performance of the supervisor's local work area, as it compares with other similar areas. And still you find the supervisor is not communicating with his or her frontline workers. Don't look to training—look at a job reassignment. One not involving supervision.

Permit us a momentary sidetrack. Our expertise is employee communication, not corporate restructuring. But we do believe there are too many supervisors out there.

Building on statistics from the U.S. Bureau of Labor Statistics, David Gordon's research shows that in 1950 there were 12.5 supervisors for every 100 frontline employees; by 1985 that figure had grown to 14.4. On average, supervisors in private nonagricultural work are managing only 7 employees. Specifically in manufacturing, each supervisor is managing only 24 employees, about 5 fewer employees than they managed in 1950. Gordon says the ratio of supervisors to employees continues to rise into the 1990s.[3]

In our view, good supervisors are managing too few employees, poor supervisors too many. The solution is obvious.

As is so often the case, Peter Drucker urged this solution years ago.[4] Drucker recommended doubling or tripling the number of workers under each supervisor. With the cost savings, he suggested increasing the salary of remaining supervisors, and hiring clerical help so supervisors could spend less time on paperwork and more time with their crews. Then, Drucker says, supervisors would "manage" not "supervise."

If you adopt the three recommendations of this book and find supervisors are still not communicating, don't look to training—look to reassigning some of your supervisors.

References

1. K. Snyder, "Supervisor's Deaths Often Linked to Earlier Disruptions of Routine," *Mine Safety and Health*, vol. 9, 1984, pp. 2–13.

2. The Conference Board, *Employee Communications: New Top-Management Priority*, by Kathryn L. Troy, Research Report #919, 1988.

3. David M. Gordon, "Who Bosses Whom? The Intensity of Supervision and the Discipline of Labor," *American Economic Review*, vol. 80, no. 2, May 1990, pp. 28–32.

4. Peter F. Drucker, *The Practice of Management*, Harper & Row, New York, 1954, especially p. 327.

9

Making Supervisors Number One Priority

Roughly half the Fortune 500 companies have formal, written, communication policies.[1]
Here are some excerpts:

Communication is everyone's responsibility.

The uninhibited flow of pertinent and accurate information through all organizational levels is our highest communication objective.

Through communication we adapt to change and prepare for the challenges ahead.

What does any of this mean?
Does it mean communication is important? If so, it wasn't worth writing down. There are no studies where employees deny the importance of communication.
The emptiness of these words results from their failure to prioritize action. In the face of limited time and money, what do we do first? What is our most important communication task? Your communication policy should unequivocally answer that question: communicating with first-line supervisors.
Make a new communication policy that supervisors are the number one communication priority. Don't write it down, hang it on the wall, headline it in the company newspaper. That would decrease its credibility. Just do it.

But Shouldn't Communication
Treat Everyone Equally?

No. This is wrong. The best way to reach frontline employees, as we've shown, is through their supervisors. Communicating equally to everyone diminishes the relative power of supervisors, thereby weakening their effectiveness as a force for change.

The idea that communication should treat everyone equally is a deeply held belief in most companies and is supported by the similar belief that all employees should participate in decision making. If everyone should participate in decision making, it follows that everyone should have access to the necessary information.

Over the last 20 years, these hand-in-hand beliefs about involving everyone in communication and decision making have dominated our efforts to improve employee performance.

Quality circles, employee involvement, quality of work life, autonomous work groups, worker democracy, consultative committees, team building, empowering programs, all require greater employee participation and entail greater access to information.

This has been a terrible mistake. Or at the very least, these programs have greatly underperformed expectations. The U.S. General Accounting Office surveyed Fortune 500 service and Fortune 500 industrial companies finding that 80 percent had some sort of employee involvement program.[2] The GAO researchers concluded that companies were:

> doing these (employee involvement) things because they're popular or because they're nice, but they don't see them as necessary. They are not really seen as being vital and essential initiatives designed to impact the culture or the processes of the organization. They're not likely to be supported and they're not likely to be sustained and they're not likely to have much of an impact.

Why? Not because managers are power hungry and refuse to share their clout. But rather, we believe, because these programs are based on a false assumption: Increasing participation increases performance.

There is no clear evidence that getting everyone involved in decision making improves productivity. An extremely important study by Edwin Locke and David Schweiger examined the research involving participation in decision making and productivity.[3] Overall they didn't find a relationship (Fig. 9-1).

We (professors, consultants, and executives) went to supervisors and demanded greater subordinate participation. Putting up programs trying to force it. This was a mistake. What we should have demanded was

Figure 9-1. Effect of participation on productivity: results from 40 studies. *(Source: Ref. 3.)*

---

involving more people in   22% of studies
decisions improved productivity

involving more people in decisions   56% of studies
had no effect on productivity

involving more people in decisions   22% of studies
decreased productivity

---

not participation but performance. In 1954, Peter Drucker laid this out with crystal clarity.[4] Drucker warned us not to aim for job satisfaction, happiness, feelings of involvement, or any other attitude. He told us to demand that employees take responsibility for the performance of their work area.

Had we taken Drucker's advice, and therefore never begun the whole pack of programs just listed, we would have eventually evolved to the correct leadership style. Which is clearly not: Always use participation. But rather, use participation when it is the correct style given a particular situation.

In 1973, Victor Vroom and Phillip Yetton explained that leaders must use a variety of decision-making styles, participative to authoritarian, depending on the problem they face.[5] In choosing the correct style, Vroom and Yetton explained that leaders must take into account whether subordinates share organizational goals, whether subordinates have essential information the leader needs, whether an authoritative decision would be accepted, whether the problem can be broken into parts, and other concerns.

Had we followed Drucker and demanded performance, Vroom and Yetton's facts would have stared us in the face: Sometimes you get performance using participation, sometimes you get it using dominance. Instead, we set up programs, for example, quality circles, demanding participation in each and every case.

Hand in hand with this unquestioning use of participation went communication: If everyone should be participating, then everyone should be treated as a communication equal. In this atmosphere of participation it doesn't make any sense to treat supervisors as privileged receivers and senders of information.

Worse than just not getting the performance we desired, we made enemies of our supervisors. Janice Klein first opened our eyes to what was happening in her insightful paper, "Why Supervisors Resist Employee Involvement."[6] Klein found only 31 percent of supervisors felt their companies' employee involvement programs were good for supervisors. And lethal, from a communication point of view, 55 percent of supervisors felt these programs harmed their ability to deal with employees one on one.

While not improving performance, employee involvement programs did succeed in a related wrong-headed goal: They decreased the relative power of supervisors. By the time these employee involvement pro-

Figure 9-2. Supervisor's power. *(Source: Refs. 7, 8, and 9.)*

supervisors believe union reps have more power over local work area decisions than they do	Mitchell Fields and James Thacker
only 47% of employees in U.K. metal industries are clear as to who has authority to make decisions involving everyday operation	Frank Heller
only 40% of supervisors feel they are part of management	Lester Bittel and Jackson Ramsey

grams had run their course, no one really knew who was in control on the front line. Look, for example, at some facts cut from research examining supervisor power (Fig. 9-2).[7,8,9]

Decreasing the power of supervisors was the last thing we should have done for supervisors alone have the power to change frontline employees. Programs don't change workers—supervisors do. Weakening their power was like shooting ourselves in the foot.

Changing your communication policy, making supervisors the number 1 priority, will meet with opposition. The opponents will say it is wrong, perhaps morally so, to treat supervisors as privileged communication sources and receivers.

The thinking of these opponents is rooted in the values of equality and participation discussed above. These values make good sense in government but not as the central principle in companies. Companies are about performance.

References

1. William V. Ruch, *Corporate Communications*, Quorum, Westport, Conn., 1984, p. 118.

2. General Accounting Office study quoted in "Big Companies Take Baby Steps Toward Change," *Quality Digest*, vol. 8, no. 10, October 1988, pp. 64–70.

3. Edwin A. Locke and David M. Schweiger, "Participation in Decision-Making: One More Look," *Research in Organizational Behavior*, vol. 1, 1979, pp. 265–339.

4. Peter Drucker, *The Practice of Management*, Harper & Row, New York, 1954, especially Chap. 23, "Motivating to Peak Performance," pp. 302–311.

5. Victor Vroom and Phillip Yetton, *Leadership and Decision Making*, University of Pittsburgh Press, Pittsburgh, 1973.

6. Janice A. Klein, "Why Supervisors Resist Employee Involvement," *Harvard Business Review*, September–October, 1984, pp. 87–94.

7. Mitchell W. Fields and James W. Thacker, "Union Influence on Internal Organizational Decisions: An Empirical Analysis," *Journal of Applied Social Psychology*, vol. 21, no. 9, 1991, pp. 747–753.

8. Frank Heller, "Does Formal Policy or Law as Used in Europe Contribute to Improved Employee Information and Participation?" in *Employee Consultation and Information in Multinational Corporations*, edited by Jacques Vandamme, Croom Helm, London, 1986, pp. 69–92.

9. Bittle and Ramsey, op. cit., p. 36.

10

If It's Not Face-to-Face, It's Not Communication

Margaret, the supervisor, is counting stock,
approving a customer's personal check, or
making sure the "specials" show the new
advertised price. A clerk stops her, "Say,
Margaret, what's this I hear about..."

This is the moment that matters. Can Margaret answer the question? Because Margaret's ability to answer this question, and hundreds of others like it, determines her power among her subordinates. And it is this power you will draw on when attempting to change the behavior of her frontline employees.

Not seeing that the critical communication is face to face between supervisors and their subordinates, communication has become the production of stuff. Instead of preparing supervisors for face-to-face encounters, we crank out material: employee reports, company newspaper, videos, posters, news flash sheets. And when not making stuff, we hold events: CEO presentations, team briefing meetings, closed-circuit TV shows, two-way satellite transmissions.

The real purpose behind all this is communicating the corporate message. Making sure what the senior executives want to say gets out. The problem is that what the senior executives want to say doesn't matter.

Above everything else, communication should be about changing employees. And senior executive communication doesn't do that—only communication between a supervisor and employees has the power to change the way employees act.

Change the priorities. Put the corporate message at the bottom. Instead, dedicate our communication to making absolutely sure we have equipped Margaret, and her fellow supervisors, to answer questions, to know what's happening, and to guaranteeing that her advice is listened to and acted upon by middle managers. When communication does this right, it simultaneously makes an ally, and enhances the power, of the one person who can change our employees.

The right goal for communication is not making stuff or holding events but giving supervisors what they need to adequately perform the most critical communication any company has: informal, face-to-face, verbal* interactions between supervisors and their subordinates.

One of the largest and most respected corporate communication programs is at British Telecom.[1] A summary of BT's program is shown in Fig. 10-1.

In light of this broad-ranging communication effort, how do BT's employees evaluate their company's communication compared to the national average? For the answer, see Fig. 10-2.[2,3]

Why doesn't BT's extensive communication effort result in a higher employee evaluation? Because much of the BT program does not fall within the boundary of what employees consider "communication."

Australian Hugh Mackay interviewed frontline employees in 11 companies around Sydney, asking their opinion about their company's communication.[4] Mackay found that, when it came to evaluating communication, employees almost never think about the corporate-produced stuff. It doesn't even get weighed as one of the factors. What they think about, almost exclusively, is the adequacy of their face-to-face communication with their supervisors.

When BT's frontline employees are asked, "Are you fully or fairly well informed?" they don't think to themselves, "There was that superb video featuring BT International's work with fiber optic cables in Thailand" or "Must remember the 2000-word piece in *Telecom Today* explaining the creative use of floating-rate notes in raising funds for capital expenditures." Instead, as Mackay supports, they think about

---

*Technically, communication is divided into verbal, which includes writing and speaking, and nonverbal, which includes gestures, facial expressions, tone of voice, and other nonword elements. Throughout this book, however, we have chosen the more popular usage where verbal implies spoken, as opposed to written, communication.

Figure 10-1. British Telecom Communication Program. *(Source: Ref. 1.)*

Attitude Surveys	25,000 employees participate every 2 years
Team Briefing/Meetings	voluntary monthly meetings conducted by district managers reaching about 75% of all employees
"Speak-Up" Facility	free phone number for employee questions concerning company matters
"Open Line" Facility	recorded telephone information about national and local BT news
"Walking the Job"	program encouraging managers to become more visible
Videos	uses both outside consultants and in-house facilities
Publications	70 regular publications, including: *Telecom Today* (corporate newspaper) and targeted publications: *Prospect* (marketing & sales) and *Tone* (operator services)
Training	2,000 company trainers, communication skills for managers is a high priority
Direct Mail	yearly letter from managing director reporting company performance with a "thank you" to staff
Employee Communication Manual	produced by Employee Communication Unit stipulating managers' communication responsibilities
"New Idea"	suggestion scheme

Figure 10-2. Percent of employees who say they are fully or fairly well informed. *(Source: Refs. 2 and 3.)*

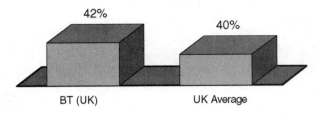

their regular, face-to-face, communication with their supervisor concerning issues in the local work area.

But only two of BT's 10 communication programs (team briefing meetings and "walking the job") even remotely touch on that critical face-to-face communication. In the eyes of frontline employees, most of these programs don't count as communication.

The point is not that BT or any other company should eliminate these programs. This communication often reaches middle and senior managers. Instead, we are saying these programs should never be the top communication priority. If your supervisors can't answer subordinates' questions about upcoming changes in the local work area—and your communication staff is busy making videos of the CEO—your priorities are upside down.

That these programs are, in fact, usually the top priority is not the fault of senior executives. It is their job to designate communication as an area needing improvement; it is the job of communication professionals to tell them how.

Many communication professionals (consultants, professors, and senior managers in human resources and public affairs) have been offering advice inconsistent with the facts. For years the research has shown face-to-face, verbal communication is the way to reach frontline employees. Look, for example, at the research conducted in the United States, United Kingdom, and Canada by the International Association of Business Communicators and TPF&C (Fig. 10-3).[5]

The widespread validity of this result is perhaps best illustrated by Hewlett-Packard. H-P employees are extremely well educated, and H-P's reputation ranks at the very top for print and video communication. Yet even here the preference for face-to-face communication with immediate managers drowns out even H-P's superlative stuff (Fig. 10-4).[6]

When Hewlett-Packard employees, having spent many years of education and entire professional careers, reading, say they want their infor-

Figure 10-3. How employees want their information. *(Source: Ref. 5.)*

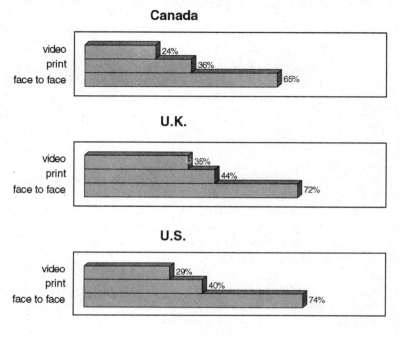

Canada

video 24%
print 36%
face to face 65%

U.K.

video 35%
print 44%
face to face 72%

U.S.

video 29%
print 40%
face to face 74%

Figure 10-4. How Hewlett-Packard employees want their information. *(Source: Ref. 6.)*

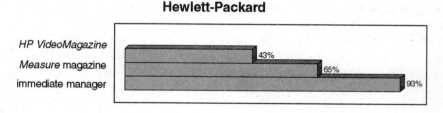

Hewlett-Packard

HP *VideoMagazine* 43%
Measure magazine 65%
immediate manager 93%

mation face to face, that should tell us something about the validity of this finding with truck drivers, bank tellers, store clerks, and miners. Most communication professionals, however, have turned a blind eye to the evidence showing a strong preference for face-to-face communication.

Eight major consultancies performing communication audits for large U.K. companies were interviewed by Anthony Booth.[7] When asked for typical recommendations given to clients, the list featured:

Employee annual reports

House newspaper

Team briefing meetings

Employee participation programs

Training managers in communication skills

None of these methods prepare supervisors for one-on-one, face-to-face communication with subordinates.

Worse still were the conclusions found by The Conference Board investigating consultants' recommendations for U.S. companies. Kathryn Troy, at The Conference Board, studied roughly 70 companies, finding the most frequent recommendation from their communication consultants were[8]:

Overhaul printed materials.

Create new communication vehicles, especially videos.

If the point is to use communication to change employees, these are bad recommendations.

If you're after improved quality or customer service, cutting costs, or implementing new technology, it would be hard to imagine anything more irrelevant than overhauling printed materials or making a video.

Even if your goal is the more ephemeral, improving morale or satisfaction, the evidence (Chaps. 1 and 2, see especially the "Pelz Effect") points not to printed material and videos but to making supervisors privileged receivers of information.

Communication is not a thing. Communication is an interaction. The goal is not to make things but to cause successful interactions. We need to equip supervisors to answer employees' questions and pressure middle managers into seeking supervisor's advice prior to making frontline changes. Communication must serve these interactions. Perhaps nothing physical is produced, or maybe something very inexpensive and puny (something that would not win an award at a communication convention). The real value is not something you hold in your hand but rather a strengthened relationship, a relationship that is a prerequisite for changing frontline employees.

Supervisor Briefing Cards

Even in cases where the primary purpose of the communication is to "inform" rather than to "change," the emphasis should still be on face-to-face communication.

One manufacturing company, a target in a dramatic and highly publicized hostile takeover, decided to make communication with frontline employees its top internal priority during the crisis. This decision was not so much a moral one, based on an obligation to tell employees what was happening, as a practical one, based on the desire to avoid drops in quality, falling behind in orders, increasing absenteeism, or worsening safety. In this situation what is the best way to reach frontline employees?

Begin by remembering the theory, receiver orientation, and ask the question: Under what circumstances will the receivers make themselves available for this information?

The most likely scenario is that a supervisor will pass by, and a frontline employee will ask: "Hey, what's the story with all this takeover business?"

This is the critical moment. The success or failure of communication hinges on what happens next: Can the supervisor answer the question? Because if she can, not only have we successfully reached the front line but we've helped fortify the supervisor as someone worth talking to.

To prepare supervisors for this question, the company decided on supervisor briefing cards: small cards, 3.5 by 5 inches, fitting in a shirt pocket, printed on both sides, and laminated.

Within 12 hours of a major development, the cards were printed (desktop-published), photocopied, laminated, and delivered by air express to 3000 supervisors around the country.

Six different supervisor briefing cards were made during the several weeks of drama. The front of the first one is shown in Fig. 10-5, and the back is shown in Fig. 10-6.

The intended audience was the thousands of frontline employees. But notice two points: First, they did not communicate directly to them, and second, they relied on face-to-face communication between the supervisors and frontline employees.

They targeted the employees most credible and desired source of information, their supervisors. And they assumed the best way to reach them was through an informal, one-on-one, verbal interaction.

These cards are not a story anyone reads but a guide for a spoken conversation:

> Hey, Betty, is it true Warmco bought this company last night?
> [She reaches into her pocket, pulls out the card, and answers.]
> No, they didn't buy it. They've just got 5 percent. They could sit there with that 5 percent for years, or they could buy more. No reason to be alarmed until they have 15 percent because that means they are going for the whole thing.
> Oh, OK, thanks."

Figure 10-5. (*Front*) Supervisor briefing card.

Supervisor Briefing Card No. 1

Warmco Positioning to Buy Our Company

Nothing is certain

If we wait for certainty - there won't be any communication

we guess a 25% chance Warmco will try to buy us

more information?
call for taped message 800-555-5555

That's it. It's over. That's all they want to know. If the above happens, the communication is 100 percent successful.

Of course, the company could have gathered employees into cafeterias around the country and addressed them through a 45-minute CEO video or live closed-circuit TV broadcast. This would have involved:

Using a less credible source

Over a medium employees don't prefer

Stopping work and gathering huge groups into crowded rooms, creating ideal conditions for breeding and spreading rumors

Providing information at a time when many employees did not specifically request it, thereby, limiting comprehension and retention

Publishing a special edition of the company newspaper would be as bad or worse: repeating the errors of using a less credible source and a medium employees don't prefer.

Figure 10-6. (*Back*) Supervisor briefing card.

> price?
> - rumors are Warmco will offer our shareholders $32 a share
> - current price is $28 a share
>
> *where would Warmco get the money to buy the shares?*
>
> - borrow the money from banks
>
> *how would Warmco repay the banks?*
>
> - try to run us with a bigger profit
> - probably break us up into pieces
> - selling some pieces to other companies to repay loans
>
> *what parts would Warmco sell?*
>
> - we don't know
>
> *when will we know what's going to happen?*
>
> - Warmco now owns 5% of our company
> - they can sit on these shares or buy more
> - Warmco has said that if it buys more than 15% it promises to go all the way and get control of the company

Frontline employees don't want to read a story—they only want a question answered. They are not going to leave their area, locate a copy of the company newspaper, find the article, and sift through a couple thousand words for the answer. In the midst of all the senior executive rambling—"This is the time to pull together as a team," "not taking our eye off the ball," "living in a time of dramatic change,"—the guts of what was happening would not have made it to the floor.

If a company decides not to equip supervisors for face-to-face communication with their subordinates, the vacuum will be filled by rumors. And this is exactly the case, as roughly 40 percent of employees in the United States, United Kingdom, and Canada report using rumors as a major source of information about the company.[9] You either supply the information the way they want it—face to face—or they'll go elsewhere for it.

This is not to say all print and video should be abolished or is a waste. These methods play a valuable role in reaching senior and middle management and a handful of particularly keen supervisors and frontline employees. Keep it. But never assume, because you wrote words down on paper and delivered them to the plant, that you've communicated. Everything we know about frontline employees says all you have done is transport paper.

Communication that reaches the front line will be transmitted by supervisors to their subordinates in informal, one-on-one, verbal interactions; usually in response to an employee-initiated question. Decide, at least on one particular issue (in this example, threat of a hostile takeover) to get this right. Make your first priority, and direct your resources to, making sure supervisors are prepared for face-to-face communication with their subordinates.

References

1. Industrial Relations Services, "BT (UK)'s Employee Communications Drive," *Industrial Relations Review and Report #449*, October 10, 1989, pp. 11–14.

2. BT (U.K.) Tracking Survey, results published in preceding article (Ref. 1) by the Industrial Relations Services.

3. International Survey Research, Limited, *The Rise and Fall of Employee Morale: Attitudes of UK Employees 1977–1990*, October 1990.

4. Mackay, op. cit.

5. "How Employees Want Their Information" (bar chart), U.K. and Canadian results derived from, Foehrenbach and Rosenberg IABC/TPF&C, op. cit.; U.S. results derived from Foehrenbach and Goldfarb, IABC/TPF&C, op. cit.

6. Whitworth, op. cit.

7. Anthony Booth, *Communications Audits: A UK Survey*, published by Taylor Graham on behalf of the Primary Communications Research Centre, University of Leicester, 1986.

8. Kathryn Troy, "Internal Communication Restructures for the '90s," *IABC Communication World*, February 1989, pp. 28–31.

9. See the IABC/TPF&C studies by Foehrenbach and Rosenberg, op. cit.; and Foehrenbach and Goldfarb, op. cit.

11
Video

[Snappy-jazzy music begins.]

[Camera 1 pans office, begins zoom.]

[CEO sitting on front edge of desk, jacket off, shirt sleeves rolled up.]

[CEO turns left to camera 2.]

The world is changing...new competitors are here to stay...no longer can we rest comfortably on our past successes...but if we work together as a team...for the challenges that lie ahead.

[Camera 1 pulls back.]

[Snappy-jazzy music again.]

[Camera 2 to company logo.]

Why would anyone do this? What's the point? What behavior is expected to change? Will frontline employees throw their caps in the air, storm the front of the cafeteria lifting the plant manager (as the living representative of the CEO) onto their shoulders and begin victory laps around the factory?

Or are the expectations more modest? Will forklift drivers do more lifts? Spot welders fewer rejects? Sales clerks more consciously restock the Levis? Bank tellers begin smiling and saying "good morning"?

Before we go to the research, use your own experience: How are frontline employees going to change as a result of a video where the CEO tells them the world is changing, and they need to pull together as a team? Or one telling them return on investment is running 5 percent, well below their industry average? Or that the company has dedicated itself to the three P's (people, profits, productivity)? And, if your answer is that there will be no change, then what are we doing? Hurling words into space?

At the same time as the U.S. employee video industry was increasing at about 25 percent a year, growing into approximately a $2.5 billion industry, where the average company producing videos was spending $287,000 on them,[1,2] employees everywhere were telling us they didn't want to see one.

U.S. employees ranked videos 11th out of 14 preferred methods of communication[3]; U.K. employees ranked videos 13th out of 16 communication methods.[4] Everywhere, face-to-face communication is preferred at a rate 2.5 times more than video.

In the United Kingdom, Touche Ross conducted research with a client's video highlighting the CEO's view of the company's future problems and solutions.[5] One thousand employees viewed the video in groups of 20. Following this viewing, employees completed a questionnaire asking if video was the most appropriate way to communicate this information. Only 19 percent said yes.

Most damning of all is the Australian research. Dennis Taylor's research, displayed in Fig. 11-1, reveals the depth of employee dislike of video.[6] This Australian preference for video, 0.5 percent, is considerably lower than the usual U.S. preference of about 30 percent. This is because Taylor's sample is almost exclusively clerical and blue-collar, his scale permits checking one method only, and his question focuses specifically on information relevant to the local work area. When it comes to changing the behavior of frontline employees, Taylor comes closest to asking the question the right way, and he finds 0.5 percent of employees prefer video.

Figure 11-1. Australian employees' preferred method of receiving information about their immediate work area. *(Source: Ref. 6.)*

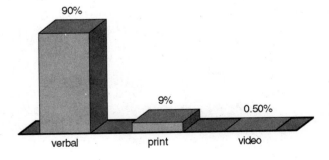

In the U.S., 43 percent of medium to large companies use video to communicate with their employees.[7] On this topic, perhaps more than any other, CEOs have received terrible advice from their communication consultants, both inside and outside the company. Vista Communications, the London based consultancy, asked British CEOs and senior executives if they felt videos were working, and 89 percent of the 402 in the sample said yes.[8] When asked what they based this positive assessment upon, the CEOs and senior executives, 51 percent, said they relied on feedback rising up through management layers. In other words, they are waiting for middle managers to write a letter saying the CEO's personal message on video was a horrible waste of time; the general manager of human resources's presentation was, say, incoherent and irrelevant; and the director of finance was, in general, not thought credible. Apparently hearing the truth about videos depends on middle managers committing hari-kari. Only 7 percent of CEOs and executives in the Vista study used employee surveys to determine the value of their videos. If they had, most would stop using them.

What's wrong with video? Everything. Videos use the wrong source (senior executives instead of supervisors), over the wrong medium (electronic instead of face to face), communicating the wrong topic (corporate not local work area issues). Violating all three facts of employee communication, the typical corporate video to employees has no chance of changing the way employees act. Videos, if existing at all, should be a bottom priority, not the fastest-growing communication technique.

Watch a Video with a Front-Line Audience

Go to the floor and watch the CEO video reporting the half-yearly financial results. Sit there among the steelworkers, truck drivers, insurance forms processors, mechanics, freight handlers, bank tellers, and cashiers. We have. Dozens of times. And observed one of two reactions: employees nearly catatonic, slumped into their chairs, eyes glazed over, motionless and silent—that's the good reaction. The other is a room full of cynical wisecracks, bursts of mocking laughter, where invariably the most jaded and bitter of employees wrestle control from the video figure and then dominate the mood and reaction of the others.

When lecturing to senior executive audiences, we frequently use a photograph of three teenage cooks sitting in the back room of a Domino's Pizza store watching a corporate video. The three teenagers, in their Domino's uniforms, hats and hair nets, are shown engaged and fascinated, eyes fixed on the corporate executive at the podium. Usually when this slide appears on the screen, our audiences spontaneously erupt into laughter. The contrived nature of this scene is so obvious it's funny. That three teenage pizza cooks would watch a corporate video with this much sincerity is instantly absurd. Yet this same audience has bought these videos to the tune of $2.5 billion.

The typical corporate video intended for frontline employees will at best do only a little harm, at worst, it will become a real headache.

GM intended to lessen support for increased wage demands by showing a film called *Road to Survival* which compared U.S. and Japanese auto industry labor costs. The union, UAW, said the film failed to show both sides of the story, leaving out the cost comparisons of U.S. and Japanese executives. The film was banned by the UAW, and GM decided against showing it.

Ford installed television sets around its plants in order to receive signals from its private TV satellite system, FCN, Ford Communication Network. In some locations, frontline employees were suspicious and thought perhaps cameras had been secretly concealed within the TVs and were spying on workers. They cut the cables.

If video were a powerful communication tool changing the behavior of large numbers of frontline employees, these isolated and admittedly rare incidents would be worth wearing. But it isn't a powerful tool. It's an expensive distraction from the communication that really matters, and as these examples show, it can provide headaches you just don't need.

One of videos supposed greatest strengths is often its most colossal screw-up. Video can transmit across vast distances. This means senior executives in Dallas, Saint Louis, and LA can deliver personal messages to frontline workers in England and Australia. And without a doubt, the worst audience reactions we have ever seen were in these kinds of situations. A confident, enthusiastic, upbeat presentation by a Dallas CEO can be easily heard as fantastically naive con-man babble to a frontline worker in Manchester or Sydney.

Here is the opening text from *Monday Morning Management*, a corporate TV program featuring the CEO of the large and successful A.L. Williams insurance company[9]:

Live from the Atlanta studies of ALW-TV, the Common Sense Network, it's *"Monday Morning Management!"*

[Enter the CEO/emcee, wearing a red sport shirt]

Good morning, everybody. My butt's on fire!

[Wild applause from studio audience]

We're not going to get fat and lazy like those other companies in America, right?

[Audience responds, "Right!"]

This ain't a dad-burned business—it's a dad-burned family. Right?

[Audience responds, "Right!"]

Even to Americans this sounds over the top. Our point is: To the British and Australians, almost all Americans sound like that. That's what they hear when all you think you're saying is, "We all need to pull together as a team," "We've overcome greater challenges in our long illustrious history," or "I know each and every one of you can call up the strength and spirit to revitalize this company." In their ear, its either embarrassingly naive or a condescending insult.

Did you think, because they spoke English, your message would necessarily carry the same meaning? As Americans hear sophistication in the English accent, romance in the French, and authoritarianism in the German, the British and Australians hear a cheerleader in ours. This message, the corporate pep talk, is not worth communicating, it won't change behavior, but, if you must and the audience is British or Australian, use print.

Video's Appropriate Use

Videos are effective under two conditions: first, communicating technical information with immediate application and, second, senior executives responding to a dramatic event of concern to all employees.

Videos work when the information is technical and application is immediate. One of our insurance clients made a video on split-dollar key-man life insurance. It was poorly scripted, badly lit and edited, and booked solid by agents dying to see it. As one agent left the room, we asked her to explain the video's popularity. She said, "The first group of agents to see this thing raised their personal income 20 percent."

The U.S. Postal Service has had a good experience communicating complex postal rate increases to 750,000 employees via its private TV satellite network. J.C. Penney has one of the United States' largest private television networks. Costing $7 million to install and $4 million yearly to operate, the network connects four studios in the Dallas headquarters to 725 Penney stores. A primary use is showing sample merchandise to managers in the stores who then place orders on a central computer. Only after managers' orders arrive does the head office buyer make a final commitment to suppliers. Penney says the TV network saves $10 million a year in travel and much more as a result of more effective buying.

When video is used this way, solving technical problems requiring immediate action, its effectiveness may even surpass face-to-face communication.

Researchers Daniel Rosetti and Theodore Surynt compared the effectiveness of video teleconferencing to face-to-face meetings.[10] The experiment involved 32 groups of 4 people. Half the groups met face to face and attempted to solve a complex problem (for example, a puzzle). The other half attempted to solve the same problem through video teleconferencing. Every individual had unique information, the sharing of which was essential to finding the solution. In 20 of the 32 groups (63 percent), video teleconferencing outperformed the face to face. Rosetti and Surynt suggest that the "cold" nature of video, typically considered a weakness, may actually be a strength, encouraging participants to get to work. They hypothesized that face-to-face meetings may allow "too much opportunity for interpersonal 'noise' and are perhaps too 'warm' for truly effective problem-solving."

A second condition under which video makes good sense occurs when a senior executive responds to a dramatic event with widespread employee interest.

October 19, 1987, the stock market crashed 508 points. Fifteen minutes after the close, Merrill Lynch's chief market analyst was on the air to 12,000 brokers in 479 offices around the country explaining the company's reaction: that the decline was overstated and there would be a snap back. Another emergency, a week later, put the Merrill executives back on air when a customer shot two brokers. In situations like this employees want to see and hear their leaders, and video rises to one of its most appropriate uses.

Methyl isocyanate (MIC), a lethal gas, leaked from Union Carbide's Bhopal, India, plant on December 3, 1984. More than 2000 people died, and tens of thousands of others were injured. In the year following this tragedy, the communication staff at Union Carbide's head office went from producing their typical 4 videos to 45. In a tragedy, leaders need to be visible, and in this situation video is irreplaceable. People outside the company expect employees to know something; husbands, wives, children, neighbors, friends, ask questions. The demand is there, and communication methods that usually don't reach employees now do.

The truth, however, is that the actual use of videos greatly overreaches these two conditions. The Conference Board surveyed 281 executives responsible for communication in their Fortune 500

manufacturing or Fortune 500 service companies.[11] Seventy percent
reported an increased use of video, 25 percent used videos monthly, and
64 percent said the major goal of these videos was improving employee
morale.

Except in dramatic events, such as the market crash or Bhopal disaster, videos have nothing to do with employee morale.

Communication researchers, Downs and Hazen, surveyed over 2000
employees in 26 U.S. companies asking them what communication-related issues affected their feelings of satisfaction.[12] Here are the top
five responses from frontline employees:

1. Supervisor trusts me.
2. Supervision given me is about right.
3. Work group is compatible.
4. Satisfaction with my job.
5. Supervisor is open to ideas.

Seeing corporate videos was not in the top 40; if the researchers had
asked, it wouldn't have appeared in the top 400. Claims that the regular
viewing of videos filled with pontificating senior executives improves
the day-to-day morale of frontline employees are totally unsustainable.

Blinded by Science

Video use increased from 300 companies in 1974 to 10,000 companies by
1988.[13] Most of this involves video cassettes. From the late eighties,
however, the action has been moving higher tech. Thirty-nine U.S. companies now operate private TV networks, enabling live broadcasts to
employees via satellite.[14] IBM, Ford, Federal Express, J.C. Penney,
Merrill Lynch, Domino's Pizza, all operate their own TV networks.

We've been this route before: assuming the solution is in the technology. Lester Thurow, at MIT, has written powerfully about management's failure to increase white-collar productivity even after massive
investments in computers throughout the 1980s.[15] For example, in banking, despite the computer revolution of the eighties, employment went
up faster than real output, and productivity actually fell. A vice president at Citibank, Richard Matteis, explained how this could happen.[16]
Bankers, Matteis says, used computers not to solve problems but to
make the paper trail electronic. Everything stayed the same, except
where an employee used to write something down, now he or she

punched the information into a keyboard. Making the paper trail electronic does not solve problems nor increase productivity.

In communication, we are repeating this mistake: electronically transforming the company newspaper into video. For the most part (there are exceptions such as the preceding J.C. Penny and U.S. Postal Service examples), we are using TV to transmit the same information we used to put in the company newspaper: half-yearly financial results, employees receiving awards, new-product launches, changes in company structure, introducing new executives, corporate strategy overviews. All the same stuff—only this time electronic.

The only real difference is that TV is much faster. But speed was never the problem with the company newspaper in the first place. The company newspaper fails to change frontline employees because it uses the wrong source (senior executives instead of supervisors) over the wrong channel (print instead of face to face) with the wrong content (corporate not local work area). So spending millions to make a real fast company newspaper is to completely miss the point.

It sounds like tremendous communication power that the CEO of Federal Express can walk out of his office, step into a studio, and instantly begin communicating to his 85,000 employees in North America and Europe through the FXTV television network. But this is illusion. Firing messages out of a head office is not necessarily communication.

Working at the Communications Institute of the Hebrew University of Jerusalem, Elihu Katz, Hanna Adoni, and Pnina Parness tested how much viewers actually retain from television.[17] The Israeli TV evening news typically contains about 14 news stories. Katz's research team telephoned 387 adults within one hour of these adults' viewing the TV evening news. Twenty-one percent of these viewers could not spontaneously recall *any* of the 14 news stories. Viewers, on average, could spontaneously remember only 2 news stories. These were not technical questions about the content, just: "Did you watch the evening news?" "Can you remember any of the stories?" Within one hour of viewing, the average person remembered 2.

Firing messages out there, fast, slow, electronically, on paper, is not what matters. Companies should be communicating to change behavior. Video (cassette, closed circuit, or satellite) violates the three facts of employee communication and therefore stands little chance of changing employees.

How about the next technological advance, two-way satellite? Will it make the difference? Ford, through its Ford Communication Network, has established two-way compressed video transmission capabilities at more than 25 of its North American locations. Won't this advance, two-way communication, overcome the limitations of traditional video? No.

Everett Rogers studied up-and-running interactive communication technologies such as the Minitel project in France, the Berkeley Community Memory Project in the United States, and interactive two-way cable television in the "wired cities" experiments in Japan, the United States, and Europe.[18] Rogers concludes that these technologies have failed to live up to their designers' expectations: greater political participation, supplying educational information, and increased awareness of community issues. Not that the technologies can't carry this information but receivers just weren't interested. What users want from these technologies is entertainment, and much of the two-way usage comes from people sharing information about sex and dating.

Turning the company newspaper into a video doesn't increase its power. Two-way satellite, where employees can ask questions of senior executives, is an electronic, live, *letters to the editor*. If your letters to the editor column in the company newspaper is having a powerful effect changing large numbers of frontline employees, then live two-way satellite may produce the desired results. But if the column isn't, moving it several notches higher tech isn't going to make any difference.

Unless these systems are used to communicate technical information requiring immediate application or intended to broadcast head office response to corporate tragedies or stunning dramatic events, the multi-million dollar investments are wasted. By "wasted," we mean something very specific: They will not change the way frontline employees do their job.

At the heart of this error in communication judgment is the belief that frontline employees really want to know what's going on in head office, that employees are deeply concerned and interested in what the executives are up to. And that if we tell them what head office is doing, if they get to see and hear head office people, it will, somehow, bind them closer to the company, increase their loyalty and devotion, and eventually cause them to improve their performance. All of this is wrong. We will tackle it head on in Part 3, but here we can say that employees couldn't care less about head office. They are not now and never will be loyal to the company. If you try to bind them closer to the corporate whole, you will fail. Whatever loyalty they have is to their supervisor and their local work area. You use that—or you don't change their behavior.

The greatest sin in the corporate use of video is that it distracts us from our real communication problems. One U.S. company has 65 staff with an annual operating budget of $8 million running its private television network; another hires about 100 individual freelance video consultants assisting in the production of corporate videos. Many companies find the time, money, and staff to film the annual shareholders' meeting and replay it in cafeterias, plants, and lobbies. And yet, we seem unable to ask a supervisor where he thinks a newly purchased lathe should be located. We forget to tell the supervisor we decided to eliminate the third shift and absorb these workers back onto first shift— she hears it first from the shop steward. We decide to close a plant but are too rushed to target supervisors with clear information about the severance package.

Companies making TV shows and running television networks need to be supremely confident that their face-to-face communication between supervisors and frontline employees is nailed down perfectly. Otherwise, their communication operates under a badly flawed set of priorities.

References

1. D/J Brush Associates of LaGrangeville, N.Y., quoted in Warren Berger, "TV for the Boardroom and the Factory Floor," *New York Times*, sec. 3, August 21, 1988.
2. D/J Brush Associates study quoted in "Downsizing, Mergers Don't Slow Corporate Video Growth," *Communication World*, December 1988, p. 12. D/J Brush Associates estimate the corporate video industry is worth $5 billion, but half the industry makes videos for people outside the company: customers, local community, or video news releases for TV stations; the other half of these videos are made for employees. So we estimate this employee segment of the market is worth about $2.5 billion. See, "Communicators See Training as the Main Use of Video Technology," *Communication World*, November, 1992, p. 12.
3. Foehrenbach and Goldfarb, op. cit.
4. The Industrial Society,*Blueprint for Success: A Report on Involving Employees in Britain*, edited by Sue Webb, London, 1989.
5. Touche Ross study in Roger Hussey: *You See What I Mean?* Touche Ross & Co., London, 1980.
6. Taylor, op. cit., p. 55.
7. D/J Brush Associates study quoted in Stephen Barr, "Smile! You're on Corporate TV," *Communication World*, September 1991, pp. 28–31.
8. Vista Communications, "Britain at Work," *The Fourth Annual Vista Survey of Communications Between the Managers and Their Staff*, Vista Communications, 1989.
9. "Broadcast News, Inc., " *Newsweek*, January 4, 1988, pp. 34–35.

10. Daniel K. Rosetti and Theodore J. Surynt, "Video Teleconferencing and Performance," *The Journal of Business Communication*, vol. 22, no. 4, 1985, pp. 25–31.

11. The Conference Board, *Employee Communications: New Top-Management Priority*, by Kathryn L. Troy, Research Report #919, 1988.

12. C. W. Downs and M. Hazen: "A Factor Analysis of Communication Satisfaction," *Journal of Business Communication*, vol. 14, no. 2, 1977, pp. 63–74.

13. Alvie L. Smith, "Bridging the Gap Between Employees and Management," *Public Relations Journal*, November 1990, pp. 20–21.

14. Fleming Meeks, "Live from Dallas," *Forbes*, December 26, 1988, pp. 112–113.

15. Lester C. Thurow, *The Zero Sum Solution: An Economic and Political Agenda for the 80's*, Simon & Schuster, New York, 1985.

16. Richard J. Matteis, "The New Back Office Focuses on Customer Service," *Harvard Business Review*, March–April 1979, pp. 146–159.

17. Elihu Katz, Hanna Adoni, and Pnina Parness, "Remembering the News: What the Picture Adds to Recall," *Journalism Quarterly*, vol. 54, summer 1977, pp. 231–239.

18. Everett M. Rogers, "Participatory Communication, Technology, and Democracy," *The World Community in Post-Industrial Society, Part 2, Continuity and Change in Communications in Post-Industrial Society*, The World Academic Conference of the Seoul Olympiad, 1988, Christian Academy, Seoul, pp. 155–164.

12
Briefing Meetings

Briefing meetings are:

Hour-long meetings run by supervisors for frontline employees.

Once a month.

Supervisors usually receive an information packet of overhead transparencies, mostly graphs representing corporate performance statistics.

Supervisors are told to also include information relevant to their local work area.

The Confederation of British Industry says 87 percent of U.K. companies with more than 2000 employees use briefing meetings to communicate with frontline employees.[1] Research by the U.K. Institute of Directors shows briefing meetings (in the United Kingdom and Australia called team briefing) are the second fasting growing communication technique (following videos).[2]

Despite their widespread use, briefing meetings cannot be recommended as a communication device for changing frontline employees.

More Meetings—Is That What Your Company Needs?

We already have quite a few meetings. According to one estimate, 11 million meetings every day in the United States alone.[3] And how effective are these meetings?

Harrison Conference Services, working with Hofstra University, asked 2000 U.S. business people about their experience with meetings.[4] The results were:

75 percent of participants were usually not clear what the meeting was supposed to accomplish.

33 percent of time spent in meetings was wasted.

Estimated cost of wasted time was $37 billion (20 to 33 percent of managers' time spent in meetings times average compensation).

For the advocates of briefing meetings, the solution to this poor record is training. Forty-nine percent of U.K. firms with team briefing run training courses in meeting and presentation skills for their supervisors.[5]

This supervisor training has little or no chance of succeeding. The Harrison-Hofstra study separated senior executives from the sample, those with titles of chairman, president, or CEO. These senior executives reported 28 percent of their time wasted in meetings; only slightly better than the 33 percent reported by all managers. With, on average, 20 years of experience, these senior executives are still wasting more than 15 minutes out of every meeting hour. It is one remarkable training course that takes supervisors off the factory floor and in a couple of sessions enables them to equal or surpass the meeting skills of CEOs with 20 years experience.

When faced with a communication problem, the knee-jerk reaction is always training. Why is the first reaction always to change the people? Why is it always the people who need fixing? Leave the people alone— fix the communication. It will prove easier, cheaper, faster to change the communication than it will ever be to change the people.

Why Supervisors Don't Want Meetings

Janice Klein's research shows 85 percent of supervisors want to communicate with their subordinates one on one—not in groups.[6]

Most supervisors we've interviewed are scared to death at the thought of standing up in front of all their subordinates and giving a presentation. Maybe scared worse than death. *The Book of Lists* reports that people's worst fear, number 1, is "speaking before a group"; "death" was number 6.[7]

And supervisors have good reason to be afraid. Think clearly about what briefing meetings mean on the front line. The least educated, most frustrated, most oppressed feeling employees in the company are going to be gathered into a group; where the least confident, least informed, least powerful member of management is going to give them a lot of statistics they don't want (data usually drawn from the company's quarterly performance report).

We have observed scores of these frontline briefing meetings run by supervisors in steel mills, mines, department stores, government departments, electrical utilities, freight companies, railroads, insurance companies, and banks. And nearly always these meetings are inches away from disintegrating into grievances sessions. The plan is for frontline employees to politely sit there and be spoon-fed reams of information about what the senior executives are thinking and doing. But, before long, a hand goes up, "If they can spend $15 million buying a bankrupt tool & die maker, why can't they keep the [profanity deleted] cafeteria clean." And now the flood gates open, "Yea, all that talk about safety is a load of [profanity deleted]. For ten years we've been writing up the wet floors caused by that leaking roof. They don't care what happens to us." The perspiring supervisor now fumbles for the next overhead showing return on assets from third quarter 1993 compared to third quarter 1992—but it's too late. The crowd has taken over.

Supervisors instinctively avoid gathering their workers into crowds, preferring informal one-on-one communication. Managers should learn from this. When Jaguar decided to improve communication through team briefing meetings, shop stewards declared a boycott, and only 20 percent of employees attended. Eventually the union backed down, but this is no way to begin a communication program. Worse, at the U.K. Post Office, the Union of Communications Workers had to be taken to the High Court, ordered by injunction to lift their boycott of team briefing meetings. Why do these tragedies happen? Because management insists on a formal program. If the communication were informal, one on one, the way supervisors want, there would be no target to aim at.

These briefing meetings make a lot of sense to college-educated managers, who got an A in their speech class, who like getting up front, and whose own subordinates typically look like members of the *Up with America* singing group. These managers can actually put up an overhead transparency of the new mission statement logo, shown in Fig. 12-1, and ask: "What does this mean to you?" And be taken seriously.

Every frontline supervisor knows the goofy square and silly question "What does this mean to you?" will get him killed. In front of his crew, he will be seen as a sold-out management flunky, mouthing company propaganda. This "communication" intended to make things better will decrease the supervisor's integrity and credibility.

Take briefing meetings out of the management textbooks and look at them on the front line. A photograph of Max, a supervisor in a steel plant, is contained in Fig. 12-2.

Figure 12-1. Mission statement logo.

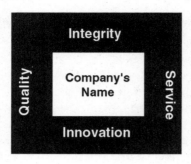

Figure 12-2. "Max" the supervisor. (*Source: Ref. 8.*)

Personnel managers told us Max has the worst employees at the plant. That's because they give him the worst employees. They also told us his crews have the highest throughput, least downtime, fewer accidents, lowest absenteeism, and best safety record.

Everywhere we found stories of Max's abilities. Maintenance workers told us about the time they were under tremendous pressure to repair a continuous casting machine in Max's area. Unfortunately Max was on vacation. At 2 a.m., they tracked him down in a bar hundreds of miles away. The mechanics held the phone to the ailing machine while Max listened. Max then directed an hours' worth of repairs by phone.

Max's company is setting up team briefing meetings. Here is a small section from the 40-page training manual given to Max to help him prepare:

> Throughout the month you should collect snippets of information on team progress. Put these snippets in your briefing folder. Toward the end of the week begin practicing your brief, either at home, or at work. Always remember IMPACT: Imagination, Motivation, Progress, Accountability, Consensus, and Teamwork.

Have another look at Max (Fig. 12-2). Max isn't going to collect "snippets" of information and put them in his briefing folder. Two or three days beforehand, Max isn't going to begin practicing his brief at home or at the plant. It is unlikely Max will remember what "IMPACT" stands for. And only a fool would try to make him. It is because of supervisors like Max that anything at all comes out of our factories, stores, and offices. He draws his respect from his unsurpassed knowledge of the operation and the belief of all his crew that he could do any one of their jobs—blindfolded.

We seem intent on destroying Max's mythical stature, and changing his image into a mealy mouthed company stooge. We have taken our world, the classroom or boardroom, and assumed it is just like his. It isn't. If you want to improve Max's communication with his subordinates, acknowledge his contribution by treating him as a privileged receiver of information and give him a greater say in the operation of his work area. Don't try turning him into a facilitator, team builder, discussion leader, or presenter of company propaganda and statistics.

And here we have something important to say: Max's problem is not that he does not know how to communicate. His problem is that too often he is not told anything worth communicating.

We spent two weeks with Max. During this time, the Human Resources Department hired a new person for his area. Max had no input. The maintenance schedule for machinery in his area was significantly altered, and no one asked his advice. One day, bewildered, his crew turned to Max for answers when the steel looked, smelled, and ran differently. Max knew nothing. We later learned these changes resulted from company experiments with pulverized coal injection in the blast furnace. At the end of the two weeks, we watched as Max sat in a training room, shoulder to shoulder with his crew, including the new hire, and was told for the first time of company plans to initiate "continuous improvement" techniques in his area. When communicating this important change, the company treated Max and the new hire who had worked in the plant one week identically.

Improving communication in Max's area has nothing to do with briefing meetings. Forget about forcing Max to hold meetings, and begin forcing middle managers in engineering, marketing, supply, planning, and personnel to get out there asking Max's opinion of upcoming changes, adapting and responding to his ideas, and always to treat him as superior to his subordinates.

But without these formal programs, the proponents say, there will be no communication. Unless we force supervisors to hold these meetings, they don't tell employees what's happening.

Here we need to think clearly. If what you mean is that, without briefing meetings, supervisors will not fill employees full of corporate statistics, you are correct. Supervisors will not informally, one on one, communicate to their subordinates the average daily units produced, direct and indirect labor hours, unit costs with and without overhead allocations, return on assets compared to return on sales, absenteeism figures, and management verses shop floor rates of contributions to the *I Have An Idea* suggestion scheme. You are right. Supervisors will not communicate this information. But why do you want them to? This information won't change behavior.

On the other hand, if a supervisor has just been consulted regarding the purchase of Komatsu bulldozers, the general manager of credit cards has apologized to supervisors for poor service and promises his staff will now answer all phone calls before three rings, the supervisor has had a private session covering the severance package for soon-to-be laid off workers, they'll tell that. You couldn't stop supervisors from communicating that information. If you supply supervisors with privileged information relevant to the local work area, you don't have a communication problem. The real communication problem in large companies is not that the supervisors refuse to tell subordinates what they know but that they don't know anything worth telling.

Polaroid Struggling with Briefing Meetings

Polaroid, at one of its largest plants, decided to improve communication.[9] Polaroid launched "What's Happening" monthly briefing meetings conducted by first-line supervisors for their subordinates.

During five years of What's Happening the program has undergone many changes. Figure 12-3 contains a summary of Polaroid's experience.

It is impossible to have anything but admiration for a company trying this hard. Polaroid is determined to improve communication. What is needed is better advice.

Figure 12-3. Polaroid's *What's Happening.*

1. **First-Line Supervisors Required to Hold Monthly *What's Happening* Meetings**

    supervisors complained they had nothing to talk about

    frontline employees said meetings were a waste of time

2. **Presentation Packets Prepared for All Supervisors**

    executives required to submit data for the packets, typical packet included overhead transparencies covering:

    > safety notices
    > attendance report
    > building information
    > monthly productivity
    > monthly quality variances
    > training & development
    > announcements

    supervisors complained information was:

    > old
    > not relevant to local work area
    > wordy and overly complex (for example, full page single spaced typed memos photocopied onto overheads)

3. **Plant Manager Began Pre-Briefing Session Exclusively for Supervisors**

    plant manager went through the presentation packet, overhead by overhead, explaining the information

    plant manager required supervisors' briefings to be included in supervisors' performance appraisals

    supervisors seemed not threatened by linking briefings to performance appraisal

    > 75% didn't attend the plant manager's pre-briefing sessions

    supervisors attending said hour long pre-briefings were mechanical and boring

    questions and discussions were rare

    middle managers complained they were excluded

    middle managers were then invited to pre-briefing sessions, but their attendance was no better than supervisors, 75% didn't come

4. **More Modifications Planned**

    frontline employees to be invited to plant manager's pre-briefing sessions

    middle managers attendance hopefully increased by allowing them to chair some pre-briefing meetings

    supervisors begin training courses designed to improve meeting, presentation, and statistical interpretation skills

The goal of What's Happening is unobtainable. First-line supervisors are never going to give informative and interesting presentations on company performance to frontline employees. Never.

Let's go back to the beginning. Why did Polaroid feel it needed What's Happening? Because the plant manager, like plant managers everywhere, was inundated with complaints of poor communication.

But unlike most plant managers, this one decided to personally interview more than 800 employees. Specific complaints heard by the plant manager included: "Nobody ever gets back to us," "We can't get clear answers to our questions," and "We hear things through the grapevine that our supervisors don't even know."

The mistake came in assuming these complaints concerned company or plant-wide information. When a frontline employee says "Nobody ever gets back to us," she doesn't mean there is no answer to some hypothetical question about inventory turnover this year compared to last. She means that her high-speed film splicer is going down for preventative maintenance every 200 hours. She knows that machine like the back of her hand and is certain that the scheduled downtime for maintenance is too frequent. But when she and her supervisor ask about changing the maintenance schedule, "Nobody ever gets back to us." Formal briefing meetings with dozens of overhead transparencies prepared by executives don't fix the problem.

Give Up on Briefing Meetings

In 1978, IBM (U.K.) decided to launch briefing meetings. They found the meetings were:

Not relevant to local needs and interests

Too detailed, formal, and rigid

Unable to get presenters' commitment

In 1980, IBM (U.K.) decided to stop them.

This should have sent alarm bells ringing everywhere. When companies with the human resource prowess of IBM and Polaroid can't get these briefing meetings to work, what possible chance have the rest of us got?

Give up on your formal briefing program. You are going to kill yourself trying to make it work, and it never will. In a study of 20 U.K. companies practicing team briefings, Vista, an employee communication consultancy, found about one-third of the employees did not even know they were receiving briefing meetings.[10] Holding meetings does not mean communication.

Take the enormous effort involved in running one of these briefing programs and put it into creating informal face-to-face communication between supervisors and their subordinates concerning performance in the local work area.

How?

When critical changes affect the local work area, communicate directly with supervisors (as described in Chaps. 1 and 10).

For less critical changes, test middle management transmission by calling supervisors and checking if the information is getting to them (Chap. 4).

Force middle managers to communicate downward by measuring and publishing supervisors' evaluation of communication with their immediate managers (Chap. 4).

Send an unmistakable message that supervisors are the most important receivers by allowing supervisors to evaluate the quality of service from head office departments (Chap. 5).

Require supervisors' opinions before making major capital equipment purchases or changes to operations (Chap. 6).

Important information that supervisors must communicate to front-line employees, (for example, severance packages) should be formally tested (Chap. 7).

None of these ideas, nor the ones coming up in Part 3, assume employees want information about the company as a whole. These ideas assume employees want information about their local work area, informally, one on one, from their supervisors.

These ideas are grounded in the three facts of employee communication. Briefing meetings are not. No amount of supervisor training is going to make up for this deficiency. Communication should work. It should change behavior. It should target supervisors as privileged receivers of information and rely on face-to-face communication about performance within the local work area.

References

1. Confederation of British Industry, *Employee Involvement—Shaping the Future for Business*, 1990.
2. Institute of Directors study in "Communicating When It Really Matters," *Director*, September 1988, pp. 139–140.
3. Ruch, op. cit., p. 191.
4. Harrison-Hofstra study reported in John N. Sheridan, "A $37 Billion Waste: That's the Annual Cost of Poorly Planned and Poorly Run Business Meetings," *Industry Week*, September 4, 1989, pp. 11–12.
5. Confederation of British Industry, op. cit., p. 19.
6. Klein, op. cit., p. 91.

7. *The Book of Lists* result reported in Lesley J. Nonkin, untitled, *Vogue*, vol. 177, May 1987, pp. 161–163.

8. The individual in the photo is not the real "Max." The supervisor pictured is from another company. We did this to avoid embarrassing Max's company.

9. Ruth G. Newman, "Polaroid Develops a Communications System—But Not Instantly," *Management Review*, vol. 79, no. 1, January 1990, pp. 34–38.

10. Andrew Jack, "When Team Briefings Tell Only Half the Story," *Financial Times*, July 19, 1991, p. 10.

13

Company Newspaper

When it comes to communicating change, the company newspaper has done enormous damage:

> Did we communicate the severance benefits connected to the terminations?
> No problem. It's in the company newspaper.

> Are you sure employees understand how and when the merger is taking place?
> All the details are in the company newspaper.

> The company's new strategy targeting high-net-worth individuals with extra customer service. Are employees on board?
> Got it covered in the company newspaper.

As if the company newspaper were a powerful communication tool.

The company newspaper has absolved managers from the responsibility of designing real communication. Communication that reaches the front line and changes behavior.

To improve communication, consider banning all company newspaper articles informing frontline employees of upcoming changes. This ban would deprive senior managers of the illusion that an article in the company newspaper was communication. It would force them to say aloud, which is the case anyway, that there is no communication.

Frontline Employees Don't Read

"Up to 10 percent of workers are either functionally illiterate or, just, marginally literate." This is the opening sentence in The Conference

Board Report, *Literacy in the Work Force*.[1] And the report goes on to show that even if they can read, it doesn't mean they understand. According to Conference Board quoted studies, three out of four young people, 21 to 25 years old, were unable to understand a long feature story in a newspaper.

How do we explain the paradox that, on the one hand, the U.S. market for remedial textbooks teaching employees how to read is worth an estimated $500 million[2] and, on the other, that 86 percent of U.S. executives rely on print to communicate important internal changes to employees?[3]

Even assuming employees can read and understand, we know they don't turn to printed material when faced with problems. Research by Mark Peterson and his team shows that when employees are searching for solutions, they first ask questions of their supervisors and coworkers and only as a last resort turn to any written material.[4]

Employee claims that they do read are often exaggerated. In The Netherlands, companies produce a document called the "social report" detailing changes in human resource plans and policies. Hein Schreuder wanted to know if employees actually read these reports.[5] Fifty-three percent of Dutch employees said they read the report "rather thoroughly" when they were answering the question on a written questionnaire. However, when interviewed, face to face, the percent saying they read the report dropped to 28 percent. The prospect of a follow-up question cut the number saying they had read it almost in half.

That we so frequently decide to reach the front line by print seems strange when you realize that managers don't want their information that way—they want it face to face. Look, for example, at the research summaried in Fig. 13-1.[6,7,8]

If college-educated managers, working in an almost exclusively symbolic world, chose face-to-face communication, why do they think a truck driver or forklift operator would prefer 30 column inches of 8-point type?

And why are we all pretending? Pretending that information moves through companies by print. Anyone spending more than one week in a large company knows that important information moves verbally. Confirming this common-sense conclusion is a flow study of how messages move from the top to the shop floor at GM's Automotive Components Group.[9] Tracking particular messages and randomly interviewing executives, managers, and supervisors, the GM study shows the flow of messages was dominated by verbal, not print, communication.

If you read the company newspaper and are shocked or surprised at its content—all this means is that you are completely unconnected to anyone with power.

Figure 13-1. Managers' preference is verbal. *(Source: Refs. 6, 7, and 8.)*

75% of managers' communication is face to face	Fred Luthans and Janet Larson
only 9% of their communication time is devoted to reading	Jane Hannaway
when communication involves ambiguous problems, managers' first preference is face to face, followed by telephone, with written information preferred last	Richard Daft and Robert Lengel

Our recommendation is banning any company newspaper articles intended to communicate change to frontline employees. This ends the charade that an article in the company newspaper is communication. This excuse, the company newspaper, is too easy. It hides the truth. We need to force managers to sit at the executive board table and announce out loud that there are no plans for communicating the change upon which the company is betting its future.

Company Newspapers Can't Do What They're Supposed To

The Conference Board asked 281 executives from Fortune 500 manufacturing and Fortune 500 service companies what they expected their company newspaper to accomplish.[10] The executives responded: improve morale, communicate internal changes, and move employees toward greater quality.

Improve Morale

Employees barely want it. How could it possibly improve morale? The IABC/TPF&C studies show U.S. employees ranked the company newspaper 10th out of 14 preferred sources of communication (supervisors were first).[11] The Industrial Society found U.K. employees ranked company publications 10th out of 16 preferred sources (supervisors were first).[12] Eighty-four percent of U.S. employees say the company newspaper has nothing to do with their day-to-day work.

No one is happy with the company newspaper. A study conducted by consulting firm William M. Mercer, Inc., asked CEOs what they wanted to see in the company newspaper. The answer was articles on quality.[13] Employees were also asked what articles they wanted. The answer was more information about future changes to the local work area. So how are publications doing? Examining 1251 articles in publications from 65 U.S. companies, the Mercer study found 5 percent were about quality and 7 percent were about upcoming changes. What fills the company newspaper, according to the Mercer study, are stories about current programs and activities (such as safety programs), community or public relations news, and personal news such as service anniversaries and retirements. Information that neither CEOs nor employees want.

In light of these facts, it is frightening that 90 percent of the executives in The Conference Board study said the primary goal of the company newspaper is to improve morale.

Morale is improved by better communication between employees and their supervisors. The effect of the company newspaper is too minuscule to be seriously considered.

Communicate Internal Changes

Companies with the least understanding of employee communication rely exclusively on the company newspaper to communicate changes. Those with greater understanding use printed communication as a back up. General Motors, for example, falls into this later category.

Perhaps no other private company has done more to share its communication knowledge than General Motors. Current and former GM managers Ron Actis, Allan Csiky, and particularly Alvie Smith (in his book *Innovative Employee Communication*) have made a deep contribution by sharing their experience and research. GM's research was among the first to reveal that communication should come from the supervisor, face to face, with issues relevant to the local work area.

But even GM cannot wean itself from a dependence on printed publications. The GM response is that these publications are a backup, just in case the face to face fails. Like getting into your car and backing up the seat belt with a piece of thread laid across your lap. And worse because, when pressed for time, managers will hurriedly skip the belt and rely exclusively on the thread.

This is why we recommend banning print as a means of communicating change to frontline employees. Take one more step than GM. Force managers to state the truth: "There was no communication at all." Because that's what communicating in the company newspaper adds up to.

Move Employees toward Improved Quality

Philip Crosby says approximately 20 percent of our costs are wasted through poor quality.[14] Few people are more poorly placed to address this issue than the editor of the company newspaper. Nearly all editors can show you scars from whippings delivered by senior managers infuriated by some tiny hint of criticism deducible from an unintended and immaterial comment written about their department.

Editors of the company newspaper are in no position to begin investigative journalism into waste and mismanagement in the company. And they don't. Ian Spurr studied 4105 articles published in 102 U.K. company newspapers.[15] Spurr found not many of the articles had anything to do with quality, and, when they did, it was almost always positive. Spurr's research is summarized in Fig. 13-2.

Unless you're talking about completely uncritical accolades, commendations, and kudos, the company newspaper is no place to pursue quality. This horn blowing delights the particular people involved but has little or no effect on the organization as a whole. As we will show in Part 3, the world of the frontline employee is his or her local work area. If the story is not about them, it might as well be about another company altogether.

The company newspaper cannot do what it is supposed to. It has no significant effect on morale, it is positively harmful when used to communicate internal change (because it provides a false sense that communication has actually occurred), and it lacks the power to expose the most serious quality issues (waste and mismanagement). That 90 percent of executives intend their company newspaper to increase morale, 86 percent to communicate internal changes, and 85 percent to move employees toward greater quality[16] shows an enormous lack of understanding of what company newspapers can actually do.

Communication professionals have failed to expose these inadequacies. Worse, in company after company, in the United States and United Kingdom, communication consultants are continually recommending

Figure 13-2. What company newspapers say about their organizations.
(Source: Ref. 15.)

organization is.........	number of articles
successful	514
unsuccessful	10
competent	115
incompetent	10
caring toward employees	115
not caring toward employees	0

more print. Research from The Conference Board, and Anthony Booth, shows one of the most frequent recommendations from communication consultants is increasing and overhauling company newspapers.

These recommendations have obviously been taken to heart by executives because, according to one estimate, over 215 million copies of company newspapers are published each year in the United States alone.[17] This is almost 3.5 times the combined circulation of all U.S. daily newspapers.[18]

And all of it violating the three most established facts of employee communication: Employees want information from their supervisor (not head office sources), face to face (not print), about their local work area (not the company as a whole).

Don't Eliminate the Company Newspaper

Don't eliminate it—understand what it does. The company newspaper communicates information about managers to other managers. It does not change the behavior of large numbers of frontline employees.

Following a lecture, we were approached by a frustrated CEO saying:

> But what you say just isn't true. As a young apprentice in this company, I read every issue of the company newspaper, and it helped form my ambition to someday become a leader here.

Such instances are undoubtedly true, but here we are reminded of a story told by a philosophy professor.

> It is said that Plato was in a corner of the Athens marketplace lecturing a couple dozen young boys. As the lecture went on, hour after hour, the boys, slowly, one at a time, began slipping away. A citizen passing by noticed Plato was now lecturing only one remaining boy. The citizen unable to control himself interrupted, "Plato, you absent-minded philosopher, you have failed to notice that all the boys are gone except one." Plato responded, "No, it is you who have failed to notice. I was only lecturing this boy at the beginning."

The company newspaper may occasionally touch a frontline employee. One of these rare individuals may someday make a singular contribution. And this may justify its existence and expense. But let's get this straight: The company newspaper is not an effective tool for changing the behavior of large numbers of frontline employees.

Almost every large company has a company newspaper. Almost none target supervisors as privileged receivers of information concerning upcoming changes. This is a serious flaw in our communication priorities and a condemnation of the communication advice given to senior executives.

Publications Miss the Point

Thinking that a publication will improve communication is to misunderstand the entire communication problem.

When supervisors say communication is bad, they are not pointing an accusatory finger at some deficiency in the company newspaper. Exasperated by poor communication, supervisors aren't thinking about publications in any shape or form. What they mean is:

> The heavy-duty stamping press is down for days with serious wear damage. Weeks earlier, tested oil samples resulted in a contamination report, but the report was not shared with the supervisor.

> The supervisor scheduled her crew roster assuming a half-day PM (preventative maintenance) on the mechanical spray painters. Maintenance changed the schedule but didn't tell the supervisor.

Assembly workers passing the parts supply depot noticed pallet loads of new titanium alloy frames. Apparently these will replace the currently used steel frames. They asked their supervisor what's up. She had no idea.

This is what supervisors mean by bad communication. The day-to-day, work-related information isn't getting to them, or their suggestions for change are ignored. This has absolutely nothing to do with any publications. Publications are irrelevant to the communication problems threatening performance.

As consultants, we are often deluged with questions: Should the publication be monthly or bimonthly? spot or full color? sent to employees' homes or distributed in the plant? The painful, but true, answer is, it doesn't matter. And more importantly, this isn't what you should be thinking about.

References

1. The Conference Board, *Literacy in the Work Force*, Report #947, by Leonard Lund and E. Patrick McGuire, 1990.

2. Estimate is made by publishers Simon & Schuster, quoted in "Can America Compete?" *The Economist*, January 18, 1992, pp. 65–68.

3. The Conference Board, *Employee Communications: New Top Management Priority*, Report #919, by Kathryn L. Troy, 1988.

4. Peterson, op. cit.

5. Hein Schreuder, "Employees and the Corporate Social Report: The Dutch Case," *The Accounting Review*, vol. 55, no. 2, April 1981.

6. Fred Luthans and Janet K. Larsen, "How Managers Really Communicate," *Human Relations*, vol. 39, no. 2, 1986, pp. 161–178.

7. Jane Hannaway, "Supply Creates Demands: An Organizational Process View of Administrative Expansion," *Journal of Policy Analysis and Management*, vol. 7, no. 1, 1987, pp. 118–134.

8. Richard L. Daft and Robert H. Lengel, "Organizational Information Requirements, Media Richness and Structural Design," *Management Science*, vol. 32, no. 5, May 1986, pp. 554–571.

9. Patrick J. McKeand, "GM Division Builds a Classic System to Share Internal Information," *Public Relations Journal*, vol. 46, November 1990, pp. 24–26.

10. The Conference Board, Report #919, by Kathryn L. Troy, op. cit.

11. IABC/TPF&C study by Julie Foehrenbach and Steve Goldfarb, op. cit.

12. The Industrial Society, op. cit., p. 42.

13. Gary W. Kemper, "The Real Scoop," *Industry Week*, June 17, 1991, pp. 68–69.

14. Philip Crosby quoted in Thomas M. Rohan, "Sermons Fall on Deaf Ears," *Industry Week*, November 20, 1989, pp. 35–36.

15. Ian Spurr, "Are House Journals Just Hot Air?" *Involvement & Participation*, IPA, autumn 1990, pp. 14–17.

16. The Conference Board, Report #919, by Kathryn L. Troy, op. cit.

17. Arnold Deutsch, *The Human Resources Revolution: Communicate or Litigate*, McGraw-Hill, New York, 1979, p. 132.

18. U.S. Bureau of the Census, *Statistical Abstract of the United States: 1991*, 111th ed., Washington, D.C., 1991, p. 561.

14
Suggestion Schemes

Here is an idea. Go to any major corporation, meet with the vice president of any large department (say, marketing) and suggest:

  Give all managers in corporate marketing a form where they write down any idea they have for improving marketing

  Bypass the VP-marketing, handing the forms directly to the CEO and board

  CEO and board pick the best idea, with a cash prize for the winner

Any self-respecting VP of marketing would resign. It's an insult. It assumes the VP of marketing doesn't know marketing. Worse, subordinates become unclear: Who exactly is running the marketing department?

Obviously distasteful at the corporate level, this idea is warmly embraced when intended for supervisors on the front line. It's called the *suggestion scheme*. Bank of America has *Ideas in Action*, Hallmark has *Creative Thinking*, British Airways call their program *Brainwaves*; in the United States alone there are an estimated 6000 formal suggestion programs.[1] Is this worth doing? No.

Supervisor As Idiot

We were working with an international freight forwarding company—trucking division—when we learned our best lesson about suggestion schemes.

The *Keep On Truckin* suggestion scheme committee brought us a suggestion they thought deserving of implementation. The suggestion called for building a large driver assignment board intended to improve communication at shift startup.

Traditionally, 50 or 60 drivers mingled at the depot office as supervisors wove through the crowd finding their respective drivers. When found, the supervisor gave the driver a truck and route number, a pouch of consignment notes (paperwork), the truck's lot location, and keys.

After observing this haphazard event, we gave our enthusiastic support to the suggested driver assignment board. The board was 4 by 8 feet, with 50 to 60 clipboards hanging from hooks with each driver's name printed above. The clipboard contained all the necessary startup information, the pouch of paperwork, and truck keys.

Typically, supervisors see their drivers for only a short time each day, and this assignment board would eliminate the routine communication and allow more concentrated communication with the fewer drivers experiencing problems.

Board went up, the suggesting employee got his $500 check, photo with general manager shaking hands appeared in company newspaper, and talk began of expanding the boards to depots nationwide.

Subsequent months of interviews (related to a different project) meant we were frequently in the depot. To our surprise, we never saw any supervisors using the driver assignment board. We repeatedly asked why and were told it didn't work. Frustrated with our persistent questioning, one supervisor decided the "communication experts" needed an education and blurted, "The board's a dumb idea. How could we possibly tell if they were drunk."

Witnessing more shift startups, and now watching more closely, we realized that supervisors, along with transferring routine information, were also checking the driver's eyes, smelling his breath, and noticing his posture. On several occasions, drivers were sent home and instructed to take an unpaid sick day.

More scientifically, research by Barbara Mensch and Denise Kandel shows that 4 percent of transport operatives *admit* to drinking alcohol on the job.[2]

Suggesting that truck drivers, particularly on night shift, should march into the depot office, yank the clipboard with keys off the driver assignment board, and go hop into a truck is an absurd and dangerous idea. Certified by the Ph.D. consultant in communication, the general manager gave $500 for an idea that may eventually have killed an employee or innocent person.

What looks like inefficiency is often only evidence of our status as foreigners in their world. How many of you, our readers, immediately realized that the driver assignment board would encourage drunken driving? Where did anyone (including us at one time) get the idea that supervisors were idiots and, despite years of experience, know little or nothing about how to communicate with their own subordinates?

Suggestion schemes see the supervisor as someone needing bypassing, they rely on written communication formalized through committees, and they reward individuals instead of groups. It would be hard to think of a worse prescription for improving communication.

Supervisors, like managers, do need to improve. In our view what is required is more pressure to perform. In Part 3, we show how to apply this pressure by communicating the relative performance of the local work group. But we strongly disagree that supervisors also need to be told how to communicate.

Employee participation programs, quality circles, consultative committees, team briefing, suggestion schemes—are all founded on the premise that supervisors don't know how to communicate. These structure are meant to remedy supervisor inadequacies.

Demanding group communication when supervisors prefer one on one, establishing written methods when supervisors prefer verbal, approaching supervisors as communication deficient—and we couldn't figure out why we didn't get their support. When supervisors didn't climb aboard, we assumed yet another inadequacy: paranoid fear of sharing power. Ignoring their preferences, approaching them as power-mongering defects, supervisors responded by systematically destroying every one of our grandiose programs.

It is clear we have missed the lesson: Supervisors should be targeted as privileged receivers of information, the method for communicating to frontline employees should be the one supervisors prefer (informal, face to face), and behavior is changed only when the communication is about the employees' local work area.

Questioning Suggestion Schemes' Claimed Benefits

General Motors says their suggestion schemes save $700 million annually[3]; British Rail, £6 million[4]; British Telecom, £10 million.[5] The average savings from a single adopted suggestion in the United Kingdom is £1250[6]; in the United States, $7103.[7]

It is unclear whether these savings would still exist after all costs. British Telecom is one of the few companies to explain that their £10 million in savings from their New Idea scheme is before £2 million in expenses. More complex, however, is adding in the opportunity costs. Assuming that supervisors and managers would have done nothing with this time and money, the suggestion scheme supporters imply that subordinates' setting the agenda is more productive than superiors' doing so.

Our informal experience with suggestion schemes (admittedly in only a handful of companies) has been negative. A majority of suggestions were obscenities and spoofs, with large numbers of suggestions coming from a handful of employees (one scheme chairman described them as "wacked-out crazies no one else would listen to"). And always one suggestion appears over and over: double-sided photocopying.

One client adopted the double-sided photocopying suggestion. Failed to add in costs of additional time, paper jams, difficulty in reading; included no enforcement plan; divided their annual photocopy paper costs in half, claiming this as the savings; and gave one-tenth of this savings to the suggestor as a reward. This, we fear, is typical of suggestion schemes.

The strongest argument for suggestion schemes is usually the success of Japanese manufacturers. For example, Toyota, Nissan, and Honda average 27 suggestions per worker a year (with a 90 percent adoption rate)[8], while in the U.S. auto industry the average is 1 suggestion for every 37 workers (with a 20 percent adoption rate).

However, these comparisons are misleading because what Westerners mean by a "suggestion" is completely different from what's meant in Japan.

Begin by looking at Matsushita (operating in the West under brand names Panasonic, National, Technics, and Quasar), the leader of the suggestions-per-employee race in Japan throughout most of the 1980s. Matsushita's 210,000 employees make over 6.5 million suggestions, or about 30 suggestions per employee per year.[9]

The hint that *suggestion* might mean something different in Japan appears when you realize that suggestion scheme committees in U.K. companies meet approximately two-thirds of a day each week to administer 0.2 suggestions per employee a year.[10] The load on the Matsushita suggestion scheme committees would be 160 times greater than their U.K. counterparts. One can only imagine legions of Matsushita suggestion scheme committees sorting, evaluating, implementing, and awarding the millions of suggestions.

The Japan Human Relations Association (the group collecting suggestion scheme data in Japan) helps explain the difference. The English word *suggestion*, according to the J.H.R.A., implies something having "effect" or "result." But the corresponding Japanese word *teian* means something closer to "participation" or "reinforcement."[11] The Japanese don't have suggestion schemes in the Western sense; they have *teian*. The J.H.R.A. also says that almost 90 percent of their "suggestions" have nothing to do with effect or result and are completely unrelated to profit. The purpose of these suggestions is not to change operations but rather to serve as testimonials of one's commitment to the group.

This difference is evidenced by the average award of $2.50 given to Japanese employees whose suggestions are adopted, while the average U.S. award is $492.[12]

The Toyota practice of weekly posting employees' names and the number of suggestions they've made further demonstrates the primary function of encouraging group cohesion.

As the Japan Human Relations Association explains:

> This must appear to be a very silly system to foreigners! And, frankly speaking, it is a waste for companies seeking efficiency and economical rationalization. However, this is the rationale of the Teian system.[13]

It is the goal of the Japan Human Relations Association to achieve suggestion participation rates of more than 80 percent of all employees (currently at 72 percent).[14] Once achieved, they intend to concentrate more on suggestions in the Western sense, those having some result or effect.

If suggestions are things like "One should come to work well rested and prepared to do one's best," then one sees how Matsushita could have more than 6.5 million of them without abandoning electronics altogether and becoming the world's largest suggestion scheme committee. With suggestions like that, you simply give the employee his or her $2.50, put a mark next to his or her name, and press on.

The Japanese system of *teian* is something we don't need. We have enough symbolic communication already. What we desperately do need to borrow from the Japanese, however, is their practice of radical information gathering upward from the front line (as much as three times more than typical in U.S. companies) prior to management decision making.[15]

Exclude Japan and look at rates of employee participation across several Western countries. If suggestion scheme participation bestows significant productivity advantages, it is not clear how to explain a U.S. participation rate almost 3 times greater than Austria's; 2.5 times greater than West Germany; and almost 20 percent more than Sweden's (Fig. 14-1).[16]

Enough Symbolic Communication

Suggestions schemes are not real communication but symbolic. Giving the appearance of communication. We don't need more symbolic communication—we're already choking on it: videos, briefing meetings, satellite TV, company newspaper, elected consultative committees, team building.

Figure 14-1. Suggestions per 100 employees. *(Source: Ref. 16.)*

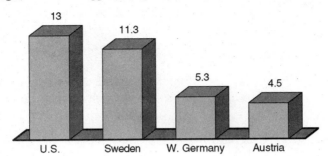

The suggestion scheme's real reason for existence is the photo in the company newspaper. CEO handing Mr. Joe Smith, arc furnace operator, a check for $1500 for his suggestion concerning appropriate cool-down temperature. The CEO believes employees will interpret this photo as hard evidence of good communication. They won't.

In U.S. companies with active suggestion schemes, each year only 3 percent of employees make a suggestion that is adopted[17]; in the United Kingdom only 1 percent.[18] During our 10 years of interviewing frontline employees and their supervisors, not one has ever voluntarily mentioned, in any context, the company suggestion scheme. It's too irrelevant to be considered.

If you ask employees about the suggestion scheme, what you get is cynicism. Supporting evidence exists. The average processing time for a U.S. suggestion committee to get back to an employee with an answer is about 130 working days (little over six months).[19] When the U.K. Association for Suggestion Schemes introduced a £50 annual fee, their membership fell from 1900 companies to 100.[20]

If the purpose of your suggestion scheme is improving upward communication from frontline employees, eliminate it.

Many senior executives want to eliminate their schemes but fear it sends the wrong signal. A signal that management is closing a communication channel. This fear is exaggerated.

Sixty U.S. companies and twenty U.K. companies shutting down their suggestion schemes were investigated by Christopher Miller and Michael Schuster.[21] These companies were beginning gain-sharing plans where employees share in performance improvements by receiving cash bonuses. Gain sharing required the elimination of the suggestion schemes. Dismantling suggestion schemes proved surprisingly easy, as Miller and Schuster explain: "Most individual suggestion plans had functioned so ineffectively that employees felt no loss at their removal." The reasons no one fought for these schemes, according to Miller and Schuster, included:

Long delays in responding to ideas

Very small bonus payments to employees

Bonuses even for bad ideas to encourage continued employee interest

Alienation of employees whose ideas were rejected

Administration costs required to maintain the system

Eliminating a purely symbolic form of communication does not send the wrong signal. Just the opposite.

A bureaucratic structure with forms to complete, committee meetings, prizes, and pictures in the company newspaper, has nothing to do with frontline communication. What's needed is improved face-to-face communication with supervisors concerning the day-to-day running of the local work area.

> Someone decided to replace the old Crown forklifts with Yale, but no one asked the supervisor's advice.
>
> The sales clerks are huddled around a mysterious new piece of equipment in the administration office. Turning to their supervisor, they ask, "What the heck is this?" It's an electronic counterfeit detector—but the supervisor can't answer because she doesn't know.
>
> Customers are screaming about receiving damaged merchandise, the packaging supervisors have been complaining for months the new corrugated cartons are too weak, but no one listens.

These are the failures that matter. This is what improving communication is about. And this improvement cannot happen through suggestion schemes.

References

1. Michael E. Trunko, "Open to Suggestions," *HR Magazine*, February 1993, p. 85–89.

2. Barbara S. Mensch and Denise B. Kandel, "Do Job Conditions Influence the Use of Drugs?" *Journal of Health and Social Behavior*, vol. 29, June 1988, pp. 169–184.

3. Smith, op. cit., p. 132.

4. Bill Goodwin, "Looking a Gift Horse in the Mouth," *The Engineer*, April 4–11, 1991, pp. 28–29.

5. Goodwin, ibid., p. 28.

6. Jean Balcombe, *Successful Suggestion Schemes: Update 1988*, U.K. Association for Suggestion Schemes, The Industrial Society, 1988.

7. National Association of Suggestion Systems and Japan Human Relations Association, "Statistical Result of Suggestion Systems in 1990," *1990 NASS and JHRA Statistical Report*, Chicago and Tokyo, 1990.

8. Robert J. Stramy, John J. Nora, and C. Raymond Rogers, *Transforming the Work Place*, Princeton Research Institute, Princeton, N.J., 1986, p. 4; quoted in Smith, op. cit., p. 77.

9. Kenjiro Yamada, "1986 Annual Statistical Report on Suggestion Systems in Japan," *HR: Human Relations*, Japan Human Relations Association, Tokyo, 1986, p. 4.

10. Balcombe, op. cit., p. 17.

11. Bunji Tohzawa, "A Comparison Between Japanese and Overseas Suggestions Systems," *HR: Human Relations*, Japan Human Relations Association, Tokyo, 1988.

12. National Association of Suggestion Systems and Japan Human Relations Association, op. cit.

13. Tohzawa, op. cit., p. 6.

14. Yamada, op. cit. p. 3.

15. Pascale, "Zen and the Art of Management," op. cit.

16. Swedish Institute for Staff Suggestions, SIFV, in Valentin Klotz, "Staff Suggestion Schemes," *International Labour Review*, vol. 127, no. 3, 1988, pp. 335–353.

17. National Association of Suggestion Systems and Japan Human Relations Association, op. cit.

18. Balcombe, op. cit., p. 10.

19. Brenda Funderburk, "Suggestion Systems: Ours vs. Theirs," *Sonoco News*, no. 5, September 1981, quoted in Ruch, op. cit., p. 185.

20. Goodwin, op. cit. p. 28.

21. Christopher S. Miller and Michael H. Schuster, "Gainsharing Plans: A Comparative Analysis," *Organizational Dynamics*, summer 1987, pp. 44–67.

15
Employee Attitude Surveys

About 50 percent of large U.S. and 65 percent of large U.K. companies use employee attitude surveys.[1,2] Only about half are satisfied, anything happens as a result, according to researchers at A. Foster Higgins & Co.[3]
These surveys suffer from two faults:

Companies have no idea what they are looking for, so the survey becomes a fishing expedition.

Nothing happens. After tabulating results, executives say, "Hmmm, that's interesting." File it and wait two years for the next survey.

To see executives fishing, attend a meeting where the questionnaire is built.

I'm curious to know if...

Wouldn't it be interesting to find out whether...

I wonder what employees think about...

This goes on and on as each executive voices his or her pet curiosity. Each curiosity becomes a question. The questionnaire becomes a colossus. The Hyatt Hotels employee attitude survey has 100 questions; Hewlett-Packard, 120 questions; and Ford, 198 questions.
Employee attitude surveys, intended as an upward communication tool, become yet another instance of management arrogance: Employees' take 45 minutes or an hour from work to answer a hundred or two management curiosities.

And what is the output? Reams of computer printout, means and standard deviations galore, managers flipping through, circling this and that, going "hmmm."

Some companies publish a version of the survey results especially for employees. But what does this mean to an employee? Receiving hundreds of bar charts, answering questions she didn't ask, where responses are usually aggregated to a level so far above the employee's work area that she doesn't know who or what the respondents were referring to.

Employee attitude surveys are worth doing, but only under two conditions: You know exactly what you are looking for and you have actions ready to launch based on learning employee opinions. When these conditions are met, surveys have only four or five questions, and aligned with each question is a planned response. For an example, see Fig. 15-1.

Communicating results to employees then becomes not a huge bunch of bar charts but four or five actions the company has taken as a result

Figure 15-1. The company cafeteria offers good value for money?

average score	planned response
above "7"	announce two year extension of existing caterers
"4" to "7"	announce caterers to go on temporary contract; question repeated in one year, if score not "7" or above, contract will be suspended
below "4"	announce catering contract suspended, begin search for new contractor

(strongly agree = 10; strongly disagree = 1)

of employee opinions. This is communication. Employees can see what happened.

Why Are We Asking These Questions?

Here are some questions pulled from our files of employee attitude surveys:

> Do employees in your area work well together?
>
> Do you find your work challenging and interesting?
>
> Does the company do a good job serving its customers?

Why did any company ask these questions? What's the planned response? If no response is planned, then why ask?

If, as we suggest, these questions were intended not as starting points for action but rather to satisfy management curiosity (where the output is not action but "hmmm"), then you don't need an employee attitude survey. The answers to these questions are available without surveying any of your employees.

Together, let's try an experiment. Open the results sections of your most recent employee attitude survey. Find questions similar to the ones in Fig. 15-2, and see if we can accurately predict your employee scores.

If you see enough survey results from enough companies, patterns emerge. These patterns are caused by forces external to, and greater than, most individual organizations; for example, see Fig. 15-3.

Unless your company is radically different and different in unpredictable ways, the answers to your management curiosities are out there, obtainable without taking your employees away from their work and dragging them through a hundred or more questions.

Why Are We Asking These People?

One large bank recently surveyed attitudes among their 30,000 employees. One question asked employees to evaluate management. The results showed that only 48 percent of employees felt senior management was doing a good job.

Courageously, the bank's executives decided to share the survey results with all employees. One can only imagine the embarrassment

Figure 15-2. Predicted answers to survey questions.

question	prediction % answering favorably
Do employees in your area work well together?	80% at all levels of company
Do you find your work challenging and interesting?	80% senior managers 60% middle managers 30% frontline employees
Does the company, in your opinion, do a good job serving its customers?	75% at all levels
Has senior management made the future direction of the company clear to you?	60% middle managers 40% frontline employees
What is the biggest barrier to improved customer service or product quality?	insufficient staff; pressure to meet unrealistic quantity targets

suffered by executives publicly admitting that less than half the employees have confidence in their ability. And imagine the concern among employees themselves upon discovering that most have no confidence in their corporate leaders.

The real tragedy, however, was asking these people this question in the first place. Roughly half the employees are tellers, almost one-half of these tellers are 25 years old or younger, and most of these tellers have worked for the bank less than 18 months.

Figure 15-3. Employee scores caused by forces external to the company.

external forces	effect on employees	effect on scores
psychological	people attribute the reasons for success to themselves; reasons for failure to external events and people beyond their control (psychologists call this attribution theory)	scores where employees evaluate their own area will be high; evaluating regional management lower; head office lowest
economic	employees praise management for increased business activity; blame management for cutbacks	morale and confidence scores move up in booms, down in recessions
business	there is inherent uncertainty in business that many employees don't understand; consequently information and assurances they want often can't be given	senior managers always receive a low score for not providing enough information about future plans

The question becomes, why are employees with about a year of banking experience being asked to evaluate the competence of senior executives? What standard did they use? Did they perhaps compare the bank's executives with what they know about executives at other large banks, for example, Citibank, or did they perhaps apply a more international criteria and evaluate their executives in comparison to Lloyds in the United Kingdom, or executives at the Royal Bank of Canada?

And what was the plan? What did the executives intend doing with the results? If 80 percent or more expressed confidence, award themselves a bonus; if 50 percent or below, quit?

Not only is this self-flagellation unnecessary, it is also unfair. Did anyone tell the executives (or the employees) that 48 percent of employees' expressing confidence in senior management might not be a bad score. Among U.K. frontline employees only 34 percent express confidence in their company's management, and among U.S. frontline employees, only 30 percent.[4,5]

Within the same survey, the bank asked employees about their new staff wardrobe: seventy percent felt the wardrobe was reasonably priced, 78 percent said it was attractive, and 84 percent thought it comfortable to wear. This is a perfect question to ask frontline employees. It's specific, within their area of expertise, and capable of a clear management response.

The questions on your survey should be about the local work area, and the questions should be specific and result in specific management action.

When Employee Attitude Surveys Make Sense

They make sense when you know what you're looking for and have a planned response.

A large oil company was moving its head office to another state. The change involved moving hundreds of employees, parting with hundreds choosing not to go, selling and buying buildings, and hiring hundreds of new employees at the new location.

Ten months before the move, the CEO asked, "I want to know if the employees believe they are prepared for the move—not what the executives think but what the employees think."

Three hours later a one-question questionnaire was on its way to all head office employees (see Fig. 15-4).

Three days later the CEO and all employees knew the answer (see Fig. 15-5).

The following Monday morning a CEO-appointed transition team began interviewing employees in the three lowest-scoring departments (which happened to include the CEO's own department). The team found three major problems:

1. *Need for a moving date.* Employees had been told they would move sometime within a three-month period. They wanted a date, even if it was later changed. Senior management came up with specific dates

Figure 15-4. Questionnaire concerning company move.

Are We Prepared?

Thinking about your job, and your department, are we becoming sufficiently prepared for the move?

not prepared at all   very well prepared

1   2   3   4   5   6   7   8   9   10

Figure 15-5. Questionnaire result.

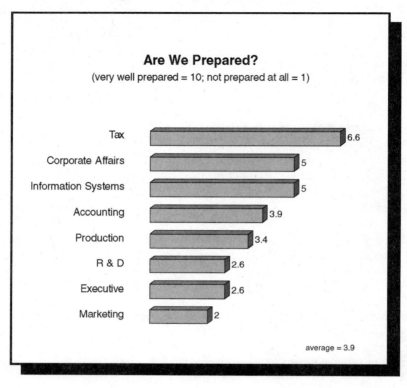

for each department along with probabilities of whether the date would change. For details, see Chap. 23.

2. *Rules on handling files.*   Some employees were told all files were going to the archives; others were told all files were going to the new building; others were told to throw away everything not absolutely essential; while still others were told by the legal department not to throw anything away no matter how obscure. The transition team nailed down five rules for handling files.

3. *Job handover procedure.*   Many employees decided to take a severance package and not make the move. These employees requested a standardized written procedure for recording the essential elements of their jobs. This would assist new employees hired to take their place. The training department responded with a handover training course and manual.

Surveys can reveal what employees think, but much more importantly they can create pressure. Managers respond to crisis. And when your department scores a 2 on a 10-point scale, shared with the CEO and all employees, concerning one of the most important changes in the company's history, that's a crisis.

The least used, but potentially the most powerful, effect of surveys is their ability to turn up the heat. Surveys, or more accurately, communicating the comparative results of surveys, can create drama, embarrassment, and urgency. The output from a survey should not be "hmmm." We're not social scientists curious about the intricacies of human nature. We're managers. Our purpose is action. The survey should help make things happen. Use it as a tool forcing managers and employees to get going.

Letting in the Academics

Letting the professors bring their questionnaires into your organization is a good idea if you are searching for the answer to questions such as:

Is the cognitive dissonance resulting from low credible messages emitted by high credible sources, individual, group, or organizationally determined?

And even then, only if you don't mind the answer being:

Little of this, little of that, depends on the situation, needs more research.

Watch frontline employees trying to answer an academic questionnaire. With contorted and confused expressions, they attempt question after question. Put yourself in their shoes by imagining someone asking you:

How do I look today?

But not me overall, all at once. First, how does my hair look?

But not my hair as a whole. Specifically, how does the color of my hair look, ignoring its shape and texture?

Now the hair's shape, ignoring texture and color.

And now just texture.

Surely, you'd think this person mad. Normal people in everyday life don't make all these fine distinctions.

Many academics grossly overestimate the precision of language as used by frontline employees.

Researchers asking employees to evaluate their boss's "consideration," "employee orientation," and "communication" found employees didn't make these distinctions.[6] Employees uniformly gave their managers nearly identical scores on each of the three variables.

Other researchers studying "performance feedback" asked employees about the "timeliness," "specificity," "frequency," and "sensitivity," of their managers' feedback.[7] None of these distinctions held. The researchers recommended: Next time just use "feedback." Even this is optimistic. Employees would probably not make a distinction between a boss's "feedback" and just plain old "communication."

In our questionnaires, we used to ask frontline employees to evaluate their boss's upward communication (did she listen and request information) and their boss's downward communication (did she inform them of changes). Even this distinction collapsed. The correlation between these upward and downward communication scores was always .8 or .9 (where 1 is perfect association).

More important than the correlations was our realization that after years of interviewing frontline employees, face to face, not one, ever, spontaneously said: "My supervisor is very good at asking us questions and getting our opinions, but terrible at passing on information she already knows."

Ask frontline employees to evaluate their supervisor's communication, and they say: "He's good," or "He's not bad," or "He's pathetic." The frontline world is not one where people paint with fine shades of grey.

We decided two questions on our questionnaire was one too many. Now we only ask: "Circle the number (1 to 10) that best describes the quality of communication with your supervisor." Academics find this crude, but our respondents don't. No frontline employees have told us the question restricted them from making a more precise evaluation of their supervisor's communication.

Many academics are on a unique mission: breaking down concepts into their component parts, drawing boxes around the parts, drawing arrows between the boxes, and putting numbers on the arrows showing the strength of the relationships. This, however, is an activity only academics do. Language on the front line doesn't work that way.

The academic questionnaire is part of a private language, spoken only by other academics. There is value in their discourse among themselves. It breeds a respect for precision, careful thinking, and substantiation. But let's not pretend it has a track record of helping managers improve their company's communication.

Questionnaires and employee attitude surveys can improve communication, but only when two conditions are met: You know exactly what you are looking for and you have a planned response ready to go as a result of the survey outcome.

References

1. Michael R. Dulworth, Delmar L. Landen, and Brian L. Usilaner, "Employee Involvement Systems in U.S. Corporations: Right Objectives, Wrong Strategies," *National Productivity Review*, vol. 9, no. 2, spring 1990, pp. 141–156.

2. Confederation of British Industry, *Employee Involvement—Shaping the Future for Business*, 1990.

3. William E. Wymer and Joseph A. Parente, "Employee Surveys: What Employers Are Doing and What Works," *Employment Relations Today*, Winter 1991/1992, p. 477–484.

4. Industrial Society, op. cit., p. 48.

5. Research by The Hay Group, quoted in Alan Farnham, "The Trust Gap," *Fortune*, December 4, 1989, pp. 56–78.

6. Michael J. Glauser, "Upward Information Flow in Organizations: Review and Conceptual Analysis," *Human Relations*, vol. 37, no. 8, 1984, pp. 613–643.

7. Larson, op. cit., p. 1083.

16
Putting Your Communication to the Test

Part 2 is the negative part of this book, arguing traditional forms of communication are not working. Video, meetings, print, suggestion schemes, and surveys have failed to reach frontline employees. Instead, our efforts should focus on face-to-face communication between supervisors and their crews.

Our claim is radical. Most communication professionals believe the problem is not enough communication. Consequently their recommendation is for more: more videos, more meetings, more print, more attitude surveys, and more technology—most recently two-way live satellite TV.

What we have isn't working. Why would we want more?

This section of the book, Part 2, begins with a description of the British Telecom communication program. Figure 16-1 tests the BT program against the three facts of employee communication. It is clear from the figure why, despite this massive effort, BT employees rate their company's communication only 2 percentage points better than the U.K. national average. BT senior management is committed to improving communication, but their communication professionals have let them down. When programs violate the three facts of employee communication, you can send your stuff out, let it fly, giving the appearance of communication, but there is no change.

Don't eliminate these programs. They reach middle and senior managers and touch a tiny number of highly motivated frontline employees (employees who may someday become corporate leaders). These pro-

Figure 16-1. Evaluating British Telecom's communication program.

	target first-line supervisors	informal face to face	communicates relative performance of local work area
attitude survey	no	no	no
briefing meetings	involved	no	it could
"Speak-Up" (call in questions)	no	no	no
"Open Line" (recorded phone news)	no	no	no
"Walking the Job" (management by wandering around)	no	yes	it could
Videos	no	no	no
publications (70 of them)	it could	no	it could
training	it could	no	no
direct mail	no	no	no
communication manual	no	no	no
"New Ideas" (suggestion scheme)	no	no	no

grams, however, will not reach the front line and will not change the way employees act.

The traditional recommendation that what's needed is more is wrong. We already have more than enough communication. The problem is the communication we have isn't doing anything. It isn't working. It isn't changing employees.

Instead of more of the same, we need to get on a whole new track. A new way of thinking.

> [Phone installer to her supervisor, Jim]
>
> Say, Jim, there's a rumor the installers in the southern district are using some fancy hand-held computers. When they're in the field, they connect the computer direct to the phone line and automatically get their next job. And when they finish, they download direct to the accounts department. Is the rumor true? Are the computers working? Are we going to get computers as well?

Jim's answer determines the quality of your company's communication. Nothing else matters. The world's greatest videos, spot color in your newspaper, new logo for the suggestions scheme, team-building-briefing meetings, opinion surveys, all are irrelevant if Jim answers:

> I don't know anything. Wouldn't surprise me if those [profanity deleted] in the ivory tower have got another stupid scheme for making our lives miserable. And when the whole bloody thing flops, you know whose [profanity deleted] will get kicked—ours.

The damage here is much greater than first appears. Employees' job satisfaction, satisfaction with their supervisor, feelings about the company, and performance, depend on one thing: believing their supervisor is well connected and has influence above (Chap. 2). Videos, newspapers, suggestion schemes, and the like have little or no effect on satisfaction, feelings about the company, and performance. So let's wake up and change our communication priorities, putting videos and all the stuff at the bottom. Let's concentrate on improving communication to supervisors, until Jim can answer:

> Ya, they are testing hand-held computers in the southern district.
>
> I've had a couple meetings with the IS boffins and told them that I'm not using those things until they come with little printers. I won't have my installers driving around in vans squinting at some tiny one-inch LCD display. When they get that right, I'm going to OK the computers for us.
>
> And I think they'll work because they'll reduce the time you installers spend hanging around, getting busy signals, trying to contact me for your next job.

When Jim answer like that, implementation of the computers goes much faster, but, more importantly, employees see their supervisor as someone connected, thereby increasing satisfaction with their supervisor and job, creating positive attitudes toward the company as a whole, and improving performance.

But shouldn't we follow General Motors' lead and use print as a back-up? Publishing a story about the hand-held computers in the division newspaper *just in case* supervisors don't tell their crews? No. Employees:

Don't read

Don't understand much of what they do read

Need the answer when they ask the question (not a month later when the paper is published)

Don't trust head office sources

Believe the company newspaper doesn't tell the whole story (see Fig. 16-2).

Worst of all, the article in the company newspaper does nothing to strengthen the relationship between the supervisor and the employee. Why talk to the supervisor? Read the divisional newspaper and you know everything he knows.

If the new hand-held computers are an important change, then all efforts should be directed at reaching frontline employees through their supervisors.

Parts 1 and 2 of this book recommend targeting supervisors and relying on informal face-to-face communication. If our words and evidence are not persuasive, then try one of these tests in your company.

Figure 16-2. Percent of employees saying official communication does not tell full story. *(Source: Ref. 1 and Ref. 2.)*

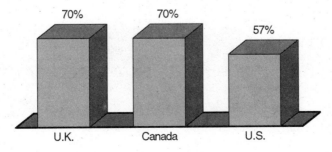

Control-Group Test

Communication should change behavior. Take a piece of your communication and see if it does.

PepsiCo, for example, encourages its divisions to give each employee a summary of the CEO's speech at the annual shareholders meeting. The eventual recipients are employees at Taco Bell, Frito-Lay, Pizza Hut, Pepsi-Cola, and Kentucky Fried Chicken.

Is it working? Everything we know about employee communication says this communication will fail because it is direct to employees, not targeted to supervisors, print instead of face to face, and about companywide, not local, issues.

It will have no effect on the way employees act. But PepsiCo could test it. Randomly divide the KFC stores in half, mailing the speech to one-half and not the other. Then it could send unannounced inspectors to the stores measuring the accuracy of the recipe mix, store cleanliness, and over-the-counter customer service. If the stores receiving the speech score higher, the communication works—keep it. But if the communication does not change employees, then why do it?

"Couldn't hurt." That's the answer most companies give. But it can hurt. This communication sends a signal to every manager that the number 1 communication priority is the CEO and downward information from head office. And worse, the communication creates an expectation among frontline employees that communication from the top is irrelevant and incomprehensible: earnings per share, return on assets, accelerated depreciation, and the rest.

And if you doubt employees think it's irrelevant, go to the back room and see how its treated: wastepaper for doodling, place mats, as a wedge to stop wobbly tables, doorstops, and paper planes.

Instead, publish in the company newspaper that any employees wanting a copy of the CEO transcript can call public affairs and have one sent to their home. Then make about 10 copies. That's all you'll need. And if you were to write down the names of the 10, you'd probably find they were to become your next generation of corporate leaders.

Testing Demand

An easier way to test communication is to stop it and see what happens.

One large bank, with 40,000 employees and 1200 branches, wanted to assess their existing communication. They initially considered doing a communication audit.

Usually an audit involves a questionnaire asking employees to evaluate the various forms of corporate-produced communication. These questionnaires typically produce an exaggerated positive response. If there is no cost involved for the receiver, in time, effort, or money, their recommendation is usually to keep it coming. A better test is just to stop it all and see what happens.

Over an eight-week period, without any warning or explanation, the bank in this example suddenly stopped all nontechnical head office communication, then counted the number of employees asking "Where is it?" For results, see Fig. 16-3.

Figure 16-3. Number of employees asking about missing communication.

Where Is It?

communication by budget size (most expensive first)	employees asking: "Where is it?" (out of 40,000 employees)
Your Bank (monthly video)	4
Transaction (company newspaper, two a month)	36
Teller-Talk (monthly newsletter specifically for tellers)	0
Report to Employees (simplified annual report)	1
Report Back: Joint Consultative Committee (one every six weeks)	0
Lend An Ear (monthly department newsletter for lending staff, approximately 2,000 employees)	12
What's Up Doc (monthly occupational health newsletter)	0
Personnel Report (monthly listing of job vacancies, promotions, and transfers)	2,112
Over-Time (monthly social committee publication)	890

These results show the bank's communication department puts its time and money into the least-noticed communication. One out of every 10,000 employees missed the corporate video enough to call and ask, "Where is it?"

These numbers demonstrate the theme coming up in Part 3: Employees care about themselves and their work area but not about the company as a whole. The communication most missed featured information about job vacancies ("Personnel Report") and fun ("Over-Time"). Only 0.09 percent of employees inquired about the missing company newspaper.

In contrast, imagine what would happen if the *New York Times* didn't come out tomorrow. What percent of its subscribers would inquire about its absence: 20 percent? 30 percent? 50 percent? Why? Because they want it. It has become part of their life. Part of their routine. The minuscule numbers above show the corporate-produced communication has not become part of employees' lives. It does not play a role and consequently is not missed. When change is important, when it really matters, don't put it there.

What Should the Communication Department Do?

The CEO should give them a new top priority: communicating change.

Take your three most important upcoming changes. For the bank in our example these are:

1. New computer system
2. Back-office paperwork moving to regional centers
3. New marketing strategy emphasizing small-business customers

Assign a communication professional to each change. Make communication professionals part of the change team. Require a communication plan for each change. The plan should target supervisors, rely primarily on face-to-face communication, and focus on implications to the local work area. Forbid any use of your traditional communication such as videos or company newspaper. This will force creativity and demand a new way of thinking.

Equip your communication professional with time and money. If necessary, take these from your current communication budget. The bank discussed here has a video production budget of more than $1.5 million, that is, $1.5 million spent on a communication device that, when suddenly stopped, was missed by 4 out of 40,000 employees. For half that amount, the company's three most important changes could be communicated to branch managers with surgical precision.

The change team needs a communication specialist. Communication is not a high priority among the head office managers overseeing change. What dominates is the "get the thing out there" mentality with its sequel, "We'll work the bugs out as we go along." This makes good sense to the head office changers. It makes chaos and frustration on the front line. Perhaps "working the bugs out as we go along" is efficient if there is only one change, but if there is a string of changes, it's disastrous. We are conditioning our employees to associate change with a screw-up. Eventually they resist before even hearing.

Clients are forever telling us, "People are naturally opposed to change." If this were true, one out of two marriages wouldn't end in divorce, the average employee wouldn't change jobs every six years, 20 percent of people would not move from one address to another every year, and no one would own a VCR, fax, or personal computer. Why do *people* change? Because they think they are changing to something better. Why do *employees* resist change? Because our changes are so poorly planned, they know it will make things worse.

The communication plan will slow change. Supervisors will accurately anticipate problems, and making adjustments takes time. But what matters is not how fast you change, but how fast you gain performance improvements relative to what existed previously. Targeting supervisors and reacting to their suggestions will slow the rate of change but greatly shorten the time it takes to surpass previous performance levels.

The clients saying people are naturally against change are the same ones saying, "The change was a good idea, but it sure took a lot longer than we expected to see the benefits." These two comments, side by side, are evidence of poor change communication. When change is properly planned and communicated, employees are not naturally antichange and benefits are not a long time coming.

Pull your staff and money off the communication that isn't doing anything, and, instead, put it where it's needed. Attach to each critical change a communication professional, a budget, and a communication plan—a plan that targets supervisors, relies on face-to-face communication, and concentrates on the local work area.

References

1. U.K. and Canadian data from Julie Foehrenbach and Karn Rosenberg, IABC/TPF&C, op. cit.
2. U.S. data from Julie Foehrenbach and Steve Goldfarb, TPF&C, op. cit.

17

Your Employees Don't Care About the Company

What they do care about is their local work area.

If communication is to change behavior, it must be about the employees' local work area. Ideally, the message should be about performance in the local work area, how this performance compares to competitors, and implicitly or explicitly, the impact on employees' job security.

Looking at what we normally communicate, one would think employees were desperate to hear about the half-yearly financial results, latest production targets, invitation for a vice president to sit on an industry council, bubblings in R&D, and the ubiquitous who runs what after the latest restructure.

We seem unable to get it through our heads: They don't care. Ask employees—they'll tell you (Fig. 17-1).[1,2,3,4]

Communication studies such as the ones in Fig. 17-1 show that what employees most want to know is the company's future plans and, in particular, the effect of these plans on their local work area.

IBM (U.K.) admits it has difficulty getting employees interested in topics beyond their local work area.[5] Research by leading employee communication consultant Roger D'Aprix shows that for employees at Weyerhaeuser, a U.S. paper company, the company is mostly an abstraction; employee allegiance is directed not to the company but to the location where they work.[6] British Telecom, noticing this trait among their employees, refers to it as their "identity problem."[7] And

Figure 17-1. Employees' limited interest in corporate topics.

topic	employees' desire to know - rank order among a list of topics	country	research by
organization's community involvement	15th out of 17 topics	USA	Rosenberg
information about the company's products and services	9th out of 12 topics	UK	Industrial Society
personal backgrounds of senior managers	18th out of 25 topics	Australia	Taylor
information about company ownership	14th out of 17 topics	New Zealand	Smith & Firth

almost everywhere senior managers are hard at work trying to figure out how to bind employees closer to their companies.

The answer is simple: You can't. Communication needs to work with the loyalties and interests employees already have, and it should not head down the futile path of trying to give employees new ones. What employees value is their local work area and their job security. Communication works, it changes employee behavior, only when it anchors itself in these values.

Here are two examples showing how senior managers can ground their messages in local work area concerns.

Communicating a Customer Service Survey in a Department Store Chain

The stores discussed here make a region within a large national retail chain. The region has 40 stores with approximately 11,000 employees.

Senior managers were deeply concerned by deteriorating scores in customer service surveys. During a 12-month period, measuring quarterly, the percent of customers very satisfied with their last purchase dropped from 87 to 86 percent, to 83 percent, ending the year at 82 percent. The sample involved customers using the store's credit card for purchases over $25 during the week prior to answering the survey questions.

The top regional manager decided the decline in scores should be communicated. Usually this sort of communication takes the form of an executive memo to all employees, most often a long spiel about how customers are number 1, the fine tradition the region has for delivering excellent customer service, and how this tradition is now in danger. Continuing with a mass of data, buried somewhere within the memo is the critical finding that service has slipped from 87 to 82 percent. Such memos end with the usual upbeat appeal for everyone to work together as a team.

All this is wrong: the wrong source, senior manager instead of the first-line supervisor; wrong method, print instead of face to face; with the wrong topic, information about the region instead of a local work area value.

The communication should be targeted to department managers (the equivalent to supervisors), such as the men's wear manager, sporting goods, or lingerie manager, with information sufficiently interesting that these managers can communicate it face to face to their hourly paid floor staff. And most important, communication should be grounded in something employees care about. Ideally this should be customer service scores for individual stores, or even better, individual departments. Unfortunately, the survey data was neither complete nor reliable all the way down to the store or department level. So, instead, senior managers linked the survey result to a related employee value, job security.

Working with a database of eight years of survey results and additional historical data concerning market share, profits, and past hiring levels, combined with projections about potential consumer spending in the upcoming 18 months, they came up with a diagram linking customer service levels to job security. The diagram was printed, front and back, on a laminated card, shirt-pocket size, handed out, and explained during sessions between senior managers and groups of department managers (Figs. 17-2 and 17-3).

Figure 17-2. (Front) Communicating customer service survey result.

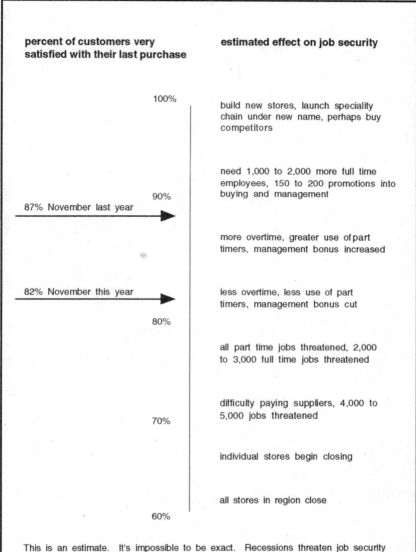

**percent of customers very
satisfied with their last purchase**

estimated effect on job security

100%

build new stores, launch speciality
chain under new name, perhaps buy
competitors

need 1,000 to 2,000 more full time
employees, 150 to 200 promotions into
buying and management

90%

87% November last year

more overtime, greater use of part
timers, management bonus increased

82% November this year

less overtime, less use of part
timers, management bonus cut

80%

all part time jobs threatened, 2,000
to 3,000 full time jobs threatened

difficulty paying suppliers, 4,000 to
5,000 jobs threatened

70%

individual stores begin closing

all stores in region close

60%

This is an estimate. It's impossible to be exact. Recessions threaten job security
even when customer service is good. Booms create some new jobs even when
service is poor. But in the long run, jobs depend on the quality of customer
service. Averaging out recessions and booms this diagram shows the relationship
between customer service and job security.

Figure 17-3. (Back) Communicating customer service survey result.

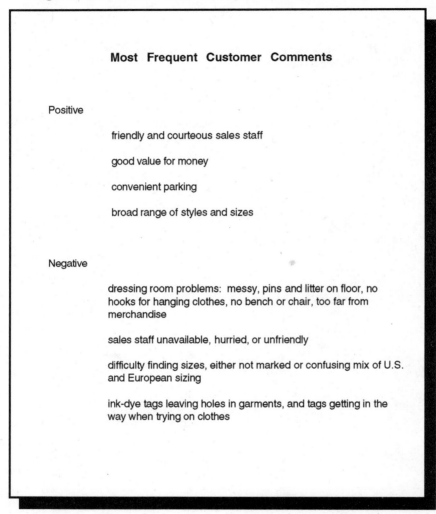

Most Frequent Customer Comments

Positive

> friendly and courteous sales staff
>
> good value for money
>
> convenient parking
>
> broad range of styles and sizes

Negative

> dressing room problems: messy, pins and litter on floor, no hooks for hanging clothes, no bench or chair, too far from merchandise
>
> sales staff unavailable, hurried, or unfriendly
>
> difficulty finding sizes, either not marked or confusing mix of U.S. and European sizing
>
> ink-dye tags leaving holes in garments, and tags getting in the way when trying on clothes

If employees were interested and concerned about the health of the region as a whole, then it would be enough to simply communicate the customer service decline from 87 to 82 percent, and employees would change, improving their customer service. But they are not concerned about the region. If they get the communication at all, they will see it as indicating problems in somebody else's department or in some other store. In their eyes it's about the company, not them.

Communication must cut through this and shake them up: *Do you care about your job? Then you better be concerned about our falling customer service.* In a factual, objective way, without the usual management rhetoric, it says, if we want to keep our jobs, we better clean up the dressing rooms and become more polite.

One senior manager objected to the communication complaining, "You're trying to scare them." Exactly. If management is scared, why shouldn't the employees be. When customer service is falling, fear is the right response. Management often tries not to scare employees. Usually this view is caused not as much by compassionate paternalism as it is by the attempt to avoid blame for their part in creating the scary situation.

This communication told the truth: Job security is related to customer service. If the truth scares them, that's good because it means we touched one of their values. And for communication to change behavior, it must touch the receivers' values. It must penetrate to the local work area and anchor itself in something they care about, in this case, their job security.

Communicating Corporatization in a Government Department

A newly elected government was quoted in a newspaper article as intending to corporatize several government departments, among them the Department of Roads and Traffic.

Unfortunately that is all the government said. One line in the newspaper. Not enough to communicate anything certain, more than enough to send employees into a panic.

Senior managers at the Department of Roads and Traffic communicated nothing because they knew nothing more than the one-line newspaper quote. Silence from senior managers convinced employees that the worst of the rumors must be true. Demand for information became a roar. Management, paralyzed, saw itself, and was seen by employees, as weak and failing to lead.

Often, senior managers feel they have nothing to communicate because of two self-imposed limitations: their habit of communicating in print and their artificial boundary that only certainty can be communicated. Get rid of these limitations, and there is much that can be said.

How to communicate when everything is uncertain is a topic we specifically discuss in Chap. 23, but here we can show an example of communication used by this government department and, most important, how the communication was made relevant to employees' local work areas.

Senior managers met with supervisors from the department's various divisions (Driver's License, Road Construction, Road and Signal Maintenance, Vehicle Licensing, and Safety). Each division had its own session.

Felt boards with stick-on statements assessing possible effects from corporatization were prepared for each division. Figure 17-4 shows a

Figure 17-4. Corporatization: What it might mean to the Drivers License Division.

competition	pay & benefits	reports
government wants competition	all Driver's License employees remain government employees	most government reports may be eliminated
perhaps auto club allowed to license members	job security, pay, and benefits for all Driver's License employees same as for any other government employee	for example: Driver's License Quarterly Budget & Personnel Report
perhaps insurance companies allowed to license customers		internal reports to Roads & Traffic senior management remain
perhaps a private licensing business will start up	**approvals**	
	greater independence from the government	**fee setting**
government could give our licensing responsibilities (and the corresponding part of our budget) to anyone giving better service for a better price	hiring and promotion within Driver's License Division may no longer require government approval	license fees probably still set by government
		training
	Driver's License Division budget may no longer require government approval	probably more expensive
government would allow competitors access to our centralized computer records		possible elimination of government subsidy for Driver's License employees attending training
	approvals still required by Roads & Traffic senior management	
		using private suppliers rather than government training college becomes an option

completed felt board accompanying the presentation senior managers gave to supervisors working in the Driver's License Division.

Look at the communication for the Driver's License Division supervisors and understand what it is not.

It is not theoretical. It is not a 5000-word treatise on the technical differences between privatization, corporatization, and operation as a government department. This would not be understood by supervisors, not communicated to frontline clerks, and would have no effect on the damaging rumors. In employees' eyes it would equal no communication at all.

This communication was not written. When senior managers write, their primary concern becomes self-defense, not communication. Second-guessing government policy, printed on Roads and Traffic letterhead, with a signature at the bottom, is not a prescription for good communication. Written communication for senior public service managers can be suicide unless filled with appropriate amounts of cooperativeness, diplomacy, reservation, and respect. First-line supervisors, unfortunately, will not penetrate the verbiage. They will get pieces of paper—not communication.

Finally, and most importantly, this communication is not intended for the entire organization. This communication is for the supervisors in the Driver's License Division. When you communicate to the entire organization, you depend on employees' taking generalized concepts and successfully applying them to their individual work area.

They won't make the transition. For example, this communication tells Driver's License supervisors that the government intends to increase competition. That alone would mean nothing. It goes on to speculate that perhaps the auto club will be allowed to license drivers. That's communication. Supervisors can see what that means. This image of people going to the auto club instead of the Driver's License Division for their license is a powerful message. A message grounded in their world. Notice also that the words *Driver's License Division* are repeated over and over. This is how they know the communication is about them. This is how they know their leaders are concerned about their situation. Mass communication does not work in large organizations.

This communication targeted supervisors, relied on face-to-face transfer, and translated the topic, corporatization, into local work area terms.

Their World Is the Local Work Area

It is impossible to underestimate the parochialism of our frontline employees. Talking about the company as a whole is an irrelevance. You might as well be speaking about another company altogether, perhaps in a foreign country. The boundary of their world is their local work area.

The unconvinced will say: Surely, then, we need to show them where their individual jobs fit in the company as a whole by showing them their role in the big picture.

The problem is, where their jobs fit in is not a high-ranking employee concern. The Confederation of British Industry found U.K. employees ranked "how my jobs fits in" 18th out of 21 desired communication topics.[8] Working with South African employees, Hill and Archer found "how my jobs fits in" ranked 7th out of 7 possible topics.[9] Research by Foehrenbach and Rosenberg shows U.S. employees rank the topic 7th out of 17 topics.[10]

And the chances of even greater parochialism in our next generation of employees looks likely. Diane Ravitch and Chester Finn, Jr., in a book called *What Do Our 17-Year-Olds Know?* tested knowledge among more than 7000 U.S. 17-year-olds, 30 percent of whom could not locate Great Britain on a map of Europe, and 35 percent of whom were unable to locate France.[11]

Don't for one moment think they are like you. Frontline employees, those making our products and delivering the services, are not the same as managers. The proof is in your hands at this very moment. Only 35 percent of Americans have read a book since graduating from high school, and only 20 percent say they have ever been in a bookstore.[12] Communicating with frontline employees as if they were managers is not receiver oriented and consequently will not change their behavior.

The boundary of their world is the local work area. Failure to realize this has taken us down several long dead-end roads.

When was the last time you heard anyone talking about *industrial democracy*? Industrial democracy, perhaps the dominant change in employee relations throughout Europe in the 1970s and early 1980s, died a quiet dignified death. Why? Not because senior managers successfully fought off attempts at worker involvement at executive levels but because employees didn't give a damn what was happening at executive levels unless it directly and immediately impacted on their local work area.

Industrial democracy was a driving concern among many politicians, union leaders, and academics but unfortunately not among many frontline employees.

Norway was a pioneer in industrial democracy. Yet as early as 1963, research by Thorsrud and Emery involving more than 1000 employees in 18 Oslo factories showed only 14 percent of these employees had any desire to participate in decisions relevant to the company as a whole.[13]

In the early 1980s, research involving the Tavistock Institute of Human Relations examined the desire for participation among 9000 employees working in 134 companies throughout 12 European countries.[14] On average, employees' desire to be personally involved in corporate long-term decision making didn't even reach the midpoint of their scale (scoring 2.3 on a 5-point scale).

Research quoted in Eric Batstone's work on industrial democracy shows that only 8 percent of worker directors in Sweden ever dissented from a board decision, and 40 percent of the time they didn't bother to report back to their shop floor constituents.[15]

In the Netherlands it has proved increasingly difficult to get shop floor workers to stand for reelection for their participative committees, called *works councils*.[16] The number of worker representatives willing to be reelected dropped from 59 percent in 1978 to 46 percent in 1984. The major reasons given for not wanting to participate were the disruption to their regular work, lack of time, and lack of interest.

Trying to get shop floor workers interested in corporate issues is like hitting your head against a brick wall; ask Cadbury Schweppes, the U.K.-based confectionery company.[17]

During the 1970s, Cadbury Schweppes took industrial democracy very seriously. At its Bournville site, employing 8500 workers, Cadbury Schweppes established 100 joint consultative committees. Employees elected 660 of their fellow workers to serve on these committees overseeing health, education and training, catering, safety, finance, amenities, suggestion scheme, and others. Operating these committees cost Cadbury Schweppes more than £50,000 a year.

Using employee surveys, Cadbury Schweppes examined what effect all this talk was having on communication. Only 11 percent of workers reported being well informed, only 12 percent said they regularly received information from their elected representatives, and 50 percent said their major source of information was workmates or gossip. When asked how communication could be improved, the number 1 response, reported by 45 percent of all employees, was that there should be increased communication from their immediate supervisor.

While the political left was struggling unsuccessfully to get workers interested in corporate-level affairs through industrial democracy, the political right decided it could bind employees closer to the company by tieing their pay to company profits.

Profit sharing, according to the theory, would make employees feel like owners, linking them closer to the company, and consequently increasing their commitment and productivity.

While employees were more than willing to take the money, it does not appear profit sharing has done much else. Michael Poole and Glenville Jenkins examined research involving 303 U.K. firms with profit-sharing schemes.[18] The results were not impressive:

Only 16 percent of employees said profit sharing made them feel more like part of the company.

Only 14 percent felt profit sharing had increased their commitment.

Only 8 percent believed employees had become more profit conscious.

83 percent reported no improvement in communication between managers and workers.

92 percent admitted putting no more effort into their work.

The truth is staring us in the face. Why not admit it? They don't care about the company. There is no great demand for information about corporate-level decisions that do not immediately impact on the employee's local work area.

We tried yanking them out of the local work area through participation on senior management committees, but that didn't work. We tried buying their corporate allegiance, linking their pay to company profits, but that didn't work. Communication will never work until we accept our employees the way they are. What employees care about is their local work area and their job security. If communication is going to change employees, it must link itself to these employee concerns.

And what exactly do we want employee to do? We want them to improve their performance. Well then, communicate performance. Especially the performance of their local work area. And give it meaning by comparing their performance to that delivered by competitors. These comparisons should be communicated to first-line supervisors. Supervisors will pass this on, face to face, to their frontline workers.

How do we know supervisors will pass it on? Because there is frontline employee demand for the information. Why do you think rumors move with such astonishing speed through huge organizations? Because there is demand for the information. The widely held belief that supervisors can't or don't communicate with their subordinates is a direct result of our refusal to give them anything worth communicating. Give them the right information, and you will not be able to stop them communicating.

During General Motors long years of declining U.S. market share (46 percent in 1979 to 35 percent in 1991[19]), GM did not communicate quality comparisons between GM cars and those manufactured by competitors to anyone outside the top 1 percent of GM's managers. These comparisons were communicated in secret "for-your-eyes-only" top-management conferences.

Beginning in 1986, the president of General Motors broke with this tradition and began talking more openly about GM's poor quality compared with other manufacturers. A 66 minute video tape discussing

GM's inferior performance was shown to 40,000, or almost half, of GM's managers.[20] And, in some isolated cases, the video tape was shown to hourly employees as well.

Sharing this information was a step in the right direction, but it was wrongly executed. If the goal was changing the behavior of shop floor employees, then this information should have targeted first-line supervisors. Among GM employees 83 percent say their most trusted and believed source of information is their immediate supervisor.[21] Seventy-three percent of GM's employees want their information face to face, and only 15 percent of GM's employees say they are interested in seeing top executives communicate on video tape. Most importantly this message of decline needed to be translated into a local work area issue.

Throughout the mid to late 1980s, the paint-line supervisors working on Chevrolet Cavaliers needed to know exactly where they stood. Tell them: The customers are screaming about your work. New Cavaliers are peeling and rusting. Show them the number of complaints. Tell them the rate of paint jobs redone on warranty. Bring in a dealer with his bulging file of irate customers and let the dealer explain the effect of their work on his business. Or buy a Honda Accord, Nissan Stanza, and Chevy Cavalier, and let an auto paint expert take them over the strengths and weaknesses of each.

GM workers needed to watch the decline of their company in terms that made sense to them. They needed to see this decline translated into their world—not labor costs per vehicle, not manhours per vehicle, not return on assets, not market share. They needed to know how the quality of the Cavalier paint job compared with the Honda Accord.

Instead of keeping this information secret, it should be the top priority of all our communication efforts: Target supervisors, with face-to-face information, concerning the relative performance of their local work area.

References

1. Karn Rosenberg: "What Employees Think of Communication: 1984 Update," *Communication World*, vol. 2, no. 5, May 1985, pp. 46–50.
2. The Industrial Society, op. cit., p. 40.
3. Taylor, Dennis, op. cit., p. 76.
4. Andrew Smith and Michael Firth, "Communicating by Employee Reports: A Survey of Employee Attitudes," *New Zealand Journal of Industrial Relations*, vol. 12, 1987, pp. 123–126.
5. Incomes Data Services, Ltd, "Employee Communication," *IDS Study*, #318, July 1984, pp. 16–19.

6. Smith, Alvie, op. cit., p. 125.

7. Industrial Relations Services, "BT (UK)'s Employee Communications Drive," *Industrial Relations Review and Report #449*, October 10, 1989, pp. 11–14.

8. The Confederation of British Industry, Brandon and Arnott, op. cit., p. 17.

9. Lorna A. Hill and Arminius A. Archer, "Communication and Labour Relations in South Africa—A Strategic Approach," *IR Journal* (South Africa), 2nd quarter, 1988, pp. 43–58.

10. J. Foehrenbach and K. Rosenberg, "How Are We Doing?" *Journal of Communication Management*, vol. 12, no. 1, 1982, p. 7, quoted in Phillip G. Clampitt, *Communicating for Managerial Effectiveness*, Sage Publications, Newbury Park, Calif., 1991, p. 87.

11. Diane Ravitch and Chester E. Finn, Jr., What Do Our 17-Year-Olds Know? Harper & Row, New York, 1987.

12. John Boswell, *The Awful Truth About Publishing*, Warner Books, New York, 1986, p. 81.

13. Thorsrud and Emery research quoted in Harriet Holter, "Attitudes Toward Employee Participation in Company Decision-Making Processes: A Study of Non-Supervisory Employees in Some Norwegian Firms," *Human Relations*, vol. 18, no. 4, November 1965, pp. 297–319.

14. Tavistock Institute research quoted in Frank A. Heller, "Does Formal Policy or Law as Used in Europe Contribute to Improved Employee Information and Participation?" in *Employee Consultation and Information in Multinational Corporations*, edited by Jacques Vandamme, Croom Helm, London, 1986, pp. 69–94.

15. Eric Batstone, "Industrial Democracy and Worker Representation at Board Level: A Review of the European Experience," in *Industrial Democracy: European Experience*, Industrial Democracy Committee, London, 1976, pp. 24 and 34.

16. Paul Kunst and Joseph Soeters, "Works Council Membership and Career Opportunities," *Organization Studies*, vol. 12, no. 1, 1991, pp. 75–93.

17. Cadbury Schweppes study in *Worker Participation in Britain*, a Social Policy Research Limited Study, London, 1974, pp. 65–72.

18. Michael Poole and Glenville Jenkins, "Human Resource Management and Profit-Sharing: Employee Attitudes and a National Survey," *International Journal of Human Resource Management*, vol. 1, no. 3, December 1990, pp. 289–328.

19. "Can GM Remodel Itself?" *Fortune*, January 13, 1992, pp. 26–33.

20. Smith, Alvie, op. cit., p. 96.

21. "Local Managers + Information = Key Internal Communicators," *Employee Relations and Human Resources Bulletin*, Report No. 1672, sec. 1, September 21, 1988, pp. 1–6.

18
Communicating Quality: Better or Worse Than Competitor's

Seventy-five percent of U.S. and U.K. companies have quality programs.[1] Most are not working. Looking at 95 U.S. companies, Rath and Strong found only 62 percent of managers said their quality programs were working.[2] Arthur D. Little's study of 500 U.S. companies found only 33 percent of managers said quality was working.[3] And worst of all, A.T. Kearney's research with 100 U.K. companies shows only 20 percent of managers believe their quality programs are successful.[4] Beginning with enthusiasm and the best of intentions, quality programs begin their decline about 18 months after inception, according to research by the Quality Improvement Company.[5]

Why? One reason is because quality is usually communicated as a corporate value, and employees don't act according to corporate values–they act according to local work area values. When it exists, the loyalty, pride, and devotion felt by employees is to the local work area, not to the corporate whole. Messages meant to change behavior must touch these feelings, feelings firmly anchored in the local work area. Telling them the company has dedicated itself to the pursuit of quality is a waste of words.

Here is an example.

A manufacturer supplying sheet metal machinery to fabricators invited us to attend a quality training session for their paint shop employees.

165

The theme of this training was the "evil of overadjustment." The intended lesson was: Too much fine-tuning can actually lessen quality. To illustrate this theme, the instructor put a funnel (held upright in a stand) on a table. Then with a piece of chalk he marked a circle on the table surface. The instructor began dropping marbles through the funnel with the goal of having them come to rest in the chalk circle.

It turns out the worst thing you can do is adjust the position of the funnel after each drop. The optimum solution is to aim the funnel the best you can and then leave it alone. Moving the funnel is a mistake because the final resting place of any particular marble is largely a random event. Making adjustments away from your best initial aim based on random information results in wild swings away from the target.

The trainer then applied the lesson to the paint shop saying:

> So, for example, take the paint-bake ovens, where the required temperature is, say, 360°C. Continual adjustment after each batch will cause the greatest departure from the desired temperature. Instead, after repeated observations, determine an upper control limit, say, 380, and a lower control limit, say, 340. And only adjust the oven temperature when it goes beyond these limits.

It was, we thought, a fascinating demonstration, but one frontline employee disagreed, heckling, "I don't think we have an overadjustment problem with our paint ovens." This brought howls of laughter. We asked why and were told, "Nobody in this place gives a damn what the oven temperature is, nobody looks at that thermometer, nobody adjusts the controls, nobody cares."

It is pointless trying to teach quality techniques to employees who have not taken responsibility for performance.

The quality experts, the Japanese, understand this. Robert Cole of the University of Michigan was researching quality programs in the early Eighties and was surprised to learn that, while Sony, Matsushita, and Sanyo all used quality programs in their Japanese plants that manufacture televisions, none used these programs in their U.S. plants.[6] The reason, according to the Japanese, "they [the U.S. factories] are not yet ready."

If employees are trying to improve performance, then quality programs make sense. But if "nobody in this place gives a damn," then pushing quality is a waste of words.

The ground must be prepared before quality can grow. Preparing the ground means having employees who are trying to do better. Do this by communicating to employees the relative performance of their local work area. How good or bad is their work compared with other similar groups? This information tugs at their self-respect and pride. It sends a message about the only thing they are likely to care about: their local work area.

The implications are important. Preaching "quality" is a mistake. Printing "quality" on every flat surface in the company (pens, notebook covers, pads, coffee cups, mobiles hanging from the ceiling, posters on every bulletin board) is wrong. Employees don't look at posters for cues how to behave. They look at other employees around them, and mostly at their supervisors.

Instead, communicate quality without ever mentioning the word. "Quality" has no pull on the front line. It is senior management talk, or to the front line, senior management babble. Tell them their performance. Tell them how well they do their job. No one will mistake that for babble.

Communicating Quality: Gas Ranges

The company in this example manufactures free standing 30-inch-wide gas ranges intended for the home appliance market. Quality preaching (posters, speeches, newspaper articles, training, buttons, pins, decals) had not worked. Instead, they decided to communicate the relative performance of the local work area. Here is what they did:

- They purchased two ranges from each of the top five producers (their range was included).
- They hired an independent product-testing firm to evaluate the quality.
- They booked a hotel conference room and brought in plant supervisors 30 at a time.
- There was a 5-minute introduction by the oven company president.
- That was followed by a 30-minute presentation from the head engineer at the product-testing firm, who ranked the gas ranges in terms of quality, 1 to 5 (their range ranked fourth).
- The room dividers opened, revealing five separate displays, one for each manufacturer.
- Each manufacturer's gas range was displayed fully assembled, and another was broken down.
- Posters around the display highlighted quality strengths and weaknesses.
- Supervisors were given 45 minutes to informally inspect all displayed ranges.

Figure 18-1. Oven quality: Communication for supervisors.

time-bake clock control knobs
not securely fastened

decorative chrome trim bent
and lifting up from frame

oven door gasket twisted,
uneven, and leaking heat

combined design/assembly flaw
causing self-cleaning automatic door lock
not to close at specified 550 degrees Fahrenheit

scratches on oven wall where
internal light installed

- A five-page summary, one page covering each range, was given to all supervisors. For a sample diagram see Fig. 18-1.

Several days after the first group of supervisors attended the quality session, senior managers randomly telephoned 100 frontline employees (not the supervisors who attended, but their subordinates) asking them what they had heard about the quality session. These calls revealed that 96 percent of frontline employees knew the quality session had occurred, 96 percent knew their company placed fourth, and 83 percent could name three or more quality faults attributed to their area.

Understand what happened here: Almost all frontline employees got the message even though nothing was communicated directly to them. There was one and only one way to learn this information: face-to-face communication with their supervisors. No articles in the company newspaper, no bulletin board announcements, no memos trickling down through middle management, and no touring, speech-making CEO. The only way to hear about the demonstration was face to face from the supervisor—and 96 percent of them got it. Why? Because the information was about the relative performance of the local work area. It was about how they do their job compared with competitors. The information was about them. That was why it flowed so easily.

If your company is constantly forcing communication—pleading, begging, training, or threatening supervisors to communicate—you have the wrong content. When the information is about the local work area, you can't stop their communicating.

In this example senior management went directly to supervisors (frontline employees and middle managers did not attend the quality sessions), with face-to-face information (supervisors were there live), about the relative performance of the local work area (how their work compared with major competitors). Unless communication conforms to these three facts, it will not change frontline employee behavior.

Communicating Quality: Freight Delivery

Over a two-year period a freight forwarding company was losing market share to a competitor. Of particular concern was the parcel or less-than-truck-load (LTL) market segment.

A quality-oriented campaign called *Fast & Fussy* had previously failed. Obscenity laws forbid us from describing how truck drivers and freight handlers altered the campaign name. This time the company decided to communicate its relative performance. Here are the details:

- They purchased two wooden crates and packed each with 72 beer glasses.
- Each crate weighed about 60 pounds.
- One crate was sent through the company to a bar in another city; an identical crate was sent to the same bar, but this one by the competitor (see Fig. 18-2).
- Bar owners recorded:

  Exact time of arrival (company and competitor)

  Breakage (how many glasses were broken)

  Customer service impression of the delivery person

- The test was repeated 20 times with 20 different bars in 20 different cities.
- In thanks for participating, bars kept the glasses.

Results: the company had 15 percent less breakage and slightly better customer service, but on the critical issue of delivery speed, it was badly beaten. Competitor delivered quicker on 16 of the 20 trials (Fig. 18-3).

These trials were run secretly. Following the last one, supervisors (the company called them "depot managers") were gathered into meetings where the CEO showed them the results. The CEO, expressing grave concern, said the trials would be repeated one month later with a different secret parcel.

Figure 18-2. Secret freight: one sent by the company, the other by the competitor.

Figure 18-3. Crate of beer glasses to bars: Delivery speed in days.

Origin/Destination	Competitor	The Company
NYC/Atlanta	2	3
NYC/Boston	2	3
NYC/Denver	4	6
-		
-		
arrived faster out of 20 trials	16 trials	4 trials

The communication caused change:

Consignment notes were put in plastic envelopes and stuck directly onto parcels instead of paperwork arriving at the depot a day or two after the parcel.

Supervisors began faxing evening floor checks to head office so it was then known which parcels had been delivered and which were still at the depot.

Management, for the first time, won union agreement permitting the movement of employees between day and evening shifts. Previously an employee hired onto the day shift stayed there as long as he or she worked for the company.

After four weeks a second secret set of trials began. This time the company selected boxes of photocopy paper, 10 reams in each box, weighing approximately 45 pounds. They sent these boxes to the same cities but this time to photocopy shops. They shipped one box by the company, one by the competitor.

Results from this second set of trials showed this time that the competitor was faster in 12 of the 20 trials. The company improved from winning 4 trials to winning 8—Not even, but closing the gap.

The communication actually did something. It changed behavior. Why? Because it was about their job, moving freight, and how well they do it compared with a competitor.

Notice: No articles in the company newspaper, no direct communication with middle managers or frontline employees, no logo, slogans, posters, training; this communication targeted supervisors with face-to-face information concerning the relative performance of the local work area.

Communicating Quality Is Forbidden

Although "quality" is the dominant idea in management today, communicating quality to supervisors and employees is almost universally forbidden. Any comparative information with competitors is kept secret, and without this, quality has no meaning. Better or worse than what?

According to the U.S. General Accounting Office, 83 percent of Fortune 1000 companies share yearly financial results with all employees, but almost none share company-competitor performance comparisons with anyone outside senior management.[7]

Even among "high information sharing" companies, The Conference Board in the United States found almost no evidence of companies willing to communicate comparative performance levels of competitors.[8] This information is regarded as proprietary and kept secret from everyone but senior executives.

None of this has escaped the attention of frontline employees. Taylor's research discovered the topic employees thought their company would most want to keep hidden from them.[9] It was not that a piece of equipment had fallen and an employee was seriously injured. It was not that management was planning plant closings and layoffs. It *was* that the company had lost a major contract to a competitor.

The single piece of information most likely to change employee behavior is our most closely guarded secret. Rather than communicate quality (better or worse than whom), companies prefer communicating quantity (how much): tons per manhour, sales per square foot, throughput, scrap rates, plant utilization, number of transactions, or calls answered. Then, in a pretence to evaluation, this quantity is compared with the quantity produced last year or last quarter. This boring data motivates no one. Your frontline employees are people, not machines, and urging them to minimize the time it takes to perform repetitive operations will not change their behavior. If you want them to listen, you must communicate the value, merit, or calibre of their work. In other words, communicate quality, not quantity, and make it meaningful by evaluating and communicating their performance compared with others.

We believe companies do not share comparative performance information because they fear embarrassing managers. Quantitative information, aggregated to the corporate level, shields individual managers from humiliation.

Denied any comparative performance information, employees assume everything is probably going just fine. A shocking 90 percent of U.K. employees believe that the quality of the products they produce are as good or better than competitors, according to research by The Industrial Society.[10] And when asked to describe the companies they work for, the most frequently mentioned words were (in order): *profitable, successful, friendly, good quality products*, and *competitive*.

Similarly the National Economic Development Office found in its study of U.K. employees that only 11 percent thought customers might be seriously dissatisfied with their company's products or services.[11]

So on they go, wrapped in their cocoon, blissfully carrying on as before, day after day, seeing no real reason to change, until the first rumors of plant closure and layoffs leak out. Then employees swing radically to the other extreme to fear and paranoia, and rumors run rampant.

As consultants, moving company to company, we find employees in one of two states: blissful ignorance or neck deep in fear. This is an inescapable byproduct of not regularly communicating relative performance with competitors. Large companies don't go bad overnight. It happens step at a time. Employees need and deserve to know where they stand.

Don't Keep Score, Don't Have Winners, Just Count Kicks

Would what we do in large companies work elsewhere? In soccer, for example, suppose we decided to eliminate the goal nets, replacing them with invisible electronic fields. Then only league executives at the control panel would know the score. Keep winners, losers, and team rankings secret. Just tell players the total number of kicks their team has this season compared with last.

While this would save bottom-performing teams some embarrassment, it would destroy everything else. Soon players would come listlessly onto the field, only half trying, rarely cooperating, unwilling to practice or try new techniques. In other words they would look like our frontline employees.

We are not going to successfully communicate quality until we communicate the relative performance of the local work area. Performing well brings pride; performing poorly, embarrassment. This pride and embarrassment will fuel performance improvements. If the communication doesn't prick these emotions, it can't change behavior. And if it doesn't change behavior, it isn't worth having.

Stop preaching "quality" as if it were some kind of religion. Realize that quality techniques will never work unless employees are trying to do better. And realize that people don't do better in a vacuum. Whatever loyalty and commitment our employees have is to their local work area. Draw on that strength—it's the only one we have. And begin communicating the relative performance of their local work area.

References

1. *The Economist*, April 18, 1992, pp. 67–68.
2. Rath & Strong study quoted in *Fortune*, May 18, 1992.
3. Arthur D. Little study quoted in *The Economist*, April 18, 1992, pp. 67–68.
4. A. T. Kearney study quoted in *The Economist*, April 18, 1992, pp. 67–68.

5. Quality Improvement Company study quoted in Kate Ludeman, "Using Employee Surveys to Revitalize TQM," *Training*, December 1992, p. 51–57.

6. The Robert Cole information taken from Robert H. Hayes, Steven C. Wheelwright, and Kim B. Clark, *Dynamic Manufacturing: Creating the Learning Organization*, The Free Press, New York, 1988, p. 259.

7. General Accounting Office study in Michael R. Dulworth, Delmar L. Landen, and Brian L. Usilander, "Employee Involvement Systems in U.S. Corporations: Right Objectives, Wrong Strategies," *National Productivity Review*, vol. 9, no. 2, spring 1990, pp. 141–156.

8. The Conference Board, *Opening the Books: Corporate Information Sharing With Employees: Report No. 167*, by David Lewin, The Conference Board, New York, 1984.

9. Taylor, op. cit., p. 50.

10. The Industrial Society, op. cit., p. 50.

11. National Economic Development Office, *Employee Views on Employment Relations*, July 17, 1987.

19

Communicating
Quality: Looking
In-House

It does not matter whether the worker wants
responsibility or not. The enterprise must
demand it of him.

Peter Drucker wrote this in 1954.[1] But how? How do you get workers to take responsibility? Communication can help. Tell supervisors how good or poor their area is compared with other similar areas. Don't communicate performance in management terms: sales per square foot, ratio of direct to indirect costs, units produced per hour. Rather, communicate performance in ways that hit at their pride and self-respect. Evaluate and compare their workmanship. By harnessing their feelings of accomplishment and embarrassment, this communication can maneuver frontline employees into a position of wanting to do better. Once they are trying, once they have begun to take responsibility for performance, then and only then can you talk to them about "quality."

The previous chapter showed how to communicate performance in comparison with other competing companies. Sometimes that is not possible. This chapter shows how to communicate performance internally, comparing one local work group to another within the same company.

Employees Not Taking Responsibility: An AT&T Example

September 17, 1991, was a terrible day for AT&T.[2]

On that Tuesday afternoon, about 4:30 p.m., the switching station in lower Manhattan had a power failure and the telephone transmission equipment began shutting down. Phone service was not 100 percent restored until midnight. The effects were dramatic:

4.5 million blocked domestic calls, 0.5 million blocked international calls

80 percent of Federal Aviation Authority communication between New York City airports blocked

Kennedy, La Guardia, and Newark airports closed for four hours

1174 canceled or delayed flights

85,000 inconvenienced passengers (one of whom happened to be the chairman of the Federal Communications Commission, AT&T's regulatory agency)

Perhaps the greatest potential danger came from clearing the airspace above New York City. While the FAA says minimum plane-to-plane spacing was maintained at all times, air traffic controllers described the clearing as "tense."

Who was to blame? To answer, more of the story needs telling.

AT&T had a power-shedding agreement with the local power authority. On peak load days, AT&T agreed to take their switching station off city power and instead draw power from its own in-house diesel generators. September 17 was a peak load day, the power authority asked AT&T to switch to internal power, and AT&T agreed to do so. The switchover occurred at 10:10 a.m., but it did not go well: The in-house generator failed, and emergency backup batteries kicked in to supply the station's power.

These backup batteries have a six-hour life span, more than enough time to repair the in-house generator or switch back to city power. On the twentieth floor of the switching station, where the batteries are located, lights were flashing and the alarm bell was ringing, warning that power was coming from the emergency backup batteries. Unfortunately no one was there to see or hear the alarms. The supervisor and his three subordinates responsible for twentieth-floor power operation were at an all-day training course in a different building. So the alarms flashed and rang on unnoticed. After six hours the batteries died, and the phone systems crashed.

Accepting blame, Robert E. Allen, chairman and CEO of AT&T, said, "I can hardly remember anything in my career that was quite as painful to me personally."[3] The FCC criticized local management, saying their decision to send the entire power staff to training on a day with a planned switch from city to in-house power was "not prudent."

In our opinion, the people most to blame are those working on the twentieth floor—it's their area. If management made a mistake and sent everyone to a training course on the same critical day, that's too bad, but it is still their area. If they don't take responsibility for the twentieth floor, no one else can because no one else is close enough.

This colossal tragedy could have been easily avoided. The supervisor or any one of his subordinates could have skipped lunch and done a walk-through of their floor. The supervisor or any subordinate could have telephoned any of the 115 employees remaining in that building and said, "Betty, hate to bother you, but could you walk up to the twentieth, have a look, and call me back."

Remember, the twentieth floor was silent (it should have been humming with the sound of the diesel generators) except for a ringing alarm bell and flashing warning light. It doesn't take an electrical engineering degree to call back saying, "Hey, something's gone wrong on your floor." The reason anything at all comes out of any company is because millions of frontline employees do take responsibility for what happens in their area—regardless of the mistakes their managers make. One reason for poor quality is that millions of others don't.

Quality programs for these employees (those who have not taken responsibility) are a waste. They are not in the game, and giving them tips on how to improve is pointless. As the Japanese said of their U.S. employees at Sony, Matsushita, and Sanyo (in the early Eighties), "They are not yet ready."[4]

Imagine that we were at the AT&T training course on that fateful Tuesday afternoon. Further imagine that we handed out a questionnaire asking the twentieth-floor employees to evaluate themselves and the quality of their work. Would they have given themselves low marks, admitting a lack of commitment and competence? No. They would have done what employees everywhere do. They would have said: "We do a pretty good job given the manpower reductions, low morale, and constant restructuring going on around us."

But this would be false. They were not doing a pretty good job. The FCC in its investigation found:

A miscalibrated safety relay-meter caused the initial failure to the in-house generators. The FCC said, "the meter had become a hair-trigger."

A critical alarm light that would have warned employees on the fourteenth floor of the power problems on the twentieth floor was burned out.

Alarm bells would have rung on the nineteenth floor except that the system was mistakenly set to "remote" instead of "local."

Power could have been restored earlier, but employees did not fully understand how to manually close the ac-dc relays in the tripped rectifiers.

Employees at the lower Manhattan switching station were not doing a pretty good job. And the whole point of this example is that they need to know that.

AT&T has 31 switching stations almost identical to the lower Manhattan one. Grade them A (excellent) to D (poor), and communicate the results to all switching station supervisors. The lower Manhattan employees needed to know that: Of the 31 stations, they were one of the worst. The employees needed to know that other employees working with similar equipment, similar manning cuts, similar chaotic restructuring, were doing a better job.

There is no guarantee this communication would have caused them to be more diligent and caring. But we can say this with complete certainty: If this communication doesn't work, no other communication will work either. If employees don't care about the performance of their local work group compared to other similar groups—at least from a communication point of view—give up. And at the very least, don't spend one penny on a quality program because it hasn't got a chance.

Communicating Relative Performance: Offshore Oil Platforms

A division within a large oil company decided to communicate the relative performance of its offshore oil platforms. There were eight similar platforms in the division. Communicating their performance required the following:

- An evaluation team (two production supervisors, two maintenance supervisors, and two head office engineers) needed to be established.

- Half the team was selected from within the division; the other half was drawn from a different division operating similar platforms in a different location.

- In preparation, the evaluation team spent four weeks informally inspecting many platforms in several divisions.

- An additional two weeks was required for the evaluation team to come up with an evaluation procedure.

- Now ready, the evaluation team arrived unannounced on platforms (platform supervisors knew an evaluation would occur but not when).

- Platforms were evaluated in three major categories (production, maintenance, and safety) on a 4-point scale (A = excellent, B = good, C = average, D = poor).

- A ranking of the eight platforms according to their scores is shown in Fig. 19-1.

- Finally, a single-page summary of major strengths and weaknesses was completed for each platform. A sampling of some remarks concerning the Rip Tow Platform is shown in Fig. 19-2.

Supervisors from all eight platforms were gathered to hear the results. The division manager showed platform rankings and described major strengths and weaknesses for each platform. Finally, each supervisor was given a nine-page handout (the overall ranking and the single-page summaries for each platform). The division manager said the evaluations would be repeated in six months and after that, yearly.

The goal of this communication was to arouse feelings. We want supervisors on Tide to feel a rush of pride, and those on Coral to feel deflated and humbled. It is these emotions, pride and embarrassment, that will

Figure 19-1. Relative performance of offshore oil platforms.

Platform Evaluation			
		production	maintenance	safety
1.	Tide	A	A	A
2.	Reef	B	A	A
3.	Island	A	A	B
4.	Crest	C	B	B
5.	Beach	C	B	C
6.	Whitewater	B	D	C
7.	Rip Tow	C	C	D
8.	Coral	D	C	D

Figure 19-2. Sample comments from "Rip Tow" evaluation.

Rip Tow

LMO valve failed to function properly when tested

volume of flared gas (15 MMSCFD) much too high

water cut of processed oil at 10% - should be closer to 5%

insufficient work order documentation concerning repairs to centrifugal compressor

bearings on MOL booster pumps in desperate need of replacement

malfunctioning alarms on main process control panel

coarse sea water filters badly clogged

...

...

---

fuel attempts to improve. And the point of this chapter is that, unless they are trying to improve, subsequent quality programs won't work.

Within the company, many critics supported the evaluations but opposed sharing the results with supervisors, and especially showing supervisors results from other platforms. Critics said, "Shouldn't this be private?" No. Shielding supervisors and frontline employees from relative performance information is what has made them so listless and uncommitted in the first place. Keeping evaluations secret cuts us off from the most powerful and efficient force known for changing human behavior—social pressure. The evaluation draws its power to change behavior from its openness. Secrecy kills it.

Interviewing frontline employees in industry after industry, what we hear most is: "It pays to keep your head down"; "Don't make waves"; "Go with the flow—even if it's wrong." Allan Frank's research with U.S. employees backs our experience, finding out that 59 percent of the time subordinates are unlikely to tell their boss about a mistake the subordinate has made.[5] Worse, 78 percent of the time subordinates are unlikely to tell their boss about a mistake the boss has made. Speaking up does not pay. Exposing the problem may simultaneously expose a contributing bad decision made by some manager somewhere. The belief on the frontline is that this manager may seek out those disclosing his or her error and punish them for the revelation. It is better in their view to let the problem manifest itself in some physical way, machine breakdowns or customer complaints, because then the managers involved cannot trace the revelation back to any so-called loud mouth frontline employee. This helps explain the Industry Week research showing 70 percent of U.S. employees "bit their tongues" at work because they feared reprisals from speaking out.[6] Or the Industry Week/Wyatt finding that while 64 percent of top managers believed their company encouraged employees to voice their opinions, only 29 percent of supervisors agreed.[7]

Solve this problem by openly communicating relative performance. Let the communication do the job of exposing poor performance. Share the performance ranking with all supervisors and higher managers. Why? To create pain and embarrassment. Make the managers responsible for those poorest-performing areas feel bad. Bad enough to force them onto the front line honestly asking advice about how to improve. Think about the research from the National Economic Development Office showing that 65 percent of U.K. frontline employees say they are rarely or never asked how their job could be done better.[8] And decide to make that style of leadership more painful for those who practice it.

All this talk of open evaluation, embarrassment, and pain will understandably make some readers uncomfortable. But this must be weighed against the tragic discomfort felt by all employees when their companies cannot improve, cannot compete, and therefore, cannot continue to exist.

If embarrassing employees is what it takes to get improvement, then do it. Nowhere is this more true than on offshore oil platforms. Tiny islands of steel, often hundreds of miles offshore, sometimes packed with a couple hundred people, and literally rumbling under the pressure of thousands of barrels of oil a day flowing at extremely high pressure and temperature through miles of piping. Mistakes in this environment costs lives. Fire on the Piper Alpha platform in the North Sea killed 165 employees; only 61 survived. On July 6, 1988, workers on Piper Alpha were repairing a backup condensate injection pump, but apparently did not appropriately tag it as under repair or adequately pass this information on to the next shift.[9] During the following shift, the primary pump failed, and workers tried starting the backup pump, not knowing it was under repair and that a pressure safety valve had been removed. During the attempted startup, a gas cloud formed and ignited. The resulting explosion escalated into a fire fierce enough to topple the entire platform into the sea. There is too much at stake here not to risk some embarrassment if that's what it takes to get improvements.

Evaluating performance, ranking local work areas, and sharing results with supervisors requires courage on the part of senior managers. One oil company executive strongly opposed to sharing the evaluation results with supervisors demanded to know, "Can you guarantee me these results will not leak to the union, local press, or regulatory agencies?" Offering no consolation, we responded, "We can almost guarantee you they will."

You can't stop this kind of information flow. It rockets through a company. That's the whole point. This is why all the usual communication baggage is unnecessary: company newspaper articles, videos, briefing meetings, overhead transparencies, speeches, posters, pins, memos, suggestion schemes, awards, training. We usually need all this stuff because we are forever trying to communicate information employees don't care about. If you get the right topic, relative performance of the local work area, you can't stop the communication.

But what about the leaks? The CEO of the oil company set the policy saying, "PR does not come ahead of performance, and nothing comes ahead of safety." Leaks occurred, and they were embarrassing for senior management.

One final point. During the two weeks when the evaluation team was building their assessment procedure, there were long, late-night arguments about criteria for determining "good" production, maintenance, and safety. For example, heated discussion arose concerning the relative importance of breakdown verses preventative verses corrective maintenance and disagreements about the best techniques for prolonging the lives of nearly depleted wells.

However, the moment the evaluation team touched down on the platforms, all that talk went out the window. The mistakes were so blatant, infraction of company policy so striking, and safety violations so obvious that only an idiot would have argued in their defense. And while there was some argument about whether a platform should be ranked fourth or fifth, no one had any doubts that Tide, Reef, and Island platforms were better than Crest, Beach, and Whitewater, and no one doubted that Rip Tow and Coral were the worst platforms in the division. Perhaps in future evaluations, with all the blatant mistakes corrected, evaluation will become more contentious. But if all the blatant mistakes are corrected, the communication will already have worked.

The evaluation did not tell senior managers much they didn't already know. Management had a pretty good idea of their best and worst platforms. The radical part was standing up and saying it out loud. Sharing the results with supervisors from the platforms. And using the communication as a tool for improving performance.

Stop Communicating Quality

"Quality" may fill senior executives and consultants full of passion and enthusiasm, but the word means nothing on the front line. It used to be "participation," then "excellence," now "quality." They've seen it all before. All this well-intended effort to get the "quality" message across—posters, pins, slogans, mission statements, speeches—turns quality into propaganda.

One consulting company claims, "We Give Every Employee a Dedication to Quality." What a strange thing to say. You don't give "dedication" to people. You use whatever dedication they have. And the dedication they are most likely to have is not to quality, or to the company, but to the local work group.

Take down the posters, call back the videos, and temporarily rein in the quality trainers.

The "quality" movement operates under an assumption that employees are trying to do better. If you assume employees are trying to do better, then all that's needed is showing them the way. And so, out come the concepts—zero defects, continuous improvement, statistical process control—and the accompanying Japanese—*kaizen*, *poka-yoka*, *kanban*.

But is the assumption correct? Are frontline employees eager to improve, ready to go, and only lacking the concepts showing them how? Probably not. Among a random sample of U.S. workers surveyed by Yankelovich and Immerwahr, 44 percent said they put no more effort into their jobs than what was required to hold on to them.[10] David Gordon, an economist at the New School for Social Research, found that increasing shop floor employees' pay did not improve their performance unless there was a corresponding increase in the number of supervisors.[11] In other words, in manufacturing plants, employees didn't improve unless they were being watched. In the United Kingdom, 31 percent of unskilled frontline employees told the Industrial Society, "I'm not interested in the company I work for. It's just a job." When the Industrial Society asked managers the same question, only 3 percent said, "It's just a job."[12]

Communication can help. Search for loyalty in the only place you are likely to find it, the local work area. Energize that loyalty by communicating their performance as it compares to other similar areas. Assume they are not eager to improve, and change that by getting your hands on their pride, self-respect, and dignity. Stop whispering and tell them the truth: "This plant is one of the best in the company." And where it applies: "This is the worst. Every other plant we have is better than this one." The best may want to stay on top. The worst may want to improve. If they don't respond, no communication can help you. If they do, dust off those "quality" manuals.

References

1. Peter F. Drucker, *The Practice of Management*, Harper & Row, New York, 1954, p. 304.

2. Most of this information is from Federal Communications Commission, *Preliminary Report by the Common Carrier Bureau on the September 17, 1991, AT&T NYC Power Outage Network Disruption*, November 8, 1991, pp. 1–18; and *Testimony of Richard M. Firestone (Chief, Common Carrier Bureau, Federal Communications Commission) Before the House Telecommunication and Finance Subcommittee*, Washington, D.C., October 1, 1991, pp. 1–12.

3. "Twin Engines: Can Bob Allen Blend Computers and Telecommunications at AT&T?" *Business Week*, January 20, 1992, pp. 56–63.

4. Quote was given to Robert Cole and described in Robert H. Hayes, Steven C. Wheelwright, and Kim B. Clark, *Dynamic Manufacturing: Creating the Learning Organization*, Free Press, New York, 1988, p. 259.

5. Allan D. Frank: "Trends in Communication: Who Talks to Whom?" *Personnel*, vol. 62, no. 12, December 1985, pp. 41–47.

6. Industry Week research quoted in Therese R. Welter, "They're Afraid of You," *Industry Week*, October 1, 1990, pp. 11–12.

7. Industry Week/Wyatt research quoted in, Matthew P. Gonring, "Communication Makes Employee Involvement Work," *Public Relations Journal*, November 1991, pp. 39–40.

8. National Economic Development Office, *Employee Views on Employment Relations*, July 17, 1987.

9. The Hon Lord Cullen, *The Public Inquiry into the Piper Alpha Disaster, Volume One*, presented to Parliament by the Secretary of State for Energy by Command of Her Majesty, HMSO, London, November 1990.

10. Yankelovich and Immerwahr study quoted in William L. Ginnodo, "How to Build Employee Commitment," *National Productivity Review*, vol. 8, no. 3, summer 1989, pp. 249–260.

11. David M. Gordon, "Who Bosses Whom? The Intensity of Supervision and the Discipline of Labor," *American Economic Review*, vol. 80, no. 2, 1990, pp. 28–32.

12. The Industrial Society, *Blueprint for Success: A Report on Involving Employees in Britain*, edited by Sue Webb, The Industrial Society, London, 1989, p. 44.

20

Communicating Customer Service Performance

Roughly 40 percent of large companies have *customer service mission statements*,[1] that is, communication trying to instill customer service as an employee value.

For most employees, customer service is not a value. Those with a deep intrinsic need to serve others go into the ministry, not into banking, department stores, and automobile manufacturing. And communication does not give employees values. You can't, as if hypodermic needle in hand, poke employees with communication and squeeze in a value.

With astounding honesty, supervisors told the American Management Association exactly whom they valued. The AMA asked 1500 managers, "Whom do we serve?"[2] Supervisors said (in order):

1. Myself
2. Subordinates
3. Employees
4. Coworkers
5. Bosses
6. Colleagues
7. Customers

Supervisors value themselves and those connected to their local work area. More appropriately, perhaps less honestly, executives ranked customers first. Middle managers ranked customers fourth.

Seeing these results, the instinctive reaction is to pump up the propaganda. Mission statements, pins, posters, slogans, training, aimed at increasing frontline respect for customers.

Propaganda is wrong. Instead, communication should link customer service to existing employee values. If employees value their local work area, then make the performance of good customer service something that reflects positively on the local work area. And poor customer service, something that reflects negatively.

Using Mystery Shoppers to Communicate Customer Service: A Banking Example

Mystery shoppers are paid individuals, who, posing as ordinary customers, shop, and report back on the quality of service. Mystery shoppers are given a transaction and sent into a bank branch. The shopper completes the designated transaction and returns to tell what happened. The shopper's experience is described on a single page, at the bottom of which appears a score (1 to 10) that reflects the shopper's subjective evaluation of the service quality.

Figures 20-1 to 20-4 show how the mystery shoppers' experiences are communicated to the bank's branch and senior managers.

This communication adheres to three principles:

1. *Communicate the performance of groups, not individuals.* Remember the energy you are trying to harness is their loyalty and dedication to the local work area. Isolating the performance of individual members is counterproductive.

2. *Praise and criticize, but do not give prizes.* This isn't a contest or some sort of game. The continued existence of your company is at stake. Treat the communication with the respect it deserves.

3. *Avoid complex measuring schemes.* Follow the advice of most academics, and you'll end up with a vastly more complicated measuring scheme. Resist. The only validity that matters is that felt by your supervisors and frontline employees. Our experience is: The less complicated the measure, the more compelling for employees and the more likely it is to change behavior. Academics are in the business of measuring precisely; you are in the business of changing behavior.

Figure 20-1. Mystery Shopper Report 1.

Essex St. Branch - May 10

Transaction

"I have $5,000 saved for a trip to Europe, I leave in 18 months, what is the best thing to do with the money till then?"

Response

greeting was a blank "yes"

I explained I was going to Europe in 18 months and asked what I should do with my $5,000 savings

teller recommended putting it in my VISA account, saying, "then when you start using your card in Europe you will be in credit"

surprised, I asked if my money would earn interest while waiting in VISA, teller said yes it would, but then went to check it out, returning with the answer, "I goofed, no it won't"

I asked for other options and was told there weren't any

I said the bank had a lot of accounts and I wondered which was best for my situation, teller answered, "they are all really much of a muchness"

teller was polite, just doesn't know much

Shopper's Subjective Evaluation   3
(10=excellent, 1=poor)

In the example discussed here, 10 mystery shops occurred for each branch in the region, a total of 11 branches. The branches were ranked-ordered according to their average evaluation score. Mystery shopper reports and ranking were bundled into a booklet given to senior managers and every branch manager in the region. Figure 20-5 shows the branch ranking.

Figure 20-2. Mystery Shopper Report 2.

Woodside Branch - May 10

Transaction

> "I have a severance check from my last job for $12,000, what
> should I do with this?"

Reply

> a polite and friendly teller said I should go to the customer service
> area, and wait for a customer service representative
>
> customer service rep said I should decide whether I was looking
> for a short term or long term investment, saying, "until you decide
> that there is nothing we can do for you"
>
> customer service rep said "you should really set up an appointment
> to see one of our Financial Management Advisers"
>
> customer service rep then gave me a business card for an adviser,
> some brochures, and a phone number to call for an appointment
>
> as I began to leave, the customer service rep leaned across the
> counter lowered his/her voice and said, "watch out for those guys,"
> "they can dazzle you with jargon," "they will put you in shares, you
> could earn 40%, but you could lose everything"
>
> the rep encouraged me to read the brochures carefully, prepare a
> written list of questions, not to be afraid to get answers, and to be
> "very careful"
>
> teller was not very knowledgeable, but seemed to me an honest
> individual, who put my interests above the bank's, and I was
> grateful for that

Shopper's Subjective Evaluation   **6**
(10=excellent, 1=poor)

The goal is to create a gratifying sense of achievement for the high performers and embarrassment for the poor ones. A teller from the Essex Street branch going out to dinner, bumping into a friend who works in the region, needs to hear, "Hey, what's going on at your branch? Did one of your tellers actually tell a customer to invest $5000

Figure 20-3. Mystery Shopper Report 3.

Hastings St. Branch - May 10

Transaction

"What are traveler's checks?"

Response

teller looked at me, gave me a bit of a glare, which I interpreted to mean that I was supposed to step up to the window area

I asked what traveler's checks were, teller responded, "I've got no idea what traveler's checks are, and you can't get them here, you must come back at a less crowded time, it takes too long, best to go to the City Center branch"

confused by that answer, I requested more information about traveler's checks

without a word the teller turned and walked away, in a few moments another teller arrived

this second teller was very polite and patient, explained what traveler's checks were and the advantages in using them

this second teller asked me to wait one moment, returning with a metal box, opened it, took out some traveler's checks in UK pounds, and showed them to me, this was very kind

one horrible teller, one great one

Shopper's Subjective Evaluation   5
(10=excellent, 1=poor)

in their Visa card?" Communication should harness the energy of social pressure, praise and blame, and make employees feel it.

It's all too comfortable out there. The attitude "This huge bank isn't going bankrupt because one customer got in a little tiff over something I said" needs to be attacked. Immediately and directly, they need to see that getting customers into a "tiff" is going to make *their branch* look bad.

Figure 20-4. Mystery Shopper Report 4.

Johnson St. Branch - May 11

Transaction

"Information about a car loan please."

Response

greeting was a pleasant, "good morning"

teller sent me to inquiry counter upstairs on first floor

Consumer Business Officer gave me a business card, asked how he/she could help

Business Officer collected the necessary forms and asked if I needed help completing them

going through the form the Business Officer explained what the various questions meant

I noticed the Business Officer was filling in the less personal parts first, like name and address, and leaving the more personal parts, income and home mortgage, for later

Business Officer said I could fill in the more personal parts at home if I wanted the additional privacy

upon noticing I had a home loan with the Royal Bank, the Business Officer said I might want to check with them as well, because sometimes they will take 1% off the interest rate for home loan customers

I had to wait 15 minutes for service in the Consumer Business area, other than that this was a perfect transaction

Shopper's Subjective Evaluation   8
(10=excellent, 1=poor)

The frontline people are too relaxed, too confident, too excusing of their own mistakes. Research by Valarie Zeithaml, A. Parrasuraman, and Leonard Berry examined managers and frontline employees in five large U.S. service companies.[3] In four of the five companies, they found frontline employees much more confident than managers that their company was living up to its advertised service promises. Similarly, the

Figure 20-5. Branch ranking based on mystery shopper evaluations.

Branch	Average Score
Johnson St.	9.1
City Center	8.9
Northgate	8.0
Gravestown	6.5
Collins Rd.	6.0
Hope Ave.	5.9
Hastings St.	5.9
Glenforth	5.0
Conroy	4.8
Woodside	4.1
Essex St.	4.0
Average	**6.2**

Opinion Research Corporation found that employees greatly overestimated the quality of service they provided when compared with customer evaluations.[4]

Most disturbing of all, however, is the research by Mary Jo Bitner, Bernard Booms, and Mary Tetreault.[5] They looked at 350 instances of poor customer service as remembered by customers (involving airlines, hotels, and restaurants). The causes of poor service fell into three categories:

43 percent of poor service incidents were due to a "system failure" (for example, canceled flight, room reservation lost, or insufficient waiters).

15 percent of poor service incidents resulted from an "inability to adequately respond to a customer need or request" (for example, airline personnel unable to escort a small child, hotel staff unwilling to quiet guests having a late night party, or waiter failing to get a customer a window table).

The shocking discovery was their third major cause of poor service:

41 percent of poor service incidents occurred as a result of "unprompted and unsolicited employee action." (For example, a customer requesting a little more time to think about their selection was told by the waitress, "If you would read the menu and not the road map, you would know what you want to order.")

More than 40 percent of all bad service, as remembered by customers, involved an employee stepping forward, teeing up, and delivering an "unprompted and unsolicited" insult into a customer's face.

We will not change that by preaching customer service as a corporate value. Change that by making them feel the consequences. Embarrass, shame, and when deserved, praise them into changing.

Tellers at the Essex Street branch in the preceding example were rude to nearly half the mystery shoppers sent to them: scolding one mystery shopper for an improperly completed deposit slip, ridiculing another for failing to understand that a three-month CD advertised at 6 percent interest would not earn the full 6 percent in only three months, laughing at another mystery shopper's account balance.

But for the tellers at the Essex Street branch, the day of reckoning arrived. They scored 4 out of 10, which was more than 2 points below the regional average and more than 5 points below the best branch. The undisputed worst of 11 branches in the region. Their treatment of customers is no longer something private between the teller and the customer; now it's something discussed by managers and tellers throughout the entire region. It's something they hear about from a friend they bump into on the way to dinner. Now their performance reflects directly back on them. This is how to make customer service something that matters to employees.

Sharing reports of poor performance with a large number of employees strikes many managers as distasteful. The time when we could think that way is gone. Customer service is critical to economic survival. Have

Figure 20-6. Economic effects of customer service.

research result	source
in general, a 1% decrease in service depresses sales by more than 1%	Shycon Associates
companies ranked by their customers as being in the top one fifth, in terms of quality, were found to have an average return on investment of 32%, and an average return on sales of 14%, approximately double those of companies ranked in the bottom fifth	Profit Impact of Marketing Strategy (PIMS)
companies ranking in the top third of perceived quality were able to sell their products or services at prices 5% to 6% higher than companies in the bottom third	(PIMS)
a 5% increase in customer retention can raise profitability by 25% to 85%	Reichheld and Sasser

a quick look at some slices of research showing the critical relationship between good service and economic performance (Fig. 20-6).[6–9]

Some researchers, such as Philip Kotler, believe customer satisfaction is the best indicator of a company's future profits.[10] Accounting firms in Sweden have gone so far as suggesting that customer satisfaction measures be included on the company balance sheet and in annual reports.[11] With the critical importance of good customer service in mind, think about the research from the Forum Corporation showing that only 14 percent of customers leave service businesses because of unhappiness with what they bought—more than 66 percent leave because of indifferent or unhelpful service people.[12]

In large companies, it's all too easy for frontline employees to believe their treatment of an individual customer is insignificant in the big scheme of things. They are wrong. Look again at the research in Fig. 20-6, or better, ask the 50,000 people who used to work at Sears.

The greatest cruelty is failing to show employees exactly how well they perform, leading them to believe that everything is OK, when often it isn't. Worst of all, our lack of evaluation and attention gives them the impression that what they do doesn't matter.

Communicating performance lets employees know where they stand, and tells them in the clearest possible way that what they do does matter.

Testing and Communicating Product Knowledge in a Department Store

They cannot deliver good service because they don't know enough about the product. Fix that tomorrow. Give them a test.

A region of a large department store decided to test the knowledge of sales assistants in their kitchen appliance departments. The region has seven stores each with its own kitchen appliance department.

Relying on the product literature, a 50-question test was written. Question types included true-false, multiple choice, and fill in the blank. Kitchen department sales assistants from all seven stores took the test. Figure 20-7 shows 3 sample questions with correct answers circled.

Senior managers and all seven kitchen appliance department managers received: the ranking based on the percent of correctly answered questions, a test with correct answers, and an explanation for each answer. Figure 20-8 shows the store ranking.

The average sales assistant missed 15 questions out of 50. More than two-thirds didn't know the dishwasher had reversible colored panels. Three-quarters thought it was still necessary to warn people with heart pacemakers about getting too close to an operating microwave. And 9 out of 10 thought the plastic shelving in GE's side-by-side refrigerators could be put in a dishwasher—they can't. Senior managers were horrified. They announced that a new test would be written and taken by all sales assistants in one month.

A flurry of activity began. Buyers put together a road show and toured the stores. Suppliers were called in to make presentations. Each sales assistant was given a product notebook, filled with a photocopy of all product literature, much of which was annotated with buyer comments. As the retest day approached, sales assistants were cramming in the lunchrooms and arguing about various product features.

The average score on the retest rose to 85 percent.

Communication can change employees. It can do so immediately and with little cost. But this requires communicating performance of the local work area and how that performance compares to other similar areas.

Figure 20-7. Testing product knowledge in kitchen appliances.

Kitchen Appliances Test

(correct answers circled)

1. The "Browner" in our Frigidaire Microwave operates by lowering the frequency of the microwaves until they eventually simulate the heating of a traditional oven. This lower frequency causes the browning of the food.

    True   (False)

2. Our gas ovens with *continuous cleaning* have special high-tech rough porous oven walls. These walls absorb splatters, spread them out, and hold them until the normal heating action of the oven, in everyday use, dries the spatter to a powder.

    (True)   False

3. The color of our Magic Chef dishwashers can be changed by: removing the panel screws; sliding out the door and lower panels; flipping the panels over showing the other color; and then replacing the panels.

    (True)   False

Employees knowing about products matters. In Sweden, Rita Martenson asked 53 bank branch managers how their customers received information about products and services.[13] Sixty-three percent of these managers said their customers' primary source of information was tellers; only 34 percent said advertising.

Further highlighting the importance of product knowledge is research by William Weitzel, Albert Schwarzkopf, and E. Brian Peach.[14] This University of Oklahoma team studied over 1000 employees working in an 80-store chain of fabric stores. The researchers asked employ-

Figure 20-8. Test results: Kitchen appliance departments.

store	% correct answers
Akers	82%
Twickingham	74%
Carriage Hills	72%
Fenimore	68%
Parktower	66%
Royal Plaza	64%
Latrobe	54%
average	**69%**

ees what caused good customer service. The employees most frequently mentioned the quality of treatment they received from management. Toward the bottom of the employee list were product knowledge issues. However, when the employee list of causes was correlated with sales, product knowledge proved to have the greatest effect.

Product knowledge is important. But don't immediately think training. Training is secondary and often irrelevant. What is most important is creating a situation where employees feel pressure to learn, where their self-respect and dignity is at stake. Sending employees off to sit in a training room is too often a waste. Turn up the heat. Create some controversy and drama.

Communicating the performance of the local work area delivers a huge additional benefit as it directs the attention of senior managers to where it's most badly needed—onto the behavior of our frontline employees. What employees don't know will shock you. What they are telling customers will terrify you. Write it down. Communicate it. This will create a crisis. And responding to crisis is what managers do best.

With the passage of every day, management attention is more urgently needed. The Hudson Institute in the United States has been comparing the abilities of our newest entrants to the workforce with the skills required by various occupations.[15] The Hudson Institute says retail sales positions require level-3 skills (writing up orders and reading merchandise information). Unfortunately, the Institute estimates only 22 percent of new employees coming onto the workforce between 1985 and 2000 will have level-3 skills. Zeithaml and her colleagues highlight the painful dilemma: While customers have ever-increasing service expectations, employees have ever-decreasing abilities. The forecast is for much worsening product knowledge among our frontline employees.

Communicating the relative performance of the local work area in this no-nonsense way produces results that scream out for management attention and demand that management divert its eyes from the lofty issues of nonstop corporate restructuring (version 2000 of the organizational chart). Communicating performance requires pushing all the boxes and arrows aside for one moment and directs attention to where we are hemorrhaging—out there—on the front line.

The Importance of Independence in Communicating Performance

The people doing the testing and communicating the performance need independence, that is, independence from the ranks of management. This independence, this arm's distance from management, gives the communication credibility. Remember, 40 percent of frontline employees believe that management communication is neither candid nor accurate.[16]

In the example immediately above, testing product knowledge in kitchen appliance departments, senior managers eventually hired the local community college to write, administer, correct, and communicate results.

Why? Because the communication needs independence to achieve credibility. Otherwise, this is what will happen:

> Hello, Mary, this is Jim [one of the kitchen appliance buyers]. Look Mary, I think we better pull any Braun appliance questions from the upcoming test. The VP has put me on a special project, top priority, and I haven't got the time to get around the stores. Better hold the Braun questions until I get back to you.

And so it will go, on and on, sucking out the legitimacy until the communication becomes a sham. Management will protect itself from embarrassment, doing so at the expense of the frontline employees, who are asked, everyday, to sell Braun products they know nothing about. If the product is on the floor, it must be in the test. That is a difficult rule for an internal employee to enforce.

The last thing managers want is an independent testing of customer service. Absolutely the last thing. One thousand four hundred managers were surveyed by the American Management Association. They

ranked the customer service measurement methods they most preferred.[17] First was "personal visits to customers by management"; last
was "observations and assessment by independent professionals" (sev-
enth out of seven tested methods).

Manipulating impressions of performance is a critical management
skill. Alliances, owed favors, contacts, loyalties, and just plain power
can all be called on. And it is in the interests, particularly of poor performers, to keep communication within this sphere.

Those insiders who try to communicate negative performance break
unwritten agreements and seriously threaten their relationships with
other managers. Breaking the agreement means one is not really part of
management. Sources of negative information are isolated and eventually silenced. For those readers who think this all a bit melodramatic or
paranoid, have a look at the important research into consumer affairs
departments conducted by Claes Fornell and Robert Westbrook.

The Fornell and Westbrook research examined the rates of customer
complaints arriving in consumer affairs departments and the subsequent influence these consumer affairs managers had in management
decision making.[18] The study involved 305 companies, all with formal
consumer affairs units.

Confirming your worst possible fears: The greater the percent of customer complaints arriving in consumer affairs departments (the average
was 47 percent of all customer communication), the less likely it was that
the consumer affairs managers would be included in marketing decisions.

The more a consumer affairs manager circulates customer complaints, the less likely he or she will participate in decisions affecting:

Warranties and/or guarantees

Quality control

Packaging and labeling

Advertising copy

Sales promotion

Pricing

Concept generation

New-product launch

A second study, by Fornell and Westbrook, went on to show that the
less influence the consumer affairs manager had in the above decisions,
the greater the company's rate of customer complaints. This second
study, adding an element of time, enabled Fornell and Westbrook to

close the circle, what they call "the vicious circle of consumer complaints." The more consumer affairs managers communicate customer complaints, the less influence they have; over time, the less influence they have, the more customers complain; and on it goes, trapped in a downward spiral.

Asking management to generate its own negative communication is asking too much. Management, as a system, is designed to eliminate, not communicate, news of its failings. And even if you could change the way managers operate, the shop floor employees wouldn't believe the information anyway. Better to establish an independent source for testing and communicating customer service performance. Use a marketing research firm and consultants, or hire a new employee who does only this and reports directly to a very senior manager, or at least use managers from a different division or location. Give the communication credibility by having it originate from an independent source.

Cutting a Direct Line from Customers to Supervisors: A Mining Example

We need to tie our first-line supervisors closer to our customers. Do that by ignoring the traditional communication channels and cut a direct link between them.

For example, by what path would a mining supervisor hear about a customer complaint, for example, an iron ore, coal, or manganese mining supervisor, supplying material to steel mill customers? These people don't see each other. For one of these supervisors to hear a customer complaint, the purchasing department at the steel mill would need to contact the mine's marketing department, who would then contact the mine's general manager, who would pass this complaint onto the department manager, who would relay it to the mining supervisor. Not likely.

From the moment the steel mill's complaint touches the mining company, it is in almost everyone's interest to water down its seriousness. Too many people contributed to the failure, and it's in their interests to get the bad news out of the organization. Customer complaints simply do not move easily through organizations, especially not all the way to the front line. This helps explain the research showing frontline employees overestimate product quality and customer satisfaction. This is particularly true in examples like this one, where the employee and customer never meet face to face.

Cut through the bureaucracy. Send the customers an evaluation and communicate the results directly to first-line supervisors. In this example, the mine asked their primary customers to rate the mine and its competitors (see Fig. 20-9).

Averaging scores across a handful of major customers, this mining company was able to determine exactly where it stood (see Fig. 20-10). The marketing managers communicated this ranking, face to face, to all mining supervisors.

Grasping the power of this tiny communication requires a little understanding of the minerals business.

When the economy is strong, and demand for steel is high, the mines are in a commanding position. Demand for steel changes quickly, but mineral supply does not. The extraordinary investments and long lead times to build a large mine are such that new supply does not easily come online. When demand rises, the mines are in the driver's seat.

Figure 20-9. Steel mill evaluates mines: completed form. (10 = excellent; 1 = poor)

Mining Companies	consistency of material	reliability of supply	flexibility in meeting changed orders
Golden Creek	8	8	5
Numbia	6	6	5
Taylorton	6	5	4
Turkstone	8	8	7
Worthington	9	10	8

Figure 20-10. Steel mill ranking of best suppliers.

1.	Worthington
2.	Turkstone
3.	Golden Creek
4.	Numbia
5.	Taylorton

The reverse is also true. When demand for steel dips, the steel mills can bring the mines to their knees. In times of low demand, the steel mills could easily destroy their least-favored mine. They rarely choose to do so because this would only strengthen the power of the surviving mines in the next upturn. However, they do not spread the pain evenly. Memories of how they were treated in the last upturn remain, and their least-favored suppliers feel more than their share of pain.

We were in the room when this ranking (see Fig. 20-10) was communicated to supervisors at the Turkstone mine. It was during the middle of an upturn, and the Turkstone mine had ranked second. We were therefore surprised by the silence and air of seriousness surrounding the news. There was no back slapping going on here.

This was an experienced group of supervisors, most having been at the mine for 10 years or more. Although this was the first time any of them had ever heard anything directly from a customer, they understood the gravity of this ranking. To be at the bottom of this list would mean the worst of the inevitable bad times ahead.

From their end, looking from the supervisors' point of view, the first sign of the downturn would be growing stockpiles and more time allocated for machine maintenance. Then it would really start: overtime cutbacks, progressing to the elimination of weekend and night shifts, then closure of selected pits, pressures for contract concessions, and eventually layoffs. Everyone would feel some of this, but the greatest pain would be reserved for the mines at the bottom of that ranking.

The atmosphere at the Turkstone mine was not one of gaiety and chest thumping; instead, it could perhaps be best described as one of relief.

The vast majority of what we communicate to employees is rubbish. It was memorable to see one page, five lines, 11 words in total, treated with such respect. We should never have let a message with so much power lie dormant for so long.

And what gives this message its power? Its indisputable relevance to the local work area.

Communicate Performance—
Not Behaviors

Far too much effort is spent communicating "what to do" and far too little communicating "how well."

Instinctively managers want to communicate what to do. Tell the employees to "answer the phone within three rings," "always ask if they want dessert," "tell customers to have a nice day," and "use their name three times during the transaction."

Telling employees what to do carries none of the risk of communicating how well they do it. Managers know the dangers of communicating performance. They are responsible for much of the failures occurring on the front line. Communicating what to do is safer. Nothing negative can splash back up, and, best of all, it looks like you are doing something because it looks like communication.

There are two problems with the obsessive communication of what to do. First, management is so far removed from the front line that it usually doesn't know what to do. Second, even if management does know, and tells them, there is no reason to believe they'll do it.

A bank in the midwestern United States decided to improve the service delivered by its tellers.[19] Helped by a team of academics, management broke down the teller-customer interaction into a desired sequence of parts. Then they built a scheme for awarding points according to the performance of each part. The scheme is shown in Fig. 20-11.

Armed with their scheme of what every teller should do, they set about, with teller knowledge, installing microphones, tape recorders, and observers to code actual teller-customer interactions. Management decided that 85 points out of the possible 100 was the minimum performance acceptable for a teller.

After 19 days of measurement, the average teller score was 61 points. When the point scheme was more fully described to tellers, their average performance rose to 72 points. When feedback was added, the average went to 78 points. With praise the added scores reached the minimum 85 points. The microphones were taken away for 20 days, then reinstalled. The baseline had again fallen to 76 points.

What's wrong? Everything.

We've spent time with tellers. Standing behind them at their windows. Not telling them what to do—how would we know? Instead, we've watched and asked them why they act the way they do. For exam-

Figure 20-11. Management's view of what tellers should do.

Part	Description	Points
1. time to service	time between customer arriving within one yard of the teller window, and the teller's first word	0-5 seconds: 12 points 6-11 seconds: 7 points >11 seconds: 0 points
2. greeting	one phrase from the list of acceptable greetings	10 points
3. expression of concern	"how are you today?" or similar statement	5 points
4. using customer's name	use of first and/or last name at least once	10 points
5. talking only to customer	no talking to anyone else unless necessary to obtain information	10 points
6. additional assistance	"can I be of further assistance" or referral to another banking product	6 points
7. minimize small talk	unnecessary self-initiated conversation	entire interaction divided into consecutive 10 second intervals for interactions under 90 seconds: 6 points if small talk less than 20% of total time for interactions over 90 seconds: 6 points if small talk less than 50%
8. responding to customer inquiries	providing appropriate information	90% or better appropriate response: 11 points 80% to 89% appropriate response: 6 points below 80% appropriate response: 0 points
9. expression of appreciation	"the bank appreciates your business" or similar	10 points
10. closing	"have a nice day" or similar	5 points
11. voice tone	tone rated unacceptable if rude, or if customer becomes angry or irritated	maintaining an acceptable tone: 15 points

total points possible = 100

ple, we noticed one teller sometimes used customer names, other times did not. We asked why.

> If I get a feeling a customer is going to be a "talker," then I don't use his or her name. If I am too open and friendly to a "talker," they'll talk. In no time, several "talkers" can stretch the line out to the sidewalk. You've got to consider the length of the line and how likely it is you have a "talker" before deciding how friendly to be.

And the teller is right. According to every banking customer service survey we have seen, nothing irritates customers more than waiting in line. Balancing the length of the line with intuitions about the customer and degrees of friendliness, is part of the reality of being a bank teller. This reality is not always visible from the leather chairs and oak table on the 42nd floor of head office.

What arrogance to think that head office managers could dictate to tellers exactly how they should behave. Did they think the inherent complexity of any human interaction could ever be captured in 11 or 15 or even 500 categories, each with their appropriate point allocation? And isn't it obvious these managers have come under the spell of their academic advisers? Taking on the unshakeable belief of so many academics that the right answer will pop out if only we measure precisely enough. And the more precise the measure, the more right the answer will be.

To be told, to the millimeter, exactly how to behave, is not only ineffective, it's an insult. If you came up with the great idea of tape recording senior managers' conversations with large corporate clients, grading their performance 1 to 100, and putting pressure on them to conform to an 11-category scheme, they would show you the door so fast you wouldn't know what happened.

Banking executives have every right to demand that customers are satisfied with the service received from tellers. They have no right, nor will they succeed, to demand that tellers act like mindless automatons. In other words, communicate performance, particularly the relative performance of the local work area—not detailed schemes of how to behave.

Several years ago, managers at K-Mart decided cashiers should close their customer interactions with, "thank you for shopping K-Mart."[20] The abbreviation "T.Y.F.S.K." was printed and attached to cash registers as a reminder. Employees sabotaged this effort by saying the letters, "T.Y.F.S.K." as bewildered customers walked away.

K-Mart managers had every right to demand that customers experience a polite and friendly cashier but no right to demand they close every episode with "thank you for shopping K-Mart." Did they think the customer so stupid as to prefer a robotic "thank you for shopping K-Mart," to a sincere smile or nod? Or did they think they could order the sincerity as well?

The U.S. Office of Technology Assessment estimates that between 25 and 35 percent of all clerical workers are now monitored electronically.[21] This is a worry. It will too often reduce evaluation to counting, encourage detailed behavior schemes, and pressure humans into acting more like the machines watching them.

Research by the Canadian team Rebecca Grant, Christopher Higgins, and Richard Irving studied both monitored and unmonitored workers in the same insurance company doing the same job, group claims processing. They found 80 percent of electronically monitored employees said "production quantity" was the most important part of their job, while 86 percent of those not monitored electronically said "customer service" was most important.

Even more disturbing, in both groups, only 13 percent of employees said they had discussions with their supervisor concerning the quality of their work.

Fred Luthans and Janet Larsen's research team studied 120 managers over a two-week period.[22] They found only 5 percent of a manager's time is spent talking with employees about how their job could be done better.

The answer is not ever fancier computer-monitored detection systems but greater efforts to get the old-fashioned human-to-human communication back on its feet.

The job of senior management is not to tell them what to do but to demand they do it better. And the shape this demand should take is communicating the relative performance of the local work area.

After communicating a ranking, based on mystery shopper evaluations, one bank branch went from the middle of the pack to first, in only a month. We went to see how they did it.

The branch had covered all posters advertising the bankwide program of giving $5 to any customer who waited in line more than five minutes. This, they said, was a disaster. A teller explained:

> When a customer waited more than five minutes, you couldn't just reach in your cash drawer, grab a $5 bill, and hand it to him. No. Any customer complaining about waiting more than the promised five minutes was told to go to the customer service counter to get his $5. There he almost always had to wait in an even longer line, only to find he then had to complete a form. Customers only complained about waiting when they were in a hurry. Putting them through this process sent them into a rage. The first thing we did to improve customer service was getting rid of that silly idea.

But abandoning this head office idea was not all they did. Tellers set up a table with a sign inviting customers to have a cup of coffee. Rarely did anyone drink the coffee. But tellers believed the invitation or perhaps the aroma made customers happy.

They decided to extend the amount of time new tellers wore "trainee" name tags. The bank mandated six months. The branch decided a year or more was better. Why?

> Customers are easier on trainees. If you get something wrong, the customer will usually smile and tell you to "take it easy—everything will be alright." The longer you can wear a trainee tag, the better.

The branch was busiest and customers most demanding between noon and 2 p.m. The tellers always took their full allocated lunch breaks no matter how busy the branch. But they discovered a technique for improving the perception of customer service:

> When we're working noon to 2, most of us will make sure we have a partly eaten apple, open yogurt container, half a muesli bar, or something like that somewhere in sight. Customers think we are working right through our lunch. Since we started doing this, complaints of slow service have dropped by half.

These techniques work. They worked on our mystery shoppers. And, according to the tellers, they work on customers as well.

Some readers will be appalled our communication resulted in these tricks. We have two responses. First, much of customer service is an illusion, and branch banking is no exception. Second, a teller who has just brewed another pot of coffee for customers, remembered to leave half his yogurt to take back to the counter, and wears a "trainee" tag months past its appropriate time is trying to improve service and is therefore considerably less likely to step forward and deliver a cutting insult into a customer's face. And Bitner and her colleagues have shown us more than 40 percent of poor customer service is exactly that.

These tellers are thinking, changing, and having fun. And that's good. Benjamin Schneider, John Parkington, and Virginia Buxton wanted to know what distinguished branches customers liked from ones they didn't.[23] They set about studying customers and tellers in 23 U.S. bank branches on the Atlantic Coast. The branches customers liked best were not those with the best marketing support, equipment and supply support, or personnel support, but instead the branches with the most enthusiastic tellers.

Why did these tellers come up with ideas for improving service? Certainly not because management told them what to do. Those customer service ideas were blatant violations of head office rules. No, those actions grew from embarrassment. Their branch performed poorly in the first wave of mystery shops. They were held up for all to see as an average to poor performer. Other branches they previously had thought no better than theirs were at the top. We pricked their pride and self-respect, and that's what caused the change. It is feeling—not intellect—that is at the source of action. Intellect may shape action once it's going, but feeling is at the beginning.

If communication is to change behavior, it must ground its message in the values of the receivers. That means they need to be told about their performance, that is, the performance of their local work area and how that performance compares to others around them.

References

1. Richard Germain and M. Bixby Cooper, "How a Customer Mission Statement Affects Company Performance," *Industrial Marketing Management*, vol. 19, 1990, pp. 47–54.

2. Barry Z. Posner and Warren H. Schmidt, "Values and the American Manager: An Update," *California Management Review*, vol. 26, no. 3, spring 1984, pp. 202–216.

3. Valarie A. Zeithaml, A. Parasuraman, and Leonard L. Berry, *Delivering Quality Service: Balancing Customer Perceptions and Expectations*, Free Press, New York, 1990.

4. Opinion Research Corporation study quoted in "Overestimating Service Quality," *Human Resource Focus*, vol. 68, December 1991, p. 12.

5. Mary Jo Bitner, Bernard H. Booms, and Mary Stanfield Tetreault, "The Service Encounter: Diagnosing Favorable and Unfavorable Incidents," *Journal of Marketing*, vol. 54, January 1990, pp. 71–84.

6. Shycon Associates study quoted in William H. Davidow and Bro Uttal, *Total Customer Service: The Ultimate Weapon*, Harper Perennial, New York, 1990, p. 36.

7. Profit Impact of Marketing Strategy (PIMS) study quoted in Davidow and Uttal, ibid., p. 40.

8. Profit Impact of Marketing Strategy (PIMS) study quoted in Zeithaml, Parasuraman, and Berry, op. cit., p. 3

9. Frederick F. Reichheld and W. Earl Sasser, Jr., "Zero Defections: Quality Comes to Services," *Harvard Business Review*, September–October, 1990, p. 105; quoted in Leonard A. Schlesinger and James L. Heskett, "The Service-Driven Service Company," *Harvard Business Review*, September–October, 1991, p. 75.

10. Philip Kotler, *Marketing Management—Analysis, Planning and Control*, 6th ed., Prentice-Hall, Englewood Cliffs, 1988, quoted in Claes Fornell, "A National Customer Satisfaction Barometer: The Swedish Experience," *Journal of Marketing*, vol. 56, January 1992, pp. 6–21.

11. See Fornell, op. cit., p. 11.

12. Forum Corporation study quoted in Schlesinger, op. cit., p. 74.

13. Rita Martenson, "Focus on the Retail Bank Market: Can You Trust Branch Managers View Of It?" *International Journal of Bank Marketing*, vol. 4, no. 4, 1986, pp. 23–38.

14. William Weitzel, Albert B. Schwarzkopf, and E. Brian Peach, "The Influence of Employee Perceptions of Customer Service on Retail Store Sales," *Journal of Retailing*, vol. 65, no. 1, spring 1989, pp. 27–39.

15. Hudson Institute research quoted in Zeithaml, op. cit. p. 165.

16. Julie Foehrenbach and Steve Goldfarb, "Employee Communication in the '90s," *Communication World*, May/June 1990.

17. Eric Rolfe Greenberg, "Customer Service: The Key to Competitiveness," *Management Review*, December 1990, pp. 29–31.

18. Claes Fornell and Robert A. Westbrook, "The Vicious Circle of Consumer Complaints," *Journal of Marketing*, vol. 48, summer 1984, pp. 68–78. (Both studies are described in this paper.)

19. Charles R. Crowell, D. Chris Anderson, Dawn M. Abel, and Joseph P. Sergio, "Task Clarification, Performance Feedback, and Social Praise: Procedures for Improving the Customer Service of Bank Tellers," *Journal of Applied Behavior Analysis*, vol. 21, no. 1, spring 1988, pp. 65–71.

20. K-Mart example from Davidow, op. cit., p. 96.

21. U.S. Office of Technology Assessment research quoted in Rebecca A. Grant, Christopher A. Higgins, and Richard H. Irving, "Computerized Performance Monitors: Are They Costing You Customers?" *Sloan Management Review*, spring 1988, pp. 39–45.

22. Fred Luthans and Janet K. Larsen, "How Managers Really Communicate," *Human Relations*, vol. 39, no. 2, 1986, pp. 161–178.

23. Benjamin Schneider, John J. Parkington, and Virginia M. Buxton, "Employee and Customer Perceptions of Service in Banks," *Administrative Science Quarterly*, vol. 25, June 1980, pp. 252–267.

21
Stop Communicating Values

With great fanfare a large U.S. manufacturing company launched its mission and future directions, organized around the "Three T's": *Trust*, *Teamwork*, and focus on *Tomorrow*.

Trust, Teamwork & Tomorrow hung on a huge banner behind the speaker's platform. The Three T's were inscribed on hats, pens, and notebook covers. A Three T booklet outlined how Trust, Teamwork & Tomorrow would be implemented. Senior manager presentations were seen live by thousands of employees and beamed by satellite to thousands more.

Following the energetic launch, employees returned from cafeterias and auditoriums to find a union-posted "Letter to Employees" on every company bulletin board. This well-documented letter revealed that for the past 18 months the company had hired private investigators to watch employees during and after work. The private investigators were watching employees who had aroused company suspicions of stealing, drug use, and fraudulent disability claims.

Attempting to rescue Trust, Teamwork & Tomorrow, public relations consultants were called in to help the company respond to the union allegation. The brief: Explain to employees that hiring private investigators to watch them does not necessarily imply a lack of trust.

A large U.K. retailer launched its customer service campaign called *Treating Customers As Family*. Included were videos, training programs, and briefing meetings beginning at the top and cascading down to all company employees. Inadvertently, a specially constituted task force simultaneously released its campaign *To Catch a Thief.*

The To Catch a Thief campaign explained that last year customers stole 1 percent of the all the stores' merchandise, which was a 15 percent increase over the previous year. To Catch a Thief gave sales assistants cash bonuses for catching shoplifters.

Despite the clash neither the training department or the security task force wanted to withdraw their respective campaigns. In the end, the training department wrote a memo to all employees explaining how it was possible to treat customers as family and potential thieves.

A particularly painful value campaign was *People Philosophy,* launched by General Motors in 1988, with its theme: *We Value G.M. People Above Everything Else.* A couple of years later GM was unloading 18 percent of what it valued most. Worse, in its 1991 announcement to close 21 plants, GM decided not to name which plants would be shut. This set GM employees against GM employees, as plants praised themselves and berated others in their efforts to avoid the axe. Now someone, somewhere, has the unenviable task of explaining how this is consistent with the People Philosophy.

The well-intended value campaign will backfire. Unavoidably, senior management will appear a bunch of hypocrites. A nonstop stream of incidents contrary to the preached value will be paraded in front of senior managers, and an explanation demanded. Instead of the value, the violations take center stage. It's a cynic's field day.

The recommendation is simple: Stop communicating values. Values are not something you communicate; values are something you do.

Communicating Values Can Harm Communication

A particularly large value campaign is Ford's *MVGP: Mission, Values and Guiding Principles.*[1]

MVGP says that Ford's success depends on its people, products, and profits. Highlighted within MVGP is the importance of: quality, customer service, continuous improvement, employee involvement, partnership, and integrity.

Communicating MVGP was an all-out effort. An explanatory MVGP booklet was sent to the home of all employees with a supportive letter from the chairman. Some part of the mission, values or guiding principles, appeared on almost every formal company document. Meetings at which the implications of MVGP were discussed involved all of Ford's 185,000 employees.

At one of these meetings, a manager of a stamping plant, discussing the effects of MVGP in his area, said:

> At this facility, we live by Mission, Values and Guiding Principles. Both the union and management support the concepts, totally. It's a way of life here; we know people and quality are number 1, and every decision is based on that.

Please, take one moment, and reread the plant manager's statement. Do you know any plant managers who speak that way?

"We live by MVGP," "both the union and management support the concepts, totally," "it's a way of life here," "people and quality are number 1." Plant managers don't normally speak that way. What's going on here?

We have not met or interviewed this individual. We have no hard evidence to suspect a meaning other than the surface one. But we do suspect another meaning.

Our interpretation is:

> Look, management often comes out with these goofy schemes. It used to be excellence, then employee involvement, now it's MVGP. The best thing is to play along with their little game, parrot back some of their mindless banalities, and get these corporate people out of your hair. Then you can get back to the real business of running a plant.

When people close to the plant, close to the front line, start talking back to you in your own value slogans, you've got real problems. This is not a sign your well-intended value campaign is working. It is a sign those close to the operation now consider you a useless bureaucrat, a head office boffin, someone needing pacifying with a slogan, an obstacle in the way of getting the real work done.

The closer one gets to the front line, the less any manager wants to communicate the Disney-like values. The value communication stalls. Frustrated with the lack of progress and bombarded with endless examples of incidents contrary to the value, senior managers up the pressure. Those not communicating the values risk poor performance appraisals, special counseling, and reduced prospects for promotion. Pushing the value campaign this way actually harms communication. The value campaign is now increasing the distance between head office and people near the front line. It has filled the communication channels with noise, demanding insincerity from anyone wishing to get ahead, while threatening to punish those not on the bandwagon. The well-intended value campaign has not helped; it has actually damaged communication within the company.

Seeing the Value Campaign through Their Eyes

BP has *OPEN:* Open thinking, Personal impact, Empowering, and Networking.

Motorolla has Total Customer Satisfaction[2] and makes the strange claim that 100,000 Motorolla employees carry a card with them at all times, reminding them:

> Our fundamental objective. Everyone's overriding responsibility. *Total Customer Satisfaction.*

What is the point? Is the assumption that employees will hear these senior management pontifications, be deeply moved, incorporate the messages into their most deeply held values, and then use them as a guide in the conduct of their day-to-day behavior? Surely this is management fantasy on the grandest scale.

Stop fantasizing and look at the reality. We were present as just under 1000 shop floor employees were gathered in the warehouse of a large U.S. manufacturing company. They were gathered to hear the new corporate mission. The CEO stepped to the microphone and explained that the mission resulted from a great deal of thought. The executive team had locked themselves away for two weeks to hammer out the company's future direction. The CEO then began explaining the tripartite mission based on "mutual respect," "good corporate citizenship," and "world best performance."

A row in front of us, we overheard one employee lean across to his supervisor and ask, "What the hell is he saying?" His supervisor translated: "A group of bigwigs from cloud cuckoo-land checked into an expensive resort, held hands, and made a wish."

No matter what was intended, that's what they heard. And when the topic is communication, what they hear is what matters.

But should we close down carefully conceived and well-intended value campaigns because of wisecracks from a handful of especially negative employees? The question denies reality. The frontline work force does not contain just a few negative employees but is cynical and negative through and through. In Canada, Hay Management Consultant found only 50 percent of employees said they had pride in their company.[3] In Australia, Towers Perrin found only 41 percent of employees had confidence in their corporate leadership.[4] Worse, in the U.K. only 27 percent of employees say they were proud of their company, and only 34 percent had confidence in senior management, according to the Industrial Society.[5] Looking at the United States, Hay Group researchers found only 30 percent of hourly-paid workers said they had confidence in top managers.[6] And 80 percent of American workers believed management could not be trusted, according to a Boston University School of Management survey.[7] In most research the trend is worsening.

Even in the very heartland of propaganda, The People's Republic of China, researchers find workers in the Guangzhou region laugh when the government tries to motivate them with "honorable titles" such as "advanced worker."[8]

Skip the research, and use your own experience. Or use ours. We have watched employees desecrate one value campaign after another. *Beliefs We Share*, turned into "bull we share"; *Working With Pride*, turned into "working for peanuts"; and *Quality in Everything We Make*, turned into "quality is everything we fake." Approaching employees with a slogan backfires, decreasing the credibility of the serious changes being attempted.

The mistake is confusing the way we market consumer goods to customers with the way to communicate change to employees. Ideas taken from marketing and advertising do not carry over to employee communication. A snappy jingle, slogan, logo or a consistent simple message, repeated over and over, may move laundry soap or toothpaste off grocery store shelves. But this model is totally inappropriate for communicating change to frontline employees.

Stop Communicating Values: Nothing Will Be Lost

The belief among senior managers that they must stand up and communicate a rock-solid corporate value can perhaps be traced back to the very influential book *In Search of Excellence*, written by Tom Peters and Robert Waterman.[9]

But Peters has moved on from the *In Search of Excellence* image of a successful company well anchored in a secure value. Peters begins his later book *Thriving on Chaos*, saying, "There are no excellent companies."[10] By this, we believe he means that the excellent company of today can easily be the inefficient and uncompetitive company of tomorrow. The new image of a successful company is, above all else, one embracing and mastering change.

Another blow to the image of a corporate value, engraved in stone, was delivered by John Kotter and James Heskett in their book *Corporate Culture and Performance*.[11] Kotter and Heskett conclude: "The statement 'Strong cultures create excellent performance' appears to be just plain wrong."

Studying the cultures and financial performance of more than 200 companies over an 11-year period, 1977–1988, Kotter and Heskett conclude: About half the time strong cultures are associated with excellent performance, and about half the time they are not. Going further, they list companies with strong cultures and poor financial performance.

H.F. Ahmanson

Citicorp

Coors

General Motors

Goodyear

K Mart

Kroger

J.C. Penney

Procter & Gamble

Sears

Kotter and Heskett say, over the long term, those cultures associated with strong financial performance do share a recurring theme: They facilitate change.

In the mid-Eighties, senior managers asked their communication consultants to help them put "growth through market share" upon the value alter. No sooner was it up there then they wanted it replaced with "customer service." Barely in place, the order came down to push "customer service" back a bit, setting "efficiency-cost cutting" in front. Now "innovation" prepares to take the step up. This canonizing and decanonizing results not from corporate fickleness or indecision but from a rational response to rapidly changing conditions. The answer, however, is to give up kneeling at the alter altogether. A strongly communicated value that everyone supposedly believes does not help us change. Employee communication should not be about the adulation of corporate values but about the hard, day-to-day business of changing the behavior of frontline employees.

Using Communication to Change Behavior

Communication from senior executives does not give values to employees. Senior managers cannot put values into employees. The image is all wrong. Values emerge up from the bottom. They are not imposed downward from the top.

Values are immaterial but are real forces emerging from the way employees do their work. Thousands and thousands of repeated behavioral episodes give birth to a particular sort of value, a value sharing the characteristics of its generating behaviors. The value then acts back down on employees, applying pressure to continue these behaviors, making the behaviors more permanent.

Figure 21-1 shows the time sequence involved in the birth of a value.

First: Employees work or interact in a particular way, some way that seems to get the job done.

Second: When this way of working is repeated thousands of times, a value emerges.

Third: Once in existence, the value acts back down on employees, an externally felt force exerting pressure for the continuation of that way of working.

Looking at Fig. 21-1, you can see why you don't want to just step up and communicate a new value. Your new value is inconsistent with what employees know works. And more, the new value has no force. The real pressure they feel comes from the old, not new, value.

The answer is also in that simple diagram. To change a value, you begin by changing the behavior. *The behavior change comes before, not after, the new value.* You don't communicate a new value to change behavior; you change behavior to get a new value. All the important action is at the bottom of the diagram, not the top.

Figure 21-1. Birth of a value.

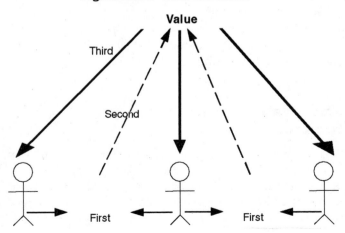

An enormous effort must be exerted to first change the behavior at the bottom. But if the new behavior is repeated thousands of times, it will give birth to a new value. The initial effort can then be lessened as the new value begins applying pressure in favor of the new behavior.

That is why the absolutely critical issue is not how to communicate a value. Instead, it is how to get the initial behavior change to occur at the bottom.

Communication plays an important role. It's what this book is all about. To kick-start the new behaviors at the bottom, target supervisors, rely on face-to-face communication, and communicate the performance of the local work area, especially how that performance compares with other similar areas.

First-line supervisors must be onside. Getting the new behavior, overriding the pressure from the old value, requires constant vigilance. Leave employees for a moment, and they will return to the old way. That sort of daily, nonstop, nagging pressure cannot be maintained from senior management levels. You are too far away. The only person who can do it is the first-line supervisor.

Achieve supervisor support for your change by targeting supervisors as privileged receivers of information. Take your case directly to them, face to face. Acknowledge their superior status by making sure they know more about the change than frontline employees. Modify your plans according to their suggestions. And force your middle managers to better serve their needs. Drive the change with face-to-face communication. Not print. Not video. And do not force supervisors to hold meetings with their subordinates.

And finally, our best advice is to try making the new behavior consistent with an already existing employee value. Get some of that pressure working for you, not against you. And what is it that employees value? Their local work area. Make the performance of the new behavior consistent with their concern, loyalty, and respect for themselves and their coworkers. Accomplish this by communicating the performance of the new behavior. Communicate how their performance of the new behavior compares with that achieved by other similar areas.

Replacing Values with Performance

When senior managers feel the need to communicate a value, they should resist and instead communicate performance.

When making radical change, employees do need to know the big picture. What is the future direction? Where is the company headed? What is required here is not a value but an objective performance standard.

Employees at Pepsi know where they are going. They are going to beat Coke. Workers at Komatsu, the Japanese earth-moving equipment manufacturer, know where senior managers are taking them: They are going to "encircle Caterpillar." Employees in General Electric businesses, not first or second in market share in their respective industries (or headed that way) know where they are going. They are going to be sold. This is not empty value talk. These are externally verifiable performance criteria, formally or informally communicated by corporate executives.

Communicating that your company is an "environmentally responsible, good corporate citizen" is meaningless. M. Cash Mathews wanted to know if formal, written, corporate codes of ethics made any difference in behavior.[12] Her research showed they didn't. Cash studied 306 manufacturing companies and found that companies with codes of ethics were just as likely to illegally dump toxic waste as companies without such codes.

Choosing to communicate performance rather than values, ICI has communicated to all employees that the company will reduce waste from its operations by 50 percent by 1995.[13] This is meaningful.

The recommendation to stop communicating values does not boil down to a prohibition against all senior management communication. But it does mean that when you feel the need to communicate, talk performance.

Senior managers at a large electrical utility were preparing to take their employees down a path of rapid change and severe pain. The utility had 22,000 employees and was the sole supplier of electricity in their state. Management decided to reduce the workforce by 30 percent, sell some power stations, and franchise parts of the retail business (meter reading, billing, and installation).

Senior managers felt the need to say something: Why was this necessary? and, Where were they headed?

Fortunately they resisted the impulse to communicate the usual management mumbo jumbo: customer driven, lean, decentralized, preparing for tomorrow, vision 2000, a mission of excellence. Instead, they decided in favor of communicating performance.

In a single day, senior management teams addressed 500 supervisors in groups of 25 and told them:

> For years, those of us working at Southern Power have believed we were the best power utility in the Tri-State region. Once this was true. It is not true today. Among the three power utilities in our area, we are third.

Senior managers then took the supervisors through four performance indicators (see Fig. 21-2). Following this discussion of performance, the senior managers explained the upcoming changes: layoffs, asset sales, and franchising.

Figure 21-2. Southern Power compared with its neighbors: (a) Average tariff; (b) electricity sold per employee; (c) power plant availability; (d) cost of generation.

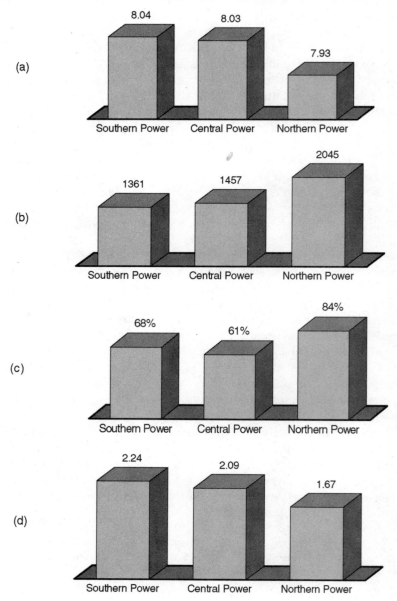

Answer the questions straight up. Why are these painful changes necessary? Because in three of the four measures of performance, we are last. We are changing because we do not do our job as well as those people right over there. And where is the company headed? It's headed to the top of those four measures.

Resist the impulse to communicate values. The value communication will harm your efforts to change employees. When communication is necessary, communicate performance.

References

1. A supportive and complementary description of Ford's MVGP campaign is contained in William L. Ginnodo, "How to Build Employee Commitment," *National Productivity Review*, vol. 8, no. 3, summer 1989, pp. 249–260.

2. Motorolla's claim that 100,000 employees carry the Total Customer Satisfaction card is made in corporate advertisements placed in *Fortune* magazine.

3. Hay Management Consultants study in Ronald J. Grey and Gail C. Johnson, "Differences Between Canadian and American Workers," *Canadian Business Review*, Winter 1988, pp. 24–27.

4. Towers Perrin, *A Day in the Life: Working in Australia in the 1990s*, Sydney, July 1992.

5. The Industrial Society, *Blue Print for Success: A Report on Involving Employees in Britain*, edited by Sue Webb, 1989.

6. Hay Group study quoted in Alan Farnham, "The Trust Gap," *Fortune*, December 4, 1989, pp. 56–78.

7. Boston University School of Management study, reported in "Complain, Complain, Complain: Worker Cynicism on the Rise," *Management Review*, June 1987, pp. 10–12.

8. Kin Hung Lam, "Motivating the Chinese Workforce," *Asia Pacific Human Resource Management*, vol. 27, no. 3, August 1989, pp. 64–73.

9. Tom Peters and R. H. Waterman, Jr., *In Search of Excellence*, Harper & Row, New York, 1982.

10. Tom Peters, *Thriving on Chaos*, Pan Books, London, 1987.

11. John P. Kotter and James L. Heskett, *Corporate Culture and Performance*, Free Press, New York, 1992.

12. The M. Cash Mathews research is quoted in Ronald E. Berenbeim, "An Outbreak of Ethics," *Across The Board*, vol. 25, no. 5, May 1988, pp. 15–19.

13. The ICI pledge to reduce waste by 50 percent is contained in their 1990 annual report.

22

If You're the Boss, Communicate Performance

> Of course we communicate performance. Every quarter I get every-one at the plant together and tell them exactly how we're doing. I tell them: average daily production, wastage and scrap rates, work-in-process levels, inventory turnover, capacity utilization and machine uptime, absenteeism, training dollars per employee,...

Stop. That's not performance—that's statistics.

Imagine the basketball team returning to the locker room after the game. The coach gathers them around, and says:

> I want to talk to you about our performance. We've had: 2965 passes so far this season, shooting percentage is 48 percent, 112 of our shots blocked, 62 percent of our time on defense, and 10 percent more fouls than this time last season. I'm sure we can do better if we continue to work together as a team. Thank you.

No one would respect a coach who communicated like that. What's missing? Praise and blame. A sincere, accurate, and passionate evaluation of performance.

This chapter is about communicating performance. Specifically about the role of the senior operating manager. By "senior operating manager," we mean a manager overseeing perhaps a dozen middle managers, perhaps 50 supervisors, and around 500 to 1000 frontline employees. We mean the most senior manager available without geographically leaving the area and heading into head office or corporate territory. Often these senior operating managers have a layer of management (department managers) between themselves and supervisors. In other words, we mean, the plant manager, site manager, mine manager, or regional manager.

In manufacturing and services, these senior operating managers have lowered themselves to communicating like accountants. With great pain and frustration, we have sat among employees and watched these senior operating managers address their work force. Out comes the stack of overhead transparencies: bar chart after bar chart, pie charts, line graphs, this quarter against last quarter, this quarter this year against this quarter last year, year to date against year to date last year, on and on. And what are the employees to think? Here is the head bean counter. What else could they think? Among supervisors and frontline employees, no one is held in lower regard than accountants. This is, of course, unfair and ignorant, but it is what they think. Why then does anyone want to paint themselves as the head bean counter?

If you are the boss (plant, district, or regional manager), communicate performance. Gather your supervisors, face to face, and tell them how well or poorly their area has performed. This should last 5 to 10 minutes. No questions, no excuses, no discussion. You are the boss. You are the judge of performance. Tell them exactly what you think.

Here are two examples.

Communicating Performance: Mining

This mine manager decided to put away all the stats and instead communicate performance.

Once a week, about 50 supervisors were gathered for a 10-minute meeting run by the mine manager, at which he told them how he felt about their performance. No questions or discussion were allowed. "If you have question," the mine manager would say, "take them to your department manager." Following the meeting each supervisor was given a one-page handout summarizing major points. This communication, shown in Fig. 22-1, is from one of these meetings. It is unmistakably from the boss.

The supervisors in the mining, mechanical, and administration departments need to know they have done well, and those in the electrical and plant departments need to know they have done poorly. And the supervisors should hear it from the top.

Figure 22-1. Mine manager's weekly review for supervisors.

Mining Department

- last week, head office asked, and I agreed, to supply JSM with a 10,000 ton over-plan order
- great work by mining department with almost no time to prepare
- tons on time (no demurrage at port)
- perfectly to spec (moisture & volatiles)
- JSM considering making our coal part of their standard blend
- nice job

Electrical Department

- completely screwed PM on SHE40
- incorrect parts ordered
- forgot to schedule crane
- assigned leckies with no shovel experience
- as a result fitters sat around all day doing nothing
- $25,000 an hour, every hour, that shovel is down
- I'm tired of this kind of work from Electrical

Mechanical Department

- first time ever all Cat 776Bs have been out of the workshop
- been a long haul getting those trucks to where they are today
- skill and patience of Mech. Dept. is greatly appreciated

Plant Department

- we are not watching the belts
- again two roller have been found frozen
- the friction could create a fire, carry it into the plant, and send the whole mine to hell
- I don't want to have to tell you this again

Admin. Department

- our new Facom computer arrived with IT's version of Basil Fawlty to help us install it
- thanks to brilliant work by our own Admin staff the machine is up and running
- there is a good chance we will all be paid with no drama

"But this happens now," our clients tell us. The mine or plant manager tells the department managers, and the department managers pass this information on to their supervisors. There is no greater and more destructive myth in communication than this one: that information trickles down through middle management to supervisors. We all know it's not true—why keep repeating it?

Negative information, in particular, does not move down. A classic experiment by C. A. O'Reilly and K. H. Roberts examined the direction unfavorable messages were most likely to travel.[1] Surprisingly, negative information moved upward to superiors more often than downward to subordinates. Superiors were likely to hear the bad news eventually anyway, so managers frequently communicated their mistakes upward; subordinates, on the other hand could be effectively kept in the dark, and they were.

Research by Larry Smeltzer helps explain why negative information does not flow to subordinates.[2] Smeltzer found that losing the support or confidence of your group (subordinates) was a greater cause of work-related stress than pressures imposed by your job or organization. Managers maintain this support by withholding, not communicating, negative information.

But skip all the studies. Go onto the shop floor and ask a supervisor: What does your plant manager think about the performance of your local work group during the last month? Prepare yourself for a blank stare.

The 50 supervisors at the mine in this example know exactly what their mine manager thinks of their work. Without any mind-numbing statistics, he tells them, face to face, if they should be proud or ashamed of their performance.

Communicating Performance: Manufacturing

The company in this example manufactures brakes. One plant in particular specializes in disc brakes for trucks. The plant manager's name is Jean, and she decided to communicate performance as it related to specific customer orders. Upon completing an order for a major customer, Jean gathers her supervisors and tells them exactly how she feels about their performance. Notes from one of these sessions are shown in Fig. 22-2. There is no fuzzy management talk here, and everyone understands: She is angry and disappointed with maintenance but pleased with research and engineering.

Typically, we have not brought supervisors in. They are kept on the outside. They see managers scurrying to and fro, they sense a disaster here or victory there, they hear bits about the boss's being angry, gossip about a lost customer. They know when something important is at stake because they feel increased pressure from above, but the outcome, that's a mystery. Then, in an insulting pretense of communication, senior operating managers gather everyone to sit through 30 or 40 overheads

Figure 22-2. Heavy-duty brakes: filling Lawton's order.

customer	order	promised delivery date	delivery
Lawtons	500 heavy duty disc brakes	May 10	300-May 13 200-May 18

- late and split delivery for one of our largest and most important customers
- disc line scheduled 8 hours for change over and set up to heavy duty
- it took them 3 days
- breakdown in plate assembly took another 18 hours of downtime

for 2 weeks before this breakdown, operators were screaming for service, but maintenance decided it was more important to stick with their CMS (computerized maintenance schedule) than listen to operators

maintenance may soon need more chairs in their computer room - if we don't start keeping our delivery promises, we will all be over there playing games on their computers

- JIT is not a big joke for Lawton's, they are taking it very seriously
- if we can't deliver on time, they'll find someone who will
- on the positive side, Research and Engineering have done brilliant work with the new conical seals
- early tests at Lawton's show new seals extend life 25% compared with our earlier model

comparing return on assets this quarter with last, leaving all the really important information to move by rumor. This is not the way a boss should communicate.

Decentralization is partly to blame. From the boss's perspective, decentralization means not trying to run a subordinate's department from a distance, not interfering in the day-to-day running. But decentralization should never mean that senior operating managers turn their backs on their responsibility for communicating performance. Don't run their department, but don't give up telling them whether they have done well or poorly. And a private little tête-à-tête with the department manager behind closed doors is the same as no communication at all, as far as supervisors are concerned. Decentralize, surely, but don't give up the role of final judge and communicator of performance.

If the senior operating manager doesn't communicate performance, who can? Not department managers. They are part of their department, fully immersed in the department's own particular brand of chauvinism, prejudice, and loyalty. Only the senior operating manager is above interdepartmental bickering and rivalries. The senior operating manager is the person with the impartiality and credibility to best communicate performance.

Employees' Greatest Fear

Their greatest fear is that what they do doesn't matter.

Never hearing praise or blame, receiving no accolades or scolding, employees, logically, come to believe that what they do doesn't matter.

Certainly their greatest fear is not that the senior operating manager is going to crack down and demand better work. Far from it. In the United Kingdom, according to The Wyatt Company, 62 percent of employees agree or partly agree that poor performance is tolerated for too long in their organization.[3] Among Australian employees, research by Verena Marshall and Ron Cacioppe found 59 percent of employees said they rarely or never receive a reprimand even when their work is below standard.[4] If you or the people around you do poor work and you never hear about it, isn't it natural to think that what you do doesn't matter?

Of course, what they do does matter. These people make the products and deliver the service. Nothing matters more. The senior operating manager needs to stand up and make that clear. The senior operating manager is the only person at the site above any and all departments. He or she is the only person who can legitimately evaluate department performance.

Break the gentlemen's agreement, the time-honored management etiquette that nothing should be said that might embarrass a department manager in front of his or her supervisors. Replace this with a new value: communicating performance.

References

1. C. A. O'Reilly and K. H. Roberts, "Information Filtration in Organizations: Three Experiments," *Organizational Behavior and Human Performance*, vol. 11, 1974, pp. 253–265.

2. Larry R. Smeltzer, "The Relationship of Communication to Work Stress," *The Journal of Business Communication*, vol. 24, no. 2, spring 1987, pp. 47–58.

3. The Wyatt Company, *Wyatt Work UK: UK Benchmark of Attitudes to Work*, London, 1989, pp. 2–19.

4. Verena Marshall and Ron Cacioppe, "A Survey of Differences in Communication Between Managers and Subordinates, *Leadership & Organization Development Journal*, vol. 7, no. 5, 1986, pp. 17–26.

23

How to Communicate When Everything Is Uncertain

We can't communicate because we don't know what's going to happen.

Wrong. You can't communicate because you have restricted yourself to only communicating certainty. If you communicate probabilities, there is much you can say.

Communicating Probabilities: An Oil Company Move

A large oil company was moving its head office to a different city and state. Ten months before the move, senior managers were concerned planning was not progressing fast enough.

Frontline employees, in their defense, said it was impossible to begin planning because they had no dates. When, they asked: does the computer become operational? will phones be plugged in? files moved? building fit out complete? furniture in place? Until they had these dates, employees said there was little they could do.

Department managers, responsible for providing dates, hesitated to commit themselves. Department managers knew that providing a date would set into motion long sequences of plans built around that date as a promise. Changing a date would send repercussions throughout the company, requiring hundreds of others to change their plans as well. The department managers responsible would wear the blame for all the added work and perhaps be held accountable for setting back the entire move. Protecting their own interests, department managers decided it was best to avoid giving a date until the last possible moment. With the benefit of more time and information, it was more likely their date would not need changing.

Escape from situations like these by communicating probabilities.

Each department head in this company was required to supply key dates. But each date was loaded with an uncertainty factor. The dates were combined into a calendar where the darkness of print for any particular date corresponded to its degree of uncertainty.

Light   75 percent chance or more this date would change

Medium   50 percent chance this date would change

Bold   25 percent chance or less this date would change

The calendar showed the upcoming 10 months. Every 2 months a new calendar was issued. Each successive calendar becoming darker and darker. Figure 23-1 shows a sample month, October, from one of the earlier calendars.

The way the calendar communicates is closer to the way planning actually occurs. Managers do not sit quietly, for weeks, in deep contemplation, planning. Then burst from the planning room, truth in hand, ready to begin implementing. Rather, the planning, thinking, and acting all occur simultaneously. This is not a defect. The scale and complexity of the change is so immense there is no other way. If all action waited for a definite plan, there would never be a beginning.

The calendar mimics the way managers plan: uncertain and changing, evolving and iterative. Doing so, the communication simply tells the truth: This is where we are today, and at this moment this is what we know.

Communicating Probabilities: Downsizing in a Packaging Equipment Manufacturer

A packaging equipment manufacturer experienced several years of declining sales. Facing up to the difficulties, senior managers began planning asset sales, plant closures, cost cutting, and layoffs. And in so doing, they began heading down a well-worn road toward communication disaster.

Figure 23-1. Company relocating: key dates in October. (The darker the print, the more certain the date.)

October

1	PABX telephone service begins operation
4	**natural gas moves**
5–8	freight access restricted due to mainframe move
12	**new hires in production begin**
18	**child care center begins operation**
22	drilling moves
25	marketing files and furniture arrive
26	**new tax dept. general manager's first day**
28	relocation consultants begin employee seminars
28	marketing moves

Communicating bad news is where we most often fail. In our experience, there are six predictable steps on the way to communication disaster:

1. During the Planning Phase, Senior Managers Decide Everything Will Be Kept Secret

This runs contrary to everything in their combined experience. No senior manager had ever seen a plan like this kept secret; regardless, the decision is made.

A task force, sworn to secrecy, begins investigating cost-cutting ideas.

2. Rumors Begin

Questions from the task force such as "Could you run this area with, say, 30 percent fewer people?" alert everyone that the cuts are going to be severe.

Senior human resource managers begin warning, "We better get out there and say something, soon."

3. Senior Managers Decide Not to Communicate Because Plans Are Not Finished

There is internal disagreement about where and how deep the cuts should be. Communication is postponed for a couple of weeks.

4. Rumors Run Wild

Finalizing plans takes not a couple of weeks but a couple of months.

Senior manager silence is interpreted as proof that the worst of the rumors must be true: "That's why they're not talking. It's too horrible to talk about. They're afraid to face us."

Employees begin confronting senior managers in elevators, saying things like:

> I've worked for this company for almost 30 years. I can tell you, this used to be a place where people mattered. But no longer. Now we are just objects to be bought and sold. Thrown in the garbage when you no longer need us. Morale here is in the dirt. Now, for the first time, people hate this company.

Senior managers find these episodes so stressful they avoid contact with employees.

Employees see that management "has gone to the bunker."

5. Plan Details Begin Leaking Out

Escalating wildly, rumors now paint a picture much worse than anything management is actually considering.

Informally, some senior managers begin damage control:

> No, I can't tell you the plan, but I can say this: We are not going to sell the entire company, and we are not going to terminate half the work force just before Christmas.

Enough damage control leaks out that some middle managers get a feeling for the parameters actually being considered. This pieced-together set of hunches moves by grapevine throughout the company.

Coming down from incredible heights, rumors now tell a story much closer to the plan actually being considered.

6. Plan Is Formally Announced

The "cowards" emerge from their "bunker" to communicate a plan that everyone, including the cleaners, has now pretty well known for weeks.

Employee anger turns to resentment:

> We can understand the cuts. We know something had to happen. But we resent the way you did it. You let rumors terrorize this place. You created tremendous and often unnecessary stress for many employees and their families. And all because you were too chicken to look us in the eye and tell us what you were thinking. We will never trust this management again.

Senior managers are a little less critical:

> We did a good job with the plan. We made the hard decisions that had to be made. The company is better positioned for the future. But the communication was a disaster.

The names of companies telling experiences like this would fill a book three times the size of this one.

There is an alternative, a junction at step 3 (Senior Managers Decide Not to Communicate). The alternative is to tell the truth: We are planning some serious cuts, but exactly where, and how deep, we are not sure; however, at this moment, this is what we are thinking. Take your options, load them with probabilities of occurring, and communicate them. Figure 23-2 shows how one company communicated its downsizing probabilities.

Teams of senior managers toured the plants giving face-to-face presentations to groups of supervisors using the information in Fig. 23-2 as a foundation.

Over four months, three briefings occurred, each providing information more definite than the one before. Not for a moment do we pretend this communication made everyone happy. Employees in Liquid Filling and Capping were severely distressed hearing they had a 50/50 chance of being sold. Employees in Transport held an immediate 24-hour strike, then an unofficial slowdown for the next three months, as a

Figure 23-2. Packaging company: probabilities of downsizing operations.

Definitely Will Occur

some business groups will be sold	some business groups will be closed	there will be layoffs among remaining groups

75% Chance Will Occur	**50% Chance Will Occur**	**25% Chance Will Occur**

Shrink & Sealing will be sold Automatic Strapping will be sold Carton & Case will be closed	Liquid Filling & Capping will be sold All remaining businesses: 15% of monthly staff laid off 15% of hourly employees laid off (50% chance % will increase) (no chance % will decrease)	Transport leased to a contractor Pharmaceuticals brought together on one site New adhesives plant opening before 1995

Definitely Will Not Occur

Sell the entire company Selling or closing PLC Systems	Selling or closing Pharmaceuticals Severance benefits lower than those offered in 1990	Selling or closing Precision Liquid Fill Any lay offs before February 7

warning to management of what would happen if they were leased to a contractor. As senior managers moved about the plants, employees mocked them by flipping coins. There is no happy way to communicate a downsizing.

Communicate probabilities when you dont know details

Using the traditional communication approach, however, the pain felt by those in Liquid Filling and Capping is often felt by everyone. And the slowdown in Transport can occur in every unit, department, and plant throughout the entire company.

Communicating probabilities is a radical approach. But given our dismal record in handling downsizing, perhaps a radical change is exactly what is needed. The research in Fig. 23-3 shows precisely how poor our downsizes have been.[1-4]

Kim Cameron and his University of Michigan colleagues found a poorly handled downsizing carries serious costs. Managers in their study said that compared to predownsizing levels, their companies had lower quality, productivity, effectiveness, morale, and trust; and higher conflict, rigidity, and scapegoating.

And there is good reason to believe that the longer communication is withheld from employees, the worse the damage gets. In a strong piece of research by David Schweiger and Angelo Denisi, evidence points to huge benefits for those companies willing to communicate early and often.[5]

The Schweiger and Denisi research involved a Fortune 500 company undergoing a merger. The CEO announced that redundant plants and jobs would be eliminated. In one plant (the experiment), Schweiger and Denisi helped managers communicate early and frequently during their planning phase. In another plant (the control), management communicated the way it normally would without any special intervention.

In both plants, Schweiger and Denisi measured the change in employee attitudes. Measuring first immediately after the downsizing announcement and then again three months later. Their results show huge benefits to be gained by communicating early and frequently (see Fig. 23-4).

As strong as the Schweiger and Denisi research is, most practicing senior managers don't need it. From experience, they know frequent communication helps employees adjust to change. The problem is the complexity of our proposed changes has increased and with it the time required in planning. What stops senior managers from communicating is not a failure to realize its importance but the simple fact that the plans are not ready.

As we see it, there is only one solution: Begin communicating probabilities.

Senior managers hesitate. They don't like the idea of communicating half-baked plans with numerical hunches attached to them. Let's then rephrase the question. The question is not "Do you want to communicate?" but rather, "Do you want to participate in the communication?" There is going to be communication one way or the other. Employees are not going to say:

Figure 23-3. U.S. companies' experience with downsizing.

researcher	sample	results
American Management Association	1,142 companies	nearly half said downsizing was "badly" or "not well" handled
Society for Human Resource Management	1,468 companies	more than half reported the same or lower levels of employee productivity after the downsizing
Right Associates (Louchheim)	1,700 human resource executives in 21 industry groups	most reported improved financial results, but only 27% reported more business, and only 29% felt the new company was a better place to work
University of Michigan (Cameron, Freeman & Mishra)	2,500 managers in 30 auto industry companies	"the way in which down-sizing occurred was more important in accounting for effectiveness than the size of the workforce reduction or the cost savings that occurred"

I think we all better sit here quietly for the next three or four months until management finally tells us for sure what they have decided.

Why do we insist on pretending the silly statement above is actually the case? Employees are going to talk.

There is going to be communication. The question is whether, as a leader, you feel the need to participate in the communication concerning the future of your company.

Figure 23-4. Downsizing: Effects of early and frequent communication. *(Source: Ref. 5.)*

Employee Attitude	Control Plant (communication in the normal way)	Experimental Plant (early and frequent communication)
stress	9% increase	no change
uncertainty	24% increase	2% increase
job satisfaction	21% decrease	7% increase
commitment	11% decrease	no change
company trustworthy, honest, caring	25% decrease	14% increase
intentions to remain	12% decrease	6% decrease
performance	20% decrease	no change

Communicating the Most Likely Scenario: A New Owner

The parent of a U.S. manufacturing company sold the company to a foreign-owned multinational. The sale was a shock to the U.S. senior management team and to the 1200 employees.

Senior managers announced the sale of the company to all employees and promised a more complete briefing in 24 hours. The problem was that the senior managers knew nothing. There was no further information from the previous or new owner. In the absence of any firm information, they turned to personal contacts (including analysts at brokerage houses) and to newspaper clippings at the public library.

The new owner had acquired many companies during the late 1980s and early 1990s, and there was a pattern. Using this information, the senior managers built a most likely scenario of changes. Figure 23-5 shows their best guess of what might happen under the new owner.

The next day briefings began using the outline shown in Fig. 23-5. Senior managers were nervous. This communication had not been approved by either the previous or the new owners. Mostly they worried about preempting the new owners and perhaps making them angry. Consequently all the communication was informal, face to face, in small groups, with nothing written.

Worried as they were, managers knew that to say nothing would invite rumors, rumors that, in the absence of any communication from senior managers, would grow exponentially, eventually painting the worst possible picture. Senior managers did not want the new owners to arrive finding the place awash in wild rumors, employees flip-flopping in emotional spasms, plants filled with poorly maintained machines, high absenteeism, and incomplete books. They did not want the new owners to interview employees and hear them say things like "Morale here is in the dirt. All the best people have split." That would invite a massacre.

Better for the emotional spasms to occur now, giving employees time to settle down and get back on their feet before the new owner's investigation team arrived. When the new owner turns to employees and says, "Perhaps this area would be more efficient if we cut the work force by 25 percent and introduced a computerized flexible manufacturing system," the employees need to respond, "It would be sad to see the people go, but it would be a great opportunity to learn more advanced processing. I'm sure the people here would be willing to give this a try." An answer like that just might save their skin.

These senior managers don't know what is going to happen. They have nothing certain to say. But they don't let the lack of certainty stop them from communicating. They communicate probabilities or in this case, the most likely scenario. As leaders, they decide not to sit back and silently watch their employees commit suicide. Instead, they admit they don't know, communicate what they think might happen, and in so doing help employees prepare for the changes ahead.

Traditional methods of communicating assume a type of manager who no longer exists: a manager with all the answers, one who knows for sure what is happening, who has events firmly under control. That is the image of management we have tried to portray. And over the

Figure 23-5. Most likely changes based on new owner's past record.

1. Reduce Size of Workforce

      cuts range from 10% to 65% of existing employees terminated
      average: 30%
      hardest hit: middle managers
      not likely that outsiders will be brought in to run the company
      very likely that younger inside managers will be promoted up into more
      senior positions

2. Production Changes

      product range will shrink
            from our existing 12 to perhaps 3 products
            much higher volumes
            introduce new high-tech production methods

      uniform report system used at all their plants
            for example: failure rates, throughput times, inventory as % of revenue
            comparisons made with their other plants
            pressure applied to meet world standard

3. Future

      linked to a huge sales and distribution network
      more international
      new technology

4. How Changes Might Happen

      new owner send a review team
            interview employees
            inspect plants
            inspect books

      after about 6 weeks changes announced
            new owner is impatient
            not many small changes over a long period
            expect big changes to happen fast, then calm

      implementing the changes
            remaining employees formed into teams
            new owner acts only as an adviser
            teams given 18 months to bring our plants up to their world standards

7. Most Important Thing For Us to Do

      show a willingness (eagerness) to change
      depth of cuts determined by our ability to change

years employees got the message. In 1976, the Confederation of British Industries asked 1038 U.K. manual workers:

> Does your company's management know for sure what's ahead for the company over the next few years?[6]

A shocking 45 percent of workers said yes; another 18 percent were unsure.

Thirteen years later, Wyatt researchers asked U.K. employees to describe their company's leaders.[7] The three most frequently mentioned attributes were: task oriented, plans for the future, and is long term oriented.   .

They think we know. They think management has the answers. That is why they can't understand your silence. We taught them we know. Now we better teach them we don't.

Given the complexity of the changes we face, the decision to restrict communication to certainty is a decision not to communicate at all. Communication must be brought into alignment with the sorts of changes we are trying to communicate: uncertain, changing, and full of probabilities.

References

1. American Management Association study quoted in David A. Heenan, "The Downside of Downsizing," *The Journal of Business Strategy,* November/December 1989, pp. 18–23.

2. Society for Human Resource Management study quoted in Ronald Henkoff, "Cost Cutting: How to do it Right," *Fortune,* April 9, 1990, pp. 40–49.

3. Frank P. Louchheim, "Four Lessons from Downsizing to Build Future Productivity," *Employment Relations Today,* winter 1991/1992, pp. 467–475.

4. Kim S. Cameron, Sarah J. Freeman, and Aneil K. Mishra, "Best Practices in White-Collar Downsizing: Managing Contradictions," *Academy of Management Executive,* vol. 5, no. 3, 1991, pp. 57–73.

5. David Schweiger and Angelo Denisi, "Communication With Employees Following a Merger: A Longitudinal Field Experiment," *Academy of Management Journal,* vol. 34, no. 1, 1991, pp. 110–135.

6. Confederation of British Industry, *Priorities for In-Company Communications,* by Michael Brandon and Michael Arnott, London, September 1976.

7. The Wyatt Company, *Wyatt Work UK: UK Benchmark of Attitudes to Work,* London, 1989, pp. 2–19.

Appendix

Examples—Summarized

Example	Description	Key point	Found in
Supervisor briefings and opinion report	Oil company communicates a change in maintenance on its offshore platforms. Senior managers hold briefing meetings for supervisors. Supervisor opinion report communicates supervisors' major worries about the change directly to the CEO.	Assumes trickle down won't work. Cuts a direct communication link between senior managers and supervisors.	Chap. 1 No figures
Transmission check	Company calls supervisors on the phone, asking them true-false questions about changes to the collective-bargaining contract. Reports scores by middle manager area of responsibility.	Puts pressure on middle managers to not only pass information on, but to add value (rewrite, provide examples, ask for questions) making the information easier for supervisors to understand.	Chap. 4 Fig. 4-2
Supervisor evaluation of manager communication	Supervisors evaluate their managers' communication. Middle managers ranked according to their scores. Ranking shared with supervisors, middle and senior managers.	Forces middle managers to divert their upward gaze directing attention back down to the front line.	Chap. 4 Figs. 4-4 to 4-7
Improving head office customer service	Branch managers in a bank evaluate the quality of service they receive from head office departments. Results published in a newsletter.	Improves cutomer service to the front line, a prerequisite before asking them to improve their service to customers.	Chap. 5 Figs. 5-2 to 5-4
Supervisor advice forms	Mining company requires proof of supervisor consultation before approving capital equipment requests.	Guarantees supervisor communication before introducing new technology.	Chap. 6 Fig. 6-3

Model for communicating a downsizing	Booklets for supervisors abandon normal rules for written communication. Few words, only facts, no justifications, no sentences or punctuation. These are not stand-alone documents; only used to guide and support verbal messages.	Much downsizing communication seems meant for the downsizers; management communicating to itself. Communication must conform to the way supervisors take information in.	Chap. 7 Figs. 7-2 to 7-4
Testing downsizing knowledge	Supervisors required to pass an exam of downsizing facts before being allowed to return to work.	Guarantees supervisors get and understand the most critical information.	Chap. 7 Fig. 7-5
Supervisor briefing cards	Company under hostile takeover threat communicates using small chunks of information, communicated frequently and directly to supervisors.	Normal communication methods (newspapers, news releases, videos, management presentations) lack credibility, are too slow, carry too much information, and fail to target supervisors.	Chap. 10 Figs. 10-5, 10-6
Employee attitude survey	Company moving to another state asks only one question, "Are we prepared?" Communicates results within a week. And has planned action ready to launch.	Stop fishing around with 100-question questionnaires resulting in no action.	Chap. 15 Figs. 15-4, 15-5
Testing demand	Large bank, without warning stops all formal nontechnical communication with employees, and then counts how many employees ask, "Where is it?"	Priorities are wrong. We can find time, staff, and money for communication that doesn't work; then ignore the communication that determines behavior (face-to-face communication with supervisors).	Chap. 16 Fig. 16-3
Communicating a customer service survey	Department store shows supervisors how results from its latest customer service survey endanger employees' jobs.	Information only changes behavior when it is grounded in local work area values—in this case, job security.	Chap. 17 Figs. 17-2, 17-3

Example	Description	Key point	Found in
Communicating corporatization	Roads and traffic department communicates an organizationwide change (corporatization).	A single message for an entire organization will not work; it will not communicate.	Chap. 17 Fig. 17-4
	Message is modified for each division; this example shows communication for the driver's license division.	Senior managers must translate the change, showing effects for each division or department.	
Communicating quality	Gas range manufacturer hires product-testing firm to compare their range with five major competitors.	Stop preaching quality as a value.	Chap. 18 Fig. 18-1
	Company communicates its fourth-place ranking to supervisors.	Simply demonstrate the quality of their work as it compares with other similar work groups.	
Communicating quality	Freight company tests delivery speed for their less-than-truck-load deliveries.	Widely communicating poor performance can bring immediate improvement.	Chap. 18 Figs. 18-2, 18-3
	Losing to their major competitor in 16 to 20 trials.		
	Results communicated to all supervisors.		
Communicating performance	Oil company evaluates and ranks offshore platforms according to quality of production, maintenance, and safety.	Use pride and embarrassment to fuel changes in employee performance.	Chap. 19 Figs. 19-1, 19-2
	Senior managers communicate results to all supervisors.		
Communicating customer service	Bank uses mystery shoppers to evaluate and rank all branches in the region.	Don't keep poor performance secret; communicate it widely, unleashing social pressure as a force for change.	Chap. 20 Figs. 20-1 to 20-5
	Results shared with all branch managers.		

Testing and communicating product knowledge	Department stores with kitchen appliance departments test product knowledge among sales assistants. Communicates results to all kitchen appliance department managers.	An independent and widely communicated measure of performance will create a a crisis, and responding to crisis is what managers do best.	Chap. 20 Figs. 20-7, 20-8
Cutting a direct line from customers to supervisors	Mine asks steel mills to evaluate them in comparison with other suppliers. Results communicated by senior managers directly to supervisors.	Information of this type will not cascade down through management layers. Take this powerful message directly to supervisors.	Chap. 20 Figs. 20-9, 20-10
Replacing values with performance	Electrical utility, beginning a downsizing, communicates that its performance on four important measures is the poorest among three neighboring utilities.	When communicating change, resist talking about values; instead, talk about performance.	Chap. 21 Figs. 21-2
Communicating performance	Mine manager gives opinion of the mine's performance during the previous week. No questions, no excuses, no marathon talk-fest. Supervisors just stand there and listen to a 5- to 10-minute appraisal of their performance.	We are communicating statistics and pretending it's performance. Statistics mean nothing on the front line. Tell them their performance, straight up: Have they done well or poorly.	Chap. 22 Fig. 22-1
Communicating performance	Plant manager in a brake manufacturing company looks at how well an order has been completed for a major customer. Communicating which departments did well and which poorly.	Decentralization has gone too far. Giving up a day-to-day interference in local work area operations should not also mean giving up communicating performance.	Chap. 22 Fig. 22-2

Example	Description	Key point	Found in
Communicating probabilities	Oil company moving its head office to another state; communicates important dates in a calendar. Darkness of print for each date corresponding to the likelihood of that date changing before the move.	The image of two distinct stages (precise planning and then implementation) is a myth. When changes are complex, the plan evolves along with the implementation. Communication must reflect this reality by communicating uncertain information.	Chap. 23 Fig. 23-1
Communicating probabilities	A packaging equipment manufacturer, planning a major downsizing, communicates the likelihood of various actions involving layoffs and plant closures.	"The plan is not ready yet" is an insufficient excuse for not communicating. Rumors, painting the worst possible picture, will fill the vacuum. Communicate simultaneously with plan development by communicating probabilities.	Chap. 23 Fig. 23-2
Communicating the most likely scenario	Manufacturing company recently sold to an overseas owner, decides to communicate the changes they believe the new owner is most likely to make.	Employees have the best chance of surviving the turmoil when their senior managers communicate early and often, even if the senior managers don't know for sure what will happen.	Chap. 23 Fig. 23-5

Glossary

Communication: Information that changes behavior.

Change: New directions requiring an improvement in employee behavior, for example: quality, customer service, new technology, and downsizing.

Frontline Employees: People who operate machines, deliver a service to customers, assemble or transport goods, process information, for example: bank tellers, retail sales clerks, stamping press operators, truck drivers, insurance form processors, and semiskilled mechanics or electricians.

Supervisors: First-line supervisors, the lowest level of management; usually nonunionized salaried people overseeing a crew of 15 to 50 frontline employees.

Managers: Middle managers; the people between first-line supervisors and senior managers.

Senior Managers: Those reporting directly to the CEO.

CEOs: Chief executive officers.

Large Companies: 500 employees or more; too big for senior executives to know the names of frontline employees.

Index

A. Foster Higgins & Co., 14, 18, 74, 134
Abel, Dawn M., 208
Adoni, Hanna, 103, 106
Ahmanson, H.F., 214
Aiken, Elaine G., 60
Albrecht, Karl, 42, 47
American Management Association, 185, 197, 234, 238
Anderson, Chris D., 208
Andrews, Douglas J., 64, 74
Archer, Arminius A., 160, 164
Arnott, Michael, 164, 238
Asea Brown Boveri (ABB), 19, 25
AT&T, 3, 176–178, 184
Auditing communication, 148–150

Balcombe, Jean, 133
Bank of America, 126
Barr, Stephen, 105
Bastien, David T., 74
Batstone, Erick, 161, 164
Bennett, James C., 74
Berger, Warren, 105
Berry, Leonard L., 190, 207
Bitner, Mary Jo, 191, 207
Bittel, Lester R., 17, 18, 31, 39, 84, 85
Bond, Michael H., 74
Booms, Bernard H., 191, 207
Booth, Anthony, 90, 95, 122
Boston University School of Management, 213, 219
Boswell, John, 164
BP, 212
Brandon, Michael, 164, 238
British Airways, 126
British Rail, 128
Brownell, Judi, 33, 39
BT (British Telecom), 62, 87–89, 95, 128, 144–145, 152

Buck Consultants, 62, 74
Bureau of the Census (U.S.), 125
Bureau of Labor Statistics (U.S.), 79
Buxton, Virginia M., 206, 208

Cacioppe, Ron, 39, 225, 226
Cadbury Schweppes, 3, 161, 164
Cameron, Kim S., 233–234, 238
Caterpillar, 58, 217
Change:
  announcing, 1–4, 233
  resisting, 151, 215
China, 213
Citicorp, 214
Clampitt, Phillip G., 16, 18, 164
Clark, Kim B., 48–49, 55, 60, 174, 184
Cole, Robert, 166, 174, 184
Communication:
  benefits, 62
  corporate relocation, 139–141, 227–228
  corporatization, 157–159
  customer service, 40–47, 154–157, 186–194, 199–201
  downsizing, 61–74, 228–235
  hostile takeover, 92–95, 235–237
  industrial relations, 28–30
  mistakes, 180–181, 223
  operational changes, 6–9
  performance, 165–174, 175–184, 202–207, 217–219, 221–225
  product knowledge, 194–197
  quality, 121, 165–184
  technology, 48–60
  values, 209–219
Communication, definition of, 87n., 245
Communication and uncertainty, 68–69, 157, 227–238

Communication by industry:
  banks, 20–23, 40–47, 186–191, 202–207
  department stores, 154–157, 194–197
  electrical utility, 217–219
  manufacturing, 23–25, 28–30, 33–38,
    92–95, 167–169, 223–225, 228–233,
    235–237
  mining, 48–60, 76–77, 199–201, 221–223
  oil, 6–9, 178–182, 227–228
  public service, 157–159
  transport, 169–171
Communication by profession:
  accountants, 64, 221
  engineers, 52–56
  marketing, 213
Communication priorities, 87, 122–123,
  150–151
Communication training, 23, 75–80
Confederation of British Industry, 107,
  115, 143, 160, 164, 238
Conference Board, 65, 74, 80, 91, 101, 106,
  118–120, 122, 124–125, 172, 174
Consultants, 89–91, 152, 183, 199
Cooper, Bixby, 207
Coors, 214
Corporate Culture and Performance (Kotter
  and Heskett), 213–214
Crosby, Philip, 125
Crossan, Des, 3, 10
Crowell, Charles R., 208
Cullen (The Hon. Lord), 184

D'Aprix, Roger, 152
D/J Brush Associates, 105
Daft, Richard L., 119, 124
Dana Corporation, 12–13
Davidow, William H., 207
Davis, Ed, 60
Davy, Jeanette A., 74
Decisions in Organizations, 20, 26
Deets, Norman, 39
Denisi, Angelo, 62, 74, 233, 235, 238
Detroit Edison Company, 14
Deutsch, Arnold, 125
Diffusion of Innovations (Rogers), 9–10
Domino's Pizza, 102, 105
Downs, Cal W., 16, 18, 102, 106
Drucker, Peter F., 79–80, 83, 85, 175, 184
Dulworth, Michael R., 143, 174

Eastern Airline, 7
Emery, 160, 164
Employee involvement programs, 82–85,
  128
Employees:
  loyalty, 104, 152–163,
  motivation, 183, 212, 225
  preferred channels, 89–90
  preferred source of information, 2–3
  preferred topics, 153

Farnham, Alan, 143
Federal Aviation Authority, 176
Federal Communications Commission,
  176–177, 184
Federal Express, 102, 103
Fields, Mitchell W., 84, 85
Finn, Chester Jr., 160, 164
Firestone, Richard M., 184
Firth, Michael, 153, 163
Fleenor, Patrick C., 39
Foehrenbach, Julie, 10, 27, 38–39, 74, 95,
  105, 124, 151, 160, 208
Ford, Bill, 57, 60
Ford Communication Network, 99, 103
Ford Motor Company, 99, 102, 134, 210,
  219
Fornell, Claes, 198, 208
Forum Corporation, 193, 208
Fowkes, Richard S., 60
Frank, Allan D., 19, 26, 180, 184
Freeman, Sara J., 234, 238
Freudenheim, M., 74
Funderburk, Brenda, 133

Gelfond, Peter A., 63, 74
General Accounting Office (U.S.), 82, 85,
  171, 174
General Electric (GE), 3, 15–16, 19, 194, 217
General Motors (GM), 3, 19, 99, 118,
  120–121, 147, 162–163, 210, 214
General Tire & Rubber, 3
Germain, Richard, 207
Ginnodo, William L., 184, 219
Glauser, Michael J., 143
Glynn, Mary Ann, 39
Goldfarb, Steve, 27, 38–39, 95, 105, 124,
  151, 208

Gonring, Matthew P., 184
Goodwin, Bill, 132
Goodyear, 214
Gordon, David M., 79–80, 183, 184
Grant, Rebecca A., 205, 208
Grey, Ronald J., 63, 74, 219

Hainey, G., 3, 10
Hallmark, 126
Hannaway, Jane, 119, 124
Harcourt, Jules, 27, 39
Harrison Conference Services, 107, 115
Hasbro, 12
Hay Group, 63, 143, 212, 129
Hay Management Consultants, 212, 219
Hayes, Robert H., 48–49, 55, 60, 174, 184
Hazen, M., 102, 106
Heenan, David A., 238
Heller, Frank, 84, 85, 164
Henkoff, Ronald, 238
Heskett, James L., 207, 213–214, 219
Hewlett-Packard (H-P), 3, 15–16, 89–90, 134
Higgins, Christopher A., 205, 208
Hill, Lorna A., 160, 164
Hofstra University, 107–108
Holter, Harriet, 164
Honda, 129
Hudson Institute, 196, 208
Hussey, Roger, 105
Hyatt Hotels, 134

IBM (U.K.), 102, 114, 152
ICI, 3, 217, 219
Immerwahr, 183, 184
In Search of Excellence (Peters and Waterman), 213
Income Data Services, 163
Industrial democracy, 160–161
Industrial Relations Services, 95, 164
Industrial Society, 3, 105, 120, 124, 143, 153, 163, 172, 174, 183, 184, 212, 219
Industry Week, 181, 184
Institute of Directors (U.K.), 107, 115
Institute of Occupational Medicine, 55, 60
International Association of Business Communicators (IABC), 3, 27, 63, 89, 95

International Harvester Company (Navister), 16
International Survey Research, Limited, 95
Irving, Richard H., 205, 208

Jablin, Fredric M., 15, 18
Jack, Andrew, 116
Jaguar, 109
Japan Human Relations Association (JHRA), 129–130, 133
Japanese, 166
  communication and decision making, 56–57
  suggestions schemes, 129–130
Jenkins, Glenville, 161, 164
Johnson, Gail C., 219
Johnson & Johnson, 16, 18
Judeikis, J., 55, 60

K-mart, 204, 208, 214
Kandel, Denise B., 127, 132
Kanter, Donald L., 4, 11
Katz, Elihu, 103, 106
Kearney, A. T., 165, 173
Kemper, Gary W., 10, 124
Kilroy, John, 74
Kingsley, E. C., 60
Kinicki, Angelo, 74
Klein, Janice A., 84, 85, 108, 115
Klotz, Valentin, 133
Komatsu, 58, 217
Kotler, Philip, 193, 208
Kotter, John P., 213–214, 219
Kroger, 214
Kunst, Paul, 164

Lam, Kin Hung, 219
Landen, Delmar L., 143, 174
Lansbury, Russell, 60
Larsen, Janet K., 119, 124, 205, 208
Larson, James R., 32, 39
Lawler, Edward E., III, 38, 39
Lawshe, C.H., 16, 18
Lengel, Robert H., 119, 124
Lewin, David, 174
Literacy, 65, 117–118, 196
Little, Arthur D., 165, 173

Locke, Edwin A., 82, 85
Longair, R., 20, 26
Lou Harris & Assoc., 4, 10
Louchheim, Frank P., 238
Ludeman, Kate, 174
Lund, Leonard, 74, 124
Luthans, Fred, 119, 124, 205, 208

Mackay, Hugh, 3, 10, 87
Marshall, Verena, 39, 225, 226
Martenson, Rita, 41, 47, 208
Marvis, Philip H., 4, 11
Mason, S., 60
Mathews, Cash M., 217, 219
Matsushita, 129–130, 166
Matteis, Richard J., 102, 106
McGuire, Patrick E., 74, 124
McKeand, Patrick J., 124
Meeks, Fleming, 106
Meetings, including "team briefing,"
    107–115
Meister, David, 53–55, 60
Mensch, Barbara S., 127, 132
Mercer, William M., 120
Merrill Lynch, 101, 102
Middle manager communication:
    as a barrier, 19–25
    networks, 27–28
    preferences, 38, 119, 223
    self-assessment of, 31–33, 38, 50–52
Miller, Christopher S., 131, 133
Miller, J., 20, 26
Mishra, Aneil K., 234, 238
Mission statements, 81, 185, 209–213
Misumi, Jyuji, 74
Mitchell, Olivia S., 63, 74
Morano, Richard, 39
Motorolla, 212, 219

Nagle, B.F., 16, 18
National Association of Suggestion
    Systems, 133
National Economic Development Office,
    172, 174, 181, 184
Newman, Ruth G., 116
Newspapers, company-produced, 117–125
Nissan, 129
Nissan (U.K.), 16
Nonkin, Lesley J., 116

Nora, John J., 133
Nystrom, Paul C., 15, 18

O'Reilly, C. A., 15, 18, 223, 225
Office of Technology Assessment (U.S.),
    205, 208
Oliver, Dale R., 39
Olney, Robert J., 74
Opinion Research Corporation, 191, 207

Parente, Joseph A., 143
Parkington, John J., 206, 208
Parness, Pnina, 103, 106
Parrasuraman, A., 190, 207
Pascale, Richard T., 57, 60, 133
Peach, Brian E., 195, 208
Peach, David A., 39
Peay, James M., 60
Pelz, Donald C. (Pelz Effect), 14–16, 18
Penney, J. C., 100, 102–103, 214
PepsiCo., 148, 217
Peters, Tom, xiii, 17, 129, 213, 219
Peterson, Mark F., 64, 74, 118
Philip Crosby Associates Inc., 23, 26
Piper Alpha (oil platform), 181
Plowman, David, 57, 60
Polaroid, 19, 112–114
Poole, Michael, 161, 164
Porter, Lyman W., 38, 39
Posner, Barry Z., 207
Post Office (U.K.), 109
Postal Service (U.S.), 100, 103
Procter & Gamble, 214
Profit Impact of Marketing Strategy
    (PIMS), 193, 207
Profit sharing, 161–162

Quality Improvement Company, 165, 174

Ramsey, Jackson E., 17, 18, 31, 39, 84–85
Rath & Strong, 165, 173
Ravitch, Diane, 160, 164
Receiver orientation, xii, 40
Reichheld, Frederick F., 193, 207
Richerson, Virginia, 27, 39
Right Associates, 70, 74, 234
Roberts, K. H., 15, 18, 223, 225

Rogers, Everett M., 3, 9–10, 11, 104, 106
Rogers, Raymond C., 133
Rosenberg, Karn, 10, 74, 95, 151, 153, 160, 163
Rosetti, Daniel K., 101, 106
Ruch, William V., 85, 115
· Rumors, 65–66, 94, 229–234

Sanders, Mark S., 60
Sanyo, 166
Sasser, Earl W., Jr., 193, 207
Scheck, Christine, 74
Schlesinger, Leonard A., 207
Schmidt, Warren H., 207
Schneider, Benjamin, 206, 208
Schreuder, Hein, 118, 124
Schuster, Michael H., 131, 133
Schwarzkopf, Albert B., 195, 208
Schweiger, David, 62, 74, 82, 85, 233, 235, 238
Scontrino, Peter M., 39
Scott, Clyde, 28, 39
Sears, 214
Senior managers:
    communication:
        clarity of incoming information, 65
        downward to employees, 1–4, 19, 86–87, 96–100, 119–122, 148, 209–219
        preferences, 38
        upward from employees, 12–14, 131–132
        video, 96–100
    employee perceptions of, 2–3, 197, 212–213, 238
    secrets, 171–172, 229
Sergio, Joseph P., 208
Service America (Albrecht and Zemke), 42
Shycon Associates, 193, 207
Sigband, Norman B., 64, 74
Smeltzer, Larry R., 223, 226
Smith, Alvie, 3, 10, 39, 106, 132, 164
Smith, André, 153, 163
Smith, Peter B., 74
Snyder, K., 80
Social report (Netherlands), 118
Society for Human Resource Management, 234, 238
Soeters, Joseph, 164
Sony, 166
Spurr, Ian, 121, 125

Steelcase, 12
Stramy, Robert J., 133
Suchan, James, 28, 39
Suggestion schemes, 126–133
Supervisors and communication:
    communication from supervisors:
        advice forms, 56
        evaluation of head office, 42–46
        evaluation of manager communication, 33–38
        opinion reports, 7–9
    communication to supervisors:
        briefing cards, 91–95
        briefings, 6
        transmission check, 28–30
Supervisors:
    credibility of, 4
    numbers of, 79–80
    power of, 17, 20, 84–85
    value of, 185–186
Surveys of employee attitudes, 134–143
Surynt, Theodore J., 101, 106
Swedish Institute for Staff Suggestions, 133

Tavistock Institute of Human Relations, 160, 164
Taylor, Dennis W., 4, 11, 97, 105, 153, 163, 172, 174
Taylor, William, 25
Tennenbaum, Allen, 38, 39
Testing, 30, 72–73, 148–150, 194–197
Tetreault, Mary Stanfield, 191, 207
Thacker, James W., 84, 85
Thorsrud, 160, 164
Thriving on Chaos (Peters), 213
Thurow, Lester C., 102, 106
Tohzawa, Bunji, 133
Touche Ross, 97, 105
Towers Perrin, 38, 39, 212, 219
Toyota, 129–130
TPF&C, 3, 27, 63, 89, 95
Troy, Kathryn L., 80, 91, 95, 106, 124, 125
Trunko, Michael E., 132

Union Carbide, 101
Union of Communications Workers (U.K.), 109
Unions, 2, 84, 109

United Auto Workers (UAW), 99
University of Michigan, 234
UNUM Corporation, 12
Usilander, Brian L., 143, 174
Uttal, Bro, 207

Vandamme, Jacques, 85
Vicious circle of customer complaints
    (Fornell and Westbrook), 198–199
Videos, 96–106
Vista Communications, 98, 105, 114
Vroom, Victor, 83, 85

Waterman, R. H., 213, 219
Wattier, Mark, 27, 39
Weitzel, William, 195, 208
Welter, Therese R., 184
Westbrook, Robert A., 198, 208
Weyerhaeuser, 152

What Do Our 17-Year-Olds Know? (Ravitch
    and Finn), 160
Wheelwright, Steven C., 48–49, 60, 174,
    184
Whitworth, Brad, 15, 18, 95
Works councils (Netherlands),161
Wyatt Company, 4, 10, 181, 184, 225–226,
    238
Wymer, William E., 143

Xerox, 37, 39

Yamada, Kenjiro, 133
Yankelovich, 183–184
Yetton, Phillip, 83, 85

Zeithaml, Valarie A., 190, 196, 207–208
Zemke, Ron, 42, 47

About the Authors

TJ LARKIN, PH.D. and SANDAR LARKIN are directors of Larkin Communication Consulting. Their company specializes in helping corporations to communicate change effectively to their employees. TJ was educated at the University of Oxford and Michigan State University. Sandar, originally from Burma, worked for the Long-Term Credit Bank of Japan before beginning a consulting business with TJ. Larkin Communication Consulting has offices in New York, London, and Melbourne.